Ethical Leadership

Ethical Leadership

Global Challenges and Perspectives

Edited by

Carla Millar

and

Eve Poole

palgrave
macmillan

First published 2011 by
PALGRAVE MACMILLAN

Palgrave Macmillan in the UK is an imprint of Macmillan Publishers Limited,
registered in England, company number 785998, of Houndmills, Basingstoke,
Hampshire RG21 6XS.

Palgrave Macmillan in the US is a division of St Martin's Press LLC,
175 Fifth Avenue, New York, NY 10010.

Palgrave Macmillan is the global academic imprint of the above companies
and has companies and representatives throughout the world.

Palgrave® and Macmillan® are registered trademarks in the United States,
the United Kingdom, Europe and other countries.

ISBN: 978–0–230–27546–1 hardback

This book is printed on paper suitable for recycling and made from fully
managed and sustained forest sources. Logging, pulping and manufacturing
processes are expected to conform to the environmental regulations of the
country of origin.

A catalogue record for this book is available from the British Library.

Library of Congress Cataloging-in-Publication Data

Ethical leadership : global challenges and perspectives / edited by
Carla C.J.M. Millar and Eve Poole.
p. cm.
ISBN 978–0–230–27546–1
1. Business ethics. 2. Leadership – Moral and ethical aspects. 3. Social
responsibility of business. I. Millar, Carla, 1941– II. Poole, Eve, 1972–

HF5387.E815 2010
174'.4—dc22   2010027578

10 9 8 7 6 5 4 3 2 1
20 19 18 17 16 15 14 13 12 11

Printed and bound in Great Britain by
CPI Antony Rowe, Chippenham and Eastbourne

Contents

Part III   Perspectives for the Future

Illustrations

Tables

Figures

Foreword

The era of irrational excess, much of it a result of either a misunder-standing or mis-pricing of risk in a variety of contexts and on multiple fronts, brought us to the brink of global economic catastrophe. One hopes it has taught us that:

- No matter the organisation – government, business, not-for-profit, or vol-untary – ethical behaviour or the lack of it has an enormous impact.
- Unfettered (no rules, and no conscience) capitalism is not sustain-able as a panacea for economic vitality and societal benefit.
- Capitalism is not 'bad' or 'must die'. The mistakes of the past must be understood, and capitalism must remake itself.

Core to the remaking of capitalism is the principle of 'doing well by doing good'. It will entail a full embrace of the idea, put into action, that ethical behaviour that facilitates and enriches social good, is not just 'virtuous', but is demonstrably 'good business'.

A critical component is encapsulated in an idea, gaining worldwide executive interest and traction, called 'Cohesive Capitalism'. This is shorthand for saying that capitalism can or should or must be the pri-mary force for bringing us together, solving the real problems of real people rather than creating disparities, discouragement, and despoli-ation of the earth's resources. The transformation from the past to a future rooted in ethical behaviour will not require a revolution. Rather, it represents a refinement in thinking and execution, and more – moral – commitment to reacting positively to social context and obliga-tion both globally and locally.

What it will mean is that corporate leaders will shoulder the respon-sibility of defining an 'ethical compass' for their organisations with sensitivity to the environments in which they operate. They will then have to be accountable for their actions. This entails living according to the course the compass prescribes by providing consistent and believ-able leadership – through personal example, and by embedding ethical behaviour in their people, processes, and practices. The goal is to bridge the gap between senior leaders, their organisations, and society as a whole: that is, creating cohesion that is virtue-based.

However, given the world's diversity of cultures, mores, perspectives, and practices, this raises a series of critical questions:

- In a business context, what is 'ethical behaviour'?
- Can the benefits of 'doing good by doing well' be quantified and measured?
- Is there a profile for leaders capable or incapable of ethical behaviour?
- What lessons about ethical behaviour can be learned from looking at leadership in developed, developing and underdeveloped countries?
- Going forward, can we create ways to
  - identify the common enablers and stumbling blocks of ethical leadership?
  - use analytics to recommend practical actions to enable leaders to behave ethically?

This book is a ground-breaking and important contribution for moving us toward a world where ethical behaviour, embodied in concepts like 'Cohesive Capitalism', becomes standard operating procedure. Its essays illustrate how leading researchers and executives are thinking about, measuring, reimagining, and laying the foundations for remaking capitalism.

It does so through three lenses:

1. **The challenge**: Who was/is responsible? Can we identify good actors and weed out bad ones?
2. **Present global perspectives**: Lessons from analysing differences in various countries based on cultural profiles, practices (as it is), and values (as it should be) levels.
3. **The future**: What sort of leadership do we need for the future?

Sharing their painstaking analysis, the contributors put forth insights into the questions posed above. These include suggestions that flow from their results on how to create and sustain a more ethical global business eco-system.

Toward Ethical Leadership

Global diversity makes the establishment of a definition of ethics in a business context a significant challenge. Cultural values about what constitutes acceptable behaviour are literally all over the map. It is a function of a multitude of variables including: geographic location; natural resources; history; the existence, nature and relationships of religions and secular authorities; leadership character; and so on.

In addition, from a purely business perspective, decision-making processes and practices are wildly divergent. The emphasis in some countries is on individual initiative, while in others it is based on collective wisdom. In addition, Western notions of making the creation of shareholder value a pillar of corporate existence are not necessarily seen as a priority value in Eastern cultures, where the good of everyone is given more credence as a corporate purpose. As the essays in the book highlight, this is not to say that no universally recognisable attributes about what constitutes ethical corporate behaviour or the characteristics of ethical leadership exist. In fact, while they may be more guidelines than hard and fast rules, a few are noteworthy.

Leadership Matters

While stating the obvious, the importance of leadership, the character and quality of individual leaders, and their ability to inspire high-performance teams cannot be over-stated. If senior executives do not appreciate, or if by nature (and training as one essay asserts) they are incapable of recognising moral issues or behaving ethically, there is no hope an organisation will act ethically. When management is insensitive to anything more than making as much profit as possible for themselves and shareholders only – regardless of the consequences to individuals, other stakeholders, countries, and society in general – research shows that corporate ethics are problematic. Simply, it really all does start at the top. This translates not only into a change in thinking, behaviour and priorities by current senior executives, but also the creation and nurturing of a corporate culture whose succession processes make ethical behaviour a primary consideration for organisational promotion.

Responsibility, Accountability, and Consistency

Senior leadership must make ethical behaviour a personal and organisational priority. The guidelines for the implementation and execution of a programme to instil ethical behaviour in organisational DNA must then be strictly adhered to. In addition, the programme will need to be constantly examined for its relevance to organisational performance, as reflected in the creation of shareholder value, and to employees and external stakeholders; relevance, too, to strategic partners, other members of a company's value chain, their places of operation, and to the changing political and macro and micro economic realities.

There are no rules about what constitutes ethical behaviour in any given place or time. However, there are certain fundamentals – 'virtues' and 'global common sense' shared across cultural and religious distinctions – that can be discerned. This starts with an acknowledgement and commitment to the belief stated previously that corporations as global citizens have obligations that extend past profit maximisation for their shareholders, which if properly executed may in fact assist in that objective. Paramount should be zealotry to solve the real problems of real people. This means substituting good deeds and hope for the creation of disparities and inequities. For too long has capitalism been allowed to pollute and squander the earth's finite resources for future generations, becoming a cause of discouragement and despair.

This discerning of the fundamentals proceeds with the knowledge that only with a clear delineation of *responsibilities*, and the strict enforcement of a system of *accountability* and *consistency*, can an organisation transform into one where ethical behaviour is a driving force for corporate actions overall. All three elements are critical. The goal is not only to create the perception of being a virtue-based organisation; it is to back up the words with actions that build trust.

It is worth looking briefly at what these highlighted terms mean. They constitute a three-legged stool. This is scientifically the most stable platform on which to build, but it cannot function if even one leg is removed.

Responsibility

In a business context, responsibility can be viewed in three areas:

- Corporate *business* responsibility – transparent governance, fair policies and practices, trusted partners, and the creation of value for investors and customers
- Corporate *social* responsibility – environmental stewardship, and the encouraging and funding of activities that make societies more educated and healthy
- Corporate *personal* responsibility – fair wages, respect for individual difference, respect for personal privacy, and respect for the need for security as well as freedom.

They are closely interrelated. They form the foundation of a virtuous engine that both epitomises and engenders ethical behaviour. The bottom line is that businesses that are transparent in their operations; treat their employees, partners and stakeholders fairly (including paying fair wages in safe workplaces, and refusing to pay or accept bribes); support causes that make the world a better, healthier and more educated place to live; and show respect for the privacy, security and safety of their customers, get paid back – in goodwill, customer loyalty, and good financial returns on their investments for their shareholders.

Accountability

Some people confuse the words *responsibility* and *accountability*. They are similar but very different. Understanding the difference is important. Being responsible means being assigned the task of overseeing something. Being accountable means that you will be judged (rewarded or punished) based on the performance of the things for which you are responsible. This is crucial in considering ethical behaviour. The research in this book points to the fact that much of our current pain is attributable to those being responsible not being accountable. Readers will see just what this means in all three sections of the book. Whether looking at the challenges present, or contemplating the future, if those responsible are not accountable, the word 'ethics' itself has very little meaning.

Consistency

The last leg on the stool is *consistency*. It should go without saying, but needs to be reiterated (and in fact can be quantified in terms of its impact), that inconsistent behaviour cannot be trusted. To paraphrase an old saying, business leaders need to know that consistency is key because trust is easy to break and almost impossible to restore. We are living during a period where even some of the world's most trusted brands have been undermined by their actions not matching their words, and where even apologies have been shown to be inconsistent with behaviour.

It is not an Impossible Dream

For ethical behaviour to permeate and have its complete beneficial impact, it must have leaders who are committed, who are willing to take responsibility, and to be held accountable, to prove over time that their organisations are trustworthy. Another way of saying this is that the remaking of capitalism, with the exercise of proper and committed leadership, can provide the cohesion whereby they can do well for everyone – employees, investors, stakeholders, customers – by doing good.

This may seem like an impossible dream. It is not. What the essays in this book demonstrate, for the first time in one place, is that:

- 'Ethical behaviour' can be generally defined.
- The benefits of 'doing good by doing well' are tangible and quantifiable.
- We can identify the character aspects of good and bad actors – enabling us to reward and nurture those with potential, and discourage those incapable of accepting the need to accommodate the greater good.
- Practical actions can be taken to align personal, organisational and societal needs, and requirements toward a higher purpose, that are win/win for business and society in general.

The essays highlight that capitalism when practised in an ethical context does not mean forgoing the opportunity of profit maximisation. In fact, the essays strongly suggest that ethical behaviour – supporting the greater good in a responsible, accountable and consistent manner at the business, social and personal levels – can conclusively be shown to be both virtuous and profitable. In other words, corporate interests and social interest can be mutually inclusive and create optimal results short and long term.

I am delighted to introduce the thoughts and insights of leading scholars and senior executives, as they share what they have learned about the power of ethical behaviour, and what it will take for ethical leaders to get us where we can and need to go.

Lord Carter of Barnes OBE

Acknowledgements

We are delighted with the spirit of cooperation between our publishers Palgrave Macmillan, Springer – the publishers of the *Journal of Business Ethics* – and Wiley's – the publishers of the *Journal of Public Affairs* – facilitating publication for the chapter authors and editors.

We are most grateful to John Wiley and Sons, the copyright holder, for granting permission to us to include as book chapters edited versions of papers from the *Journal of Public Affairs* (10.3) by the following authors: Clive Boddy et al., Keith Thomas and Allan Walker, Ricky Szeto, Kurt April et al., and James Lager.

We thank Palgrave Macmillan, the copyright holder, for granting permission to Mikko Manner, Stephen Chen, Josep Maria and Josep Lozano, Lindsay Thompson, and Fahri Karakas to publish fuller academic versions of the book chapters in the *Journal of Business Ethics*.

We acknowledge with thanks the support of the CEO and staff of Ashridge, particularly Eileen Mullins, in organising the Ashridge International Research Conference that led to the development of this book.

We are very grateful to our publisher, Virginia Thorp, for her crucial help and guidance throughout the project, without which we would not have met the tight schedule.

Last but not least, we are indebted to all ethical and unethical leaders who directly or indirectly inspired and guided us to write this book.

Carla Millar and Eve Poole
London, April 2010

Contributors

Kola Abimbola is a Lecturer in Law at the School of Law, University of Leicester, UK. His research interests are in the areas of company law, corporate social responsibility, applied ethics, evidence and proof, and forensic science. His works have appeared in the *Journal of Law and Society*, *Cardozo Law Review*, *Principia: An International Journal of Epistemology*, *Clinical Risk*, and *West Africa Review*.

Temi Abimbola is Associate Professor of Marketing at the Management and Strategic Management Group, Warwick Business School, UK. Her research interests are in the areas of market; entrepreneurial organisation; identity, reputation and branding. Her works have appeared in the *European Journal of Marketing*, *Journal of Marketing Management*, *International Marketing Review*, and *Qualitative Marketing Research: An International Journal*.

Kurt April is a Professor at the University of Cape Town (South Africa), and Research Fellow of Ashridge (UK). Outside of academia, Kurt is Managing Partner of LICM Consulting (South Africa), Owner-Director of Helderview BMW (South Africa), and Non-Executive Director of Achievement Awards Group (South Africa), Member of the Novartis DIAC (Switzerland), Member of the Talent and Diversity SAC of the World Economic Forum (Switzerland), and Head of an International D and I Advisory Faculty of the National Health Service (NHS, UK).

Nicolae A. Bibu is Professor of Management in the Management Department of the University of the West in Timisoara, Romania. He teaches management, business ethics, cross-cultural management, leadership, and entrepreneurship. His research interests are in management, cross-cultural management, entrepreneurship, and organisational change and development. He has a PhD in Management (West University Timisoara, 1997) and an MBA (Durham University, UK, 1995). He is currently coordinating PhD researchers in Management and is Head of the Management Department, Faculty of Economics and Business Administration.

Clive R.P. Boddy is currently conducting research into the influence of Corporate Psychopaths on organisations. He has been studying the effects of Corporate Psychopaths, as experienced by managers, over the past four years. He holds two UK Visiting Professorships, in Marketing and Marketing Research respectively. He is a Chartered Marketer and a Fellow of the Chartered Institute of Marketing, a Fellow of the Association of Tertiary Education Management, and a Fellow of the Australian Institute of Management.

Laura Brancu is Senior Lecturer at the Management Department, University of the West in Timisoara, Romania. She teaches cross-cultural management, business ethics, project management, and European business. She has a PhD in Management (both from the Université de Lille and the University of the West in Timisoara, 2007). Her research interests are in cross-cultural management, international business, and business ethics.

Stephen Carter is Chairman of Ashridge Business School and Chief Marketing, Strategy and Communications Officer of Alcatel-Lucent Inc. He has held a variety of senior executive roles in the media and telecommunications industry, including being founding Chief Executive of Ofcom (the UK Communications Regulator); Managing Director of NTL UK and Ireland; and Chief Executive of two marketing service businesses – J. Walter Thompson UK Limited and the Brunswick Group LLP. Most recently he served as Minister in the UK Government for the Communications, Technology and Broadcasting Sector, where he was the author of the *Digital Britain Report*, and the follow on *Digital Economy Act 2010*. Stephen was awarded a CBE for services to the Communications Industry, and is a Life Peer in the UK House of Lords.

Stephen Chen is Associate Professor of Business at Macquarie University. He obtained his MBA from Cranfield School of Management and his PhD in Management from Imperial College, London and previously has taught at City University Business School (now Cass Business School), Manchester Business School, Henley Management College, Open University (UK), UCLA and the Australian National University. His research interests are in the general areas of strategic management and international business, including corporate social responsibility in multinational firms, social entrepreneurship and management of not-for-profit organisations.

Peter Galvin is Director of the MBA programme and a professor at Curtin University of Technology where he teaches strategy and international business. He researches in the areas of innovation and business performance, competitive business strategy, product modularity and inter-organisational networks. He has published numerous articles in academic journals in these areas, and has also presented at and published in the proceedings of numerous conferences.

Fahri Karakas recently completed his PhD in Organizational Behavior at the Desautels Faculty of Management at McGill University. His thesis was on Benevolent Leadership. He has taught organisational behaviour and global leadership courses at McGill University, Canada, and Bogazici University, Turkey, and published papers in the *Journal of Business Ethics*, *Journal of Management Education*, *Organization Development Journal*, *International Journal of Organizational Analysis*, and *Journal of Business Strategy*.

Richard K. Ladyshewsky is Associate Professor of Managerial Effectiveness at Curtin University of Technology. His doctoral research in education focused on peer coaching and its relationship to clinical reasoning in novice practitioners. This research has led to strategic approaches for leadership development and professional competency in both the management and health sciences sectors. Richard is an Associate Fellow of the Australian Institute of Management as well as a Fellow of the Higher Education Research and Development Society of Australasia.

James Lager is Deputy Ethics Counsellor at the US Government Accountability Office (GAO), and Adjunct Faculty, Robert H. Smith School of Business, University of Maryland. He gained an MS in Organization Development, American University/NTL Institute for Applied Behavioral Science, 1999; and a JD at the Washington College of Law, American University, 1984. The opinions and views expressed in his chapter are the author's alone and are not intended to reflect GAO's institutional views.

Kirsten Locke works as Group Accounts Manager (National Trade Marketing) at South African Breweries (SAB) Head Office in Sandton (South Africa) – which entails developing marketing strategies, managing budgets, and being chief liaison for selected on-premises national groups. She holds an MBA from the University of Cape Town (South Africa), BComm (Hons) from the University of South Africa (UNISA), Advanced Marketing and Advertising Communications Higher Diploma from the Red and Yellow School (Cape Town), and a BComm in Marketing Management from Stellenbosch University (South Africa).

Josep M. Lozano is Senior Researcher in CSR at the Institute for Social Innovation in ESADE Business School (URL) and Professor in the Department of Social Sciences of ESADE. He is co-author of *Governments and Corporate Social Responsibility* (London, Palgrave Macmillan 2008) and author of *The Relational Company, Responsibility, Sustainability, Citizenship* (Oxford, Peter Lang 2009).

Mikko Manner received his PhD in Ecological Economics from Rensselaer Polytechnic Institute in Troy, NY USA in May 2009. He writes on this topic from both an academic and applied perspective. Mikko has an MBA from Cornell University and a BSBA from Lehigh University. He also has 13 years of business experience, having worked in public accounting for Ernst and Young, as a consultant for Deloitte and Touche and in a number of management positions for American Airlines.

Josep F. Mària, Jesuit, is Researcher at the Institute for Social Innovation in ESADE Business School (URL) and Professor in the Department of Social Sciences of ESADE. He is author of several articles on globalisation and on the role of organisations in developing countries. He was Visiting Professor at the Universidad Centroamericana de Managua (Nicaragua) and in the Centre d'Etudes pour l'Action Sociale (CEPAS) in Kinshasa (The Democratic Republic of the Congo).

Carla Millar is Professor of International Marketing and Management at the University of Twente (NL), a Fellow of Ashridge Business School, and Partner in Management Partners/Europrofile (UK). Previously, she was Dean of TSM Business School and Professor at the University of Groningen. She spent 10 years with major MNCs, followed by 15 years at the University of Greenwich and City University Business School, London (UK). Her research and consultancy interests are in International Business and Marketing, Knowledge Intensive Services, Ethics, Leadership, Branding and Reputation. Publications include the *Journal of Management Studies, British Journal of Management, Journal of Business Ethics, Management International Review, Journal of Knowledge Management,* and *International Journal of Technology Management.*

Caroline Mlambo holds an MBA from the Graduate School of Business at the University of Cape Town (South Africa), and works as the Head of Credit at Standard Bank Swaziland Limited. She holds a BSc (Agriculture) of the University of Zimbabwe. Caroline has worked predominantly in banking and worked at Barclays Bank of Zimbabwe, Barclays Bank PLC (UK), Stanbic Bank Zimbabwe Limited.

Valentin Munteanu is senior lecturer in the Management Department, University of the West in Timisoara, Romania. He teaches production management, cross-cultural management, business ethics, and project management. He has a PhD in Engineering and has done research in business ethics, production management, and project management. He is currently Deputy Dean of the Faculty of Economics and Business Administration.

Kai Peters is Chief Executive of Ashridge Business School. Prior to joining Ashridge in 2003, Peters was Dean, and previously Director of MBA Programmes of the Rotterdam School of Management (RSM) of the Erasmus University in the Netherlands. Peters is interested in strategy and leadership with an emphasis on management development. He holds degrees from York University, Toronto, and the University of Quebec in Chicoutimi (Canada), and Erasmus University (Netherlands).

Eve Poole is Deputy Director of the Public Leadership Centre at Ashridge Business School. She specialises in leadership, ethics, and learning. She holds a BA in Theology from the University of Durham, an MBA from the University of Edinburgh, and a PhD from the University of Cambridge in theology and capitalism. Her previous careers have included working for the Church of England and for Deloitte Consulting. She has published in the *Journal of Business Ethics* and in *Studies in Christian Ethics*, and has a book called *The Church on Capitalism* due out in 2010 (Palgrave Macmillan).

Elena Sărătean is a senior lecturer in the Management Department, University of the West in Timisoara, Romania. She teaches organisational behaviour, human resource management, management, leadership, and organisational behaviour. She has a PhD in Management (West University Timisoara, 2003). She has done extensive research in human resource management, cross-cultural management and organisational change.

Ricky Szeto is Associate Professor and Head (Administration) of the Department of Business Administration at Hong Kong Shue Yan University, and a Distinguished Researcher at Peking University. His research interests include business ethics, corporate governance, and creativity management. He has published numerous research papers in international refereed journals. Most recently he published *Corporate Governance and Business Ethics: A New Perspective*. He serves as Executive Director of Hung Fook Tong Holdings Limited and as Chairman of the Hong Kong Professional and Educational Service.

Keith T. Thomas is Associate Director and Head of Evaluation Services at the Centre for Learning Enhancement and Research at The Chinese

University of Hong Kong. After an earlier career in the Australian Defence Force, he moved to tertiary education in 1999. He has extensive teaching and instructional experience, initially in the military and subsequently in undergraduate and postgraduate programmes in Australia, China and Vietnam. His research interests include leadership and professional development, and learning and teaching in higher education.

Lindsay Thompson is Assistant Professor at the Johns Hopkins Carey Business School of Johns Hopkins University in Baltimore. The Moral Compass, Dr Thompson's model of ethical leadership, is designed as a tool for discernment, dialogue, decision-making, and consensus-building around values. Her current research explores the moral claims of human flourishing and social equity in a global market economy.

Allan Walker is Chair Professor of International Educational Leadership, Head of The Department of Education Policy and Leadership and Director of The Asia Pacific Centre for Leadership and Change, The Hong Kong Institute of Education. He is widely recognised in educational leadership in the Asia Pacific Region. Allan has experience as a teacher, school principal, university teacher and administrator, and consultant in a range of local and international settings. He has worked in universities in Australia, Singapore and Hong Kong.

1
Ethical Leadership in a Global World – a roadmap to the book

Carla Millar and Eve Poole

Introduction

This book is inspired by the observation of both practitioners and academics that, somehow, as the millennium has turned, we seem to have ventured onto a slippery slope where one organisational scandal erupts after another. Most people are aware of Enron in the United States and Northern Rock in the United Kingdom, and the accounting scandals that led to the introduction of Sarbanes Oxley in the United States and corporate governance codes in the United Kingdom and beyond. Since then, many firms have adopted strict ethical codes of conduct, some have even appointed chief ethics officers (Fombrun, 2004), and the number of courses and modules on 'ethics' in business schools and universities has risen dramatically. These various measures, however, did not stop the recent spate of banking scandals, and the near meltdown of the global financial system. While there were rules in place designed to make the system function smoothly and safely, it seems that those who were in charge – the leaders of organisations – took a position that allowed them to find ways around these rules, by inventing products and transactions not covered by them, or by reinterpreting them so as to permit profit maximisation. They did this without regard for the possible consequences for the rest of society, and the term 'greed' has often surfaced in analyses of what happened.

We wanted to understand the reasons for the actions that precipitated such events. We wanted to penetrate the complexities, collecting views and providing a platform for a discussion of these phenomena. We wanted to put ethical leadership under the microscope, in a global context. We ultimately hoped, through our work at Ashridge, to come up with routes to a solution to 'How to help bring ethics back into the practices of leaders, executives, and business life'. This vision led to the convening of an International Research Conference on 'Global Ethical Leadership – in Search of a Moral Compass' (Ashridge, 2009). The conference brought together a rich mixture of academics and practitioners from around the world and across disciplines. Consultants talked to theologians, historians talked to CEOs, and philosophers talked to marketers, creating an extraordinary confluence of discourse, geography, cultural similarity, and cultural difference. The event showed the value of a broad-ranging discussion of ethical leadership, and of the presence of an eclectic mix of disciplines and geographical backgrounds, and led to this book being conceived as a way to bring together a wide range of perspectives on the subject.

We are not alone in our concern for this topic. Leadership and business ethics are of increasing interest to both academics and practitioners, and the volume of research work is mounting. The world of practice is discussing seriously what changes to implement – more rules, fewer rules, codes of practice or not, and so on. There is now an increased willingness in the business world to change and adapt to new standards of behaviour. And in the United Kingdom, political scandals concerning MPs' expenses claims and 'cash for questions' has shown that the public sector is not exempt from scrutiny over sharp practice. This provides an opportunity for genuine reform that we are anxious for the world not to miss. While ethical leadership is a mysterious, somewhat magical intangible for many academics and executives, it urgently needs to be grasped and understood in this new global millennium. For so many people, uncertainties seem to be piling up, familiar anchors are disappearing, and the importance of leadership (and a multiplicity of recipes for its success) is proclaimed by ever-increasing numbers of populist management books. In contrast, in this book we do not offer prescriptions, but an open discussion and varied analyses of the issue of ethical leadership, its drivers, scope, and obstacles – particularly in a global context. We offer three perspectives in three parts of the book: theoretical challenges, practice from around the world, and a visionary look at the future.

Looking to the future, as we do in the final chapter, many issues arise. Is there a need to balance the leader's personal ethical values with the potentially manipulative task of aligning others in the organisation with such values? What underlies the ability to balance corporate responsibility obligations with more immediately pressing matters that, for instance, would argue for cost-cutting in the face of a global slowdown? And what is the influence of national institutional and cultural contexts on leadership ethics and corporate responsibility? Such quandaries emphasise that even the identification of a personal moral compass cannot guarantee that an executive's values will guide the actions of their colleagues, or that these values are the most appropriate or effective in achieving the intended results. This issue becomes particularly complex in the context of globalisation, where value systems collide and the complexity of decision-making creates new ethical dilemmas faster than the old ones can be solved.

To set the scene, in this introduction we offer a pre-theoretic set of observations, highlighting factors that seem worth investigating on the basis of their relevance to recent events, and the context and trends that attend them. We see important changes taking place at three levels: the individual, the organisation, and the environment.

The individual

At an individual level one would like to know how ethical leadership is arrived at. What makes one leader an ethical leader, the other one not? Leadership is not new, and neither are texts on how to do it well. In his famous work *The Art of War*, written around 500 BC, Sun Tzu formulated his leadership lessons for warriors (see Figure 1.1).

There are Five Fundamentals
   For deliberation
   For the making of comparisons
   And the assessing of conditions:

The Way	Causes men To be of one mind With their rulers To live or die with them And never to waver
Heaven	Ying and Yang Cold and Hot The cycle of seasons
Earth	Height and depth Distance and proximity Ease and danger Open and confined ground Life and death

Figure 1.1   Sun Tzu on Leadership

Leadership	Wisdom
(Command)	Integrity
	Compassion
	Courage
	Severity
Discipline	Organization
	Chain of command
	Control of expenditure

Figure 1.1   Continued

> Every leader is aware
> Of these
> Five Fundamentals
>
> He who grasps them
> Wins;
> He who fails to grasp them
> Loses
>
> Sun Tzu (c551–496 BC)

'Every leader is aware of the five fundamentals', but there is a difference between being merely aware and truly understanding them: 'He who grasps them wins; he who fails to grasp them loses.' *The Art of War* (Sun Tzu, 500 BC/2002) offers its five vantage points from which to study an opponent or organisational entity. If the leader studies them to a point where he has true clarity, Sun Tzu says that by this understanding he will succeed. However, if he does not, he will fail, by the very lack of such an understanding. Sun Tzu's advice marks an early attempt in the long tradition of trying to teach leadership, and his leadership blueprint includes compassion and integrity, those qualities we would expect to be prominent in the make-up of an ethical person. However, he also stresses that the guide to behaviour is 'the way' which demands loyalty to the powers that be. In effect, this demands acceptance of the corporate rather than the individual ethic. There are obvious parallels with modern dilemmas concerning the individual and the corporate ethic, as well as with the wider debate about individualism in society.

But after so many centuries of the teaching of leadership, why has it not advanced to the point where it is more commonplace and more usually successful? Clearly there are many leaders who are viewed as role models, but too often their success comes with a lack of visible commitment to clear ethical standards. Whatever has been learned seems to have neglected the ethical side of leadership. We will not rehearse here the nature versus nurture arguments (Meaney, 2001), but there is evidence that courses with the title 'ethics' can have an effect on those who take them. One such study demonstrated that the studying of ethical scandals positively impacted MBA students' ethical decision-making and their perceptions of the ethics of business people (Cagle and Baucus, 2006). Whether ethics courses do in fact deal with ethics in the purest sense has been questioned (Van Liedekerke and Dubbink, 2009), but in any case there is no conclusive evidence that an ethical education is contagious. And no matter how successful any such course proves to be, we have to recognise that, among the totality of behavioural influences, individuals in business organisations are subject to pressures that emphasise economic results irrespective of their moral value. Finance courses invariably teach future managers to believe that the purpose of business is to 'maximize shareholder value' (Jensen, 2000; Rappaport, 1998) and even an original focus on long-term shareholder value has quickly given way to short-term shareholder value maximisation: in Aspen's most recent MBA poll, 93% of the MBA students indicated that they 'strongly or somewhat agree that managers place too much emphasis on short-term performance measures when making business decisions' (Aspen, 2008, p17). This followed business practice (Handy, 2002; Mintzberg et al., 2002), to please ever more demanding institutional shareholders and investment analysts, as well as in reaction to the distortion caused by remuneratory stock options (Wolf, 2002, Emiliani, 2004). When all indicators point towards profit maximisation, moral scruple can simply be crowded out. Our supposition therefore is that a full account of what is happening will need to accommodate the various forces acting on individuals and the way they respond to them, whether through good or poor role-modelling, standard-setting, training, or inculcation, and throughout the world.

The organisation

As a further development, the structure of organisations may be encouraging a propensity for unethical behaviour. Increasingly complex global and matrix-managed organisations can confuse accountability and provide ample room for the miscreant to hide. Increasingly transactional employment contracts, enforced through objective-based performance management systems, limit staff to their role-responsibility. 'Going beyond that is not encouraged or even punished. This implies that at all levels of the organisation we are confronted with moral muteness, the unwillingness to speak out when confronted with practices which one considers to be problematic' (Van Liedekerke and Dubbink, 2009:11). Such issues are compounded when organisations operate in many different cultural contexts, with employees whose moral codes differ. In such situations 'moral muteness' may be considered a wise move for both the individual and the organisation in order to avoid disputes, and the diversity and cultural sensitivity rhetoric provides welcome shelter from these particular storms. Even corporate policies and ethical codes can backfire if these feed a reluctance to challenge questionable behaviour in case such a challenge is seen as violating a human right or affecting employability.

The transactional nature of much employment is mirrored in the worrying compartmentalisation of ethics, it being delegated to suitably vague and unenforceable codes of conduct, or collectively to the Corporate Social Responsibility (CSR) team. Where this division of labour can fall down is where it absolves individuals from the need to engage in genuine moral deliberation, because this is supposedly done elsewhere (Van Liedekerke and Dubbink, 2008:273). Distinguishing ethical, altruistic and strategic CSR, Lantos argues that altruistic CSR is not a legitimate role of business, but that ethical CSR, grounded in the concept of ethical duties and responsibilities, should be mandatory. His research suggests that strategic CSR, underpinned by senior leadership involvement, is good for business and society (Lantos, 2001).

A further organisational trend might be shorthanded 'forgetting Kotler', the marketing *eminence grise* who taught generations to delight customers, not just serve them. Many businesses interact directly with members of the public, and the growth of the service sector has been a notable feature of recent decades. The 'stars' of this growth have tended to be the technology-rich information and computing companies, with their ability to deliver standardised performance and 'solutions' on a global scale. Although their direct contact with consumers and their ability to marshall data might have been expected to engender a greater ability to deliver 'mass customisation' and tailored sensitivity to the array of customer needs, values, and preferences, the opposite seems to have been the case. Indeed, their interaction with consumers often seems similar to that of the manufacturing companies of the early marketing days, who are roundly castigated in the literature for their old-fashioned sales and product-driven approaches. Even Google (whose professed ethic 'don't be evil' is a good example of low expectations in the ethical sphere) can be criticised for allowing economic efficiency to be their default driving force. Only after prompting did they accept the need for considered ethical reflection in areas such as the handling of personal information, privacy, the acceptance of government censorship, or, allegedly, predatory activity to protect market share.

The environment

While organisations exert influence on those within them, they are themselves shaped by their surrounding environment. This environment is radically different from that of even a generation ago. Many of the essays in this collection discuss these trends, which are too numerous to be adequately summarised here, neither do we wish to rehearse the crucial effect discussions on sustainability are having on a consideration of future business models and ways of operating. However, one structural change is worth mentioning, because it has turned the face of business from the consumer towards the financial markets. Facilitated by sophisticated financial instruments, many businesses have adjusted their capitalisation, using leverage to fuel growth. In many industries, businesses are now able to differentiate themselves by their different financing positions. Those that are well financed have the opportunity to give better service to consumers, or they can use their access to resources as a basis for rewarding shareholders. This has two consequences. On the one hand, superior shareholder rewards result in an improved ability to attract capital. On the other, the actual offer to consumers can be limited to matching that of the less well-financed players, possibly with cosmetic differences and the heavy use of brand. As more businesses become dependent on strategies that only financiers understand, they become financial institutions in their own right, increasingly focusing their attention on the secondary financial markets to the detriment of the consumer. While this may have an altruistic intent about the management of risk, its effect does not tend to favour the consumer in practice. This is fundamentally changing the traditional focus of business, reinforcing the bias towards shareholder value, which can only ever be fundamentally guaranteed by exquisite and persistent customer focus. This point was also made in a recent edition of *The Economist*, which argued for the replacement of shareholder value by 'customer-driven capitalism' (*The Economist*, 24 April 2010, p. 64).

A book such as this is timely because of the widespread feeling that business has lost its moral compass. Business leaders seem to be more interested in their own remuneration than in serving their customers, and few could name more than a handful of business leaders they regard as global ethical role models. This book focuses on the role of leaders and their role in ethics, forcing back on the agenda an uncomfortable but crucial topic for our future global flourishing.

Roadmap

While it is our strong belief that leadership in the world today is not as ethical as it should or could be, this book does not pretend to give all the answers. However, it does open a number of gateways and comprises three sets of perspectives. The first part offers perspectives on the nature of the challenges faced by global leadership ethics. The second offers perspectives from around the world, widening our field of experience, and the third offers perspectives for the future. Each section will be briefly outlined here. While the chapters may be read in isolation, this chapter offers a logic to assist the reader who wishes to digest the collection as a whole.

First – Perspectives on the Nature of the Challenge. In this first part, a number of challenges that bring pressure to bear on ethical leadership are analysed: environmental pressures from the media and shareholders, the impact of the personality type of the leader for good or ill, and the impact of operational pressures at the sharp end.

Many commentators have laid the blame for the recent turmoil in world markets at the foot of unethical leaders. In support of this thesis, Boddy uses the psychopathy scale to show that psychopaths appear to be disproportionately represented in senior leadership positions. He introduces the concept of the Corporate Psychopath, a ruthless, selfish and conscience-free employee who finds it easy to gain entry to and promotion within organisations. Using new data, Boddy argues that the higher than normal incidence of this type of profile in businesses seriously affects an organisation's ability to be ethical, given the lack of moral accountability among psychopaths and their seniority, and the problems associated with screening employees for psychopathy.

One way in which organisations are increasingly giving voice to their ethical intent is through corporate social responsibility initiatives. Given their prevalence, Manner has investigated what sort of leadership correlates with exemplary corporate social performance. Given the direction of travel towards more 'applied' university topics, he finds that strong performance in this area is positively related to the CEO having a Bachelor's degree in humanities. Further, interestingly given the increasing number of women in senior leadership positions, he finds a positive correlation between exemplary performance and being female.

While he also identifies a positive correlation with breadth of career experience, he identifies negative correlations between strong socially responsible performance and the CEO having a Bachelor's degree in economics, and between performance and their level of short-term compensation. His findings suggest that CEOs have more discretion in promoting strong and exemplary social performance than in countering poor performance in this area, which offers a degree of optimism for the success of such initiatives in the future.

Chen, too, focuses on the role of the leader, examining the proposition that a major cause of recent financial accounting scandals was unethical leadership. Using computer modelling, he demonstrates the additional role played by financial analysts, by the press, and by shareholders in bolstering unethical leadership in companies. He concludes that, as well as unethical leadership, a combination of CEO narcissism, financial incentives, shareholder expectations, and media praise can do much to explain the incidence of financial accounting scandals.

Thomas and Walker add to this complexity, discussing life 'at the sharp end' in organisations, where there is little room for intellectual introspection or detailed post-hoc ethical analysis. Describing, with examples, a complex activity space, the authors show how individual biases, group dynamics, and countervailing forces shape behaviour. They also show how these collective influences can often derail well-intentioned actions by creating irrational moments that spiral out of control.

Second – Perspectives from Around the World. This second part gives an insight into the world of practice. In this part we have collected research from across the continents on how leadership is perceived and implemented, challenged and encouraged.

Mària and Lozano examine leadership in the contrasting settings of a federation of co-operatives in Nicaragua and an employer organisation in the DR Congo. The authors explore the visions, roles, and virtues of leadership, comparing two theoretical approaches and illustrating them with two cases. The theoretical approaches compare a management theory with a sociological theory of leadership, in terms of the perspective adopted, the diagnosis of the situation, the focus and style of the leader, and the outcome.

Bibu et al. use the lens of the Romanian cohort of the Global Leadership and Organisational Behaviour Effectiveness (GLOBE) project to discuss the relationship between ethical issues and the characteristics of the ideal leader within a post-communist societal context. The GLOBE project was carried out by a consortium of 12 universities from different regions of Romania. Using GLOBE data to examine Romania's societal culture profile at practice level (as it is) and at value level (as it should be), the authors explore the gaps between these levels, concluding that leadership in Romanian culture and society is changing from the traditional model towards a more modern idea of leadership. They suggest that this trend is closely linked to the changes in both organisational culture and the Romanian societal context as a whole.

Abimbola and Abimbola then offer the contrasting cases of The Body Shop in the UK and the Nigerian Stock Exchange. Using the example of The Body Shop, they use virtue ethics, new institutional theory, and the stakeholder perspective to offer a view designed to bridge the gap between leadership, the organisation, and society as a whole. They argue that micro and macro economic factors require an alignment between strategic leadership at these personal, organisational, and societal levels, defending the viewpoint that a virtue-based theory of ethical leadership is applicable and desirable in all environments.

Szeto takes us next to China, to examine the influence of Chinese folk wisdom on leadership behaviour. It has been argued that Western concepts of capitalism undermine traditional Confucian values in business dealings, and Szeto uses a survey of business managers to examine the impact of Chinese folk wisdom on ethical practices and behaviour. He finds that Chinese folk wisdom remains an effective carrier of the Chinese traditional ethical values, acting as an effective 'firewall' to guard against possible unethical practices by Chinese managers.

Finally, April et al. use empirical research conducted among MBA students in the Netherlands and in South Africa to identify the enablers and stumbling blocks for ethical leadership. Focusing on the personal challenges of leading ethically, the authors set out to understand what prevents individuals from acting courageously on their often substantial theoretical ethical knowledge, as well as what helps those who do feel able to live and act ethically. The authors use the data to suggest a range of practical actions that help leaders to behave well.

Third – Perspectives for the Future. In this last part of the book, we focus these various perspectives with a set of views about ethical leadership for the future, concluding with our own view on the topic. The role of regulation is discussed, and the tension between being ethical and being merely compliant. While long-term vision and a stakeholder orientation are characteristics of a great ethical leader, so is moral direction, and a moral compass can help leaders through the maze of uncertainty and challenge in a global world. Spiritual anchors, too, can help to capture and analyse the diverse configuration of value sets within organisations.

One remedy for unethical behaviour that is very much in vogue is the introduction of more legislation. But Lager argues that ethics is not readily susceptible to legislation, requiring clear and consistent ethical leadership beyond the limits of a compliance-based culture. He argues that ethical leadership requires the recognition that the standards of compliance set by law and regulation are merely standards and not measures of ethical conduct. He concludes that leaders should integrate ethical values into the fabric of the organisation by responsible ethical leadership, values-based training, and a genuine concern for employees and other stakeholders. Such behaviour will naturally inspire the behaviour in others that complies with most legislative and regulatory commands, while greatly enhancing productivity and brand strength.

Thompson then offers a perspective on globalisation as a labyrinth, a maze of opportunities, risks, and dilemmas with few clear directional signals. To be effective, leaders need tools for engaging with human values and moral will to create new wisdom to meet new ethical challenges. Drawing many strands together, she therefore proposes a moral compass as a model for building common moral ground, across social boundaries, values, and the competing claims of religion, ethnicity, and culture. Thompson argues that morality is a culturally situated human structure, and that moral direction is the work of leaders. Given modern complexity, contemporary leaders face the demands of new, untested challenges that preclude reliance on any single wisdom tradition for moral guidance. Thompson's moral compass is more than a metaphor, because it structures moral meaning to enable adaptive leaders to create new guiding wisdom traditions.

Karakas then introduces the spiritual dimension, discussing nine spiritual anchors as a framework for capturing and analysing diverse value compasses of leaders in organisations. Building on Schein's concept of 'career anchors', this article introduces the concept of 'spiritual anchors', patterns of deeply held spiritual motives, values, and attitudes that provide direction, meaning, wholeness, and connectedness to that person's life and work. Based on qualitative interviews, the article develops a typology of spiritual anchors, each of which can be thought of as the spiritual DNA of a person, or a fractal of that person's holistic value system.

The collection concludes with a reflection by the editors, drawing together the themes raised. In it, we look at the skills, characteristics and competences an ethical leader is likely to need in the future, and we discuss the particular ethical challenge of leading in a global and increasingly knowledge-based world. Finally, we reflect on future directions in leadership ethics.

This chapter concludes the book, a book that is distinctive because it combines academic rigour and research with a realistic sense of application. It does this through modelling and other abstract approaches as well as through research derived from the realm of practice. It is also distinctive in drawing together chapters from authors around the world to show diverse perceptions and interpretations of ethical leadership through their academic and practical work – and it draws together a perspective and positive outlook on the better prospects that exist for ethical leadership globally, in the future.

The conference at which some of the material in these chapters was first presented was held at Ashridge Business School in May 2009, chaired by Carla Millar and Marc Jones. It led to guest-edited publications in the *Journal of Public Affairs* and in the *Journal of Business Ethics*. This collection also draws from this rich source, supplementing it through additional contributions to ensure the flow and integrity of an academic book.

We trust that this book will satisfy the needs of scholars and executives from around the world who would like to read about theoretical and practical issues of ethical leadership against a global backdrop. Our Ashridge experience tells us that the 'collection' format will particularly appeal to the reading habits of an executive audience, while permitting academic readers access to a range of approaches, research, ideas, and references.

We hope that you will find it thought-provoking.

Bibliography

Agrawal, A. and Chadra, S., 'Corporate Governance and Accounting Scandals', *Journal of Law and Economics*, XLVIII (2005) 371–406.

Ashridge, Call for Papers Ashridge International Research Conference (Berkhamsted: Ashridge, 2009).

Aspen (2008), Where will they lead? MBA Student Attitudes about Business and Society, The Aspen Institute, Queenstown, MD, available at: http://www.aspen-cbe.org/documents/ExecutiveSummaryMBAStudentAttitudesReport2008.pdf) accessed 28 July 2010

Cagle, J.A.B. and Baucus, M.S., 'Case Studies of Ethics Scandals: Effects on Ethical Perceptions of Finance Students', *Journal of Business Ethics*, 64 (2006) 213–229.

Conner, K.R. and Prahalad, C.K., 'A Resource-based Theory of the Firm: Knowledge versus Opportunism', *Organisation Science*, 7(5) (1996) 477–501.

De Jongh, D., 'A Global Scan of Corporate Citizenship', *Management Today*, 25 (2009) 20–26.

Doh, J.P. and Stumpf, S.A. (eds), *Handbook on Responsible Leadership and Governance in Global Business* (Cheltenham and Northampton, MA: Edward Elgar, 2005)

Emiliani, M.L., 'Is Management Education Beneficial to Society?', *Management Decision*, 42(3–4) (2004) 481–498.

Emiliani, M.L., 'Linking Leaders' Beliefs to their Behaviors and Competencies', *Management Decision*, 41(9) (2003) 893–910.

Fombrun, C. and Foss, C., 'Business Ethics: Corporate Responses to Scandal', *Corporate Reputation Review*, 7(3) (2004) 284–288.

Gosling, M. and Huang, H.J., 'The Fit between Integrity and Integrative Social Contracts Theory', *Journal of Business Ethics*, 90(3) (2010), pp. 407–417.

Handy, C., 'What's a Business For?', *Harvard Business Review*, 80(12) (2002), pp. 49–55.

Jensen, M.C., A Theory of the Firm: Governance, Residual Claims and Organizational Reforms. (Harvard: Harvard University Press,2000).

Knippenberg, L. and de Jong, E.B.P., 'Moralising the Market by Moralising the Firm', *Journal of Business Ethics* (2010, forthcoming).

Lantos, G.P., 'The Boundaries of SCR', *Journal of Consumer Marketing*, 18(7) (2001) 595–632.

Maak, T. and Pless, N.M., 'Responsible Leadership in a Stakeholder Society: a Relational Perspective', *Journal of Business Ethics*, 66 (2006) 99–110.

McNeil, M. and Pedigo, K., 'Western Australian Managers tell their Stories: Ethical Challenges in International Business Operations', *Journal of Business Ethics*, 30 (2001) 305–317.

Meaney, M.J. 'Nature, Nurture, and the Disunity of Knowledge', *Annals of the New York Academy of Sciences*, 935 (2001) 50–61.

Millar, C.C.J.M. and Chong Ju Choi, 'The Innovative Future of Service Industries: (Anti)globalisation and Commensuration', *Service Industries Journal*, 31(1) (2011).

Mintzberg, H., Simons, R. and Basu, K., "Beyond Selfishness", *Sloan Management Review*, 44(1) (2002), pp. 67–74.

O'Leary, C. and Hannah, F.M., 'Are Students from Different Business Majors Predisposed to Different Ethical Sensitivities?', *Corporate Ownership and Control*, 6(1) (2008) 254–263.

Pless, N.M. and Maak, T., 'Responsible Leaders as Agents of World Benefit: Learnings from Project Ulysses', *Journal of Business Ethics*, 85 (2009) 59–71.

Polanyi, M., *The Tacit Dimension* (New York: Anchor Day, 1957).

Rappaport, A., *Creating Shareholder Value* (New York: The Free Press, 1998).

Schwitzgebel, E. and Rust, J. , 'The Moral Behaviour of Ethicists', *MIND*, 118 (2009) 1043–1059.

Smith, J., 'The Shareholder vs Stakeholder Debate', *MIT Sloan Management Review*, Summer (2003) 85–90.

The Economist, 24 April 2010, 65.

Tzu, S., *The Art of War*, translated by John Minford (London: Penguin Books Ltd, 500 BC/2002).

Van Liedekerke, L. and Dubbink, W., 'Twenty Years of European Business Ethics: Past Developments and Future Concerns', *Journal of Business Ethics*, 82(2) (2008) 273–280.

Van Liedekerke, L. and Dubbink, W., 'Banking in Crisis: towards a Responsible Organisation', *Ethik und Gessellschaft*, 2 (2009) 2–12.

Visser, W., 'Revisiting Carroll's CSR Pyramid: An African Perspective'. in Pedersen, E.R., and M. Huniche (eds), *Corporate Citizenship in Developing Countries* (Copenhagen: Copenhagen Business School Press, 2006), pp. 29–56.

Waldman, D.A. and Gavin, B.M., 'Alternative Perspective of Responsible Leadership', *Organisational Dynamics*, 37 (2008) 327–341.

Wolf, M. (2002), "A rescue plan for capitalism", Financial Times, 3 July.

Part I

Perspectives on the Nature of the Challenge

2
Corporate Psychopaths

Clive R.P. Boddy, Peter Galvin, and Richard K. Ladyshewsky

Introduction

As once-great companies are brought down by the misdeeds of their leaders, commentators on business ethics note that corporate scandals have assumed epidemic proportions. One writer on leadership goes as far as to say that modern society is suffering from a plague of bad leadership in both the private and public sectors (Allio, 2007). These commentators raise the intriguing question of how resourceful organisations end up with such poor leaders in the first place (Singh, 2008). Understanding the role of Corporate Psychopaths helps to answer this question. Psychopaths are people without a conscience who often end up in prison (Hare, 1999). They are one of the most studied of all people with personality disorders. A well-established, valid, and reliable method for identifying them exists, called the Psychopathy Checklist – Revised (PCL-R) (Hare, 1991; Hare at al., 1991). This checklist is used around the world, and has been called the 'gold standard' tool for identifying and assessing psychopathy (Edens, 2006; Mahmut et al., 2007; Edens et al., 2006).

Corporate Psychopaths are psychopaths who work in corporations. Were Corporate Psychopaths to end up in corporate leadership positions, this would be expected to cause very poor levels of ethical and other decision-making within corporations (Boddy, 2010a; Boddy, 2006). Recently, psychologists have come to understand that a type of psychopath exists who is not prone to violent, criminal behaviour and who therefore operates relatively undetected and successfully in society (Babiak and Hare, 2006; Board and Fritzon, 2005; Babiak, 1995; Levenson et al., 1995; Cooke et al., 2004). They have been called 'successful psychopaths' because they successfully evade contact with legal authorities. Some of these successful psychopaths work in corporations, and have been called Industrial Psychopaths, Organisational Psychopaths, Organisational Sociopaths, Corporate Psychopaths or Executive Psychopaths (Babiak, 1995; Boddy, 2006; Clarke, 2005; Babiak and Hare, 2006; Morse, 2004). Whatever they are called, these psychopathic individuals seem successful, particularly to those people who have not yet experienced the impact of their ruthlessness and lack of a conscience.

Few studies have been conducted into populations of these non-criminal or successful psychopaths (Mahmut et al., 2007). Calls for such studies have repeatedly been made. The aim of this chapter is to stimulate debate on this issue in academic circles, outside the disciplines of psychology and criminology, and to bring it to the attention of business and management academics. Because of the large-scale nature of the financial, environmental and human resources that many modern international corporations have at their disposal, many corporations are bigger in financial terms than nation-states are. Of the 100 largest economies in 2002, 50 per cent were corporations (Assadourian, 2005). Senior corporate managers, psychopathic or not, have the financial power and resources to make a major global impact on society, for good or ill.

Writers on business ethics have long been interested in the influence of ruthless leaders, such as 'Machiavellian managers' (Schepers, 2003; Singhapakdi, 1993; Buttery and Richter, 2005). It is evident that Corporate Psychopaths and Machiavellian managers share many common characteristics, together with some important differences (Paulhus and Williams, 2002; Jakobwitz and Egan, 2005; McHoskey et al., 1998). However, psychopathy is a much more developed and researched construct than Machiavellianism. Indeed, it is one of the most commonly studied constructs in psychology. For these reasons management researchers need to become more aware of it, particularly given the body of research highlighting the crucial role of business leaders in setting the ethical tone of the organisation (Klann, 2003; Jones and Millar, 2008); (Robbins, 2008; Thomas and Simerly, 1994). In terms of leadership research, bad leaders are said to be callously disregarding of the needs and wishes of other employees, and are prepared to lie, bully and cheat and to disregard or cause harm to the welfare of others (Perkel, 2005). All these traits are commonly associated with psychopathy. This is one reason why research into Corporate Psychopaths is important; it is a part of understanding bad corporate leadership and where it comes from.

The Origins of Psychopathy

Debate continues about the origins of psychopathy, but there is a growing tendency among psychologists to accept that brain structure, function, and chemical anomalies are associated with the syndrome of psychopathy (Weber et al., 2008). While a detailed treatment of these papers is beyond the remit of this chapter, it is important to note that if psychopathy is neurologically caused, this has implications for the ethics of how psychopaths should be treated (Boddy et al., 2010).

For the purpose of this discussion, Corporate Psychopaths are defined as those workplace employees who are perceived to exhibit a score of 13 or more (that is, 13 out of the total possible psychopathy score of 16) on the traits identified as psychopathic in the Psychopathy Measure – Management Research Version (Boddy, 2010b).

In terms of successful psychopaths like Corporate Psychopaths, researchers suggest that non-criminal psychopaths may have the same neuropsychological dysfunctions as criminal psychopaths, resulting in a similar lack of empathy. It has also been suggested that superior executive functioning in these non-criminal psychopaths may serve as a protective factor, decreasing their risk of being involved in illicit behaviour or detection (Mahmut et al., 2007). This superior executive functioning would be promoted by a good socio-economic family background, good education, and high intelligence, as might be formally suggested by research showing that high criminal psychopathy traits are strongly associated with the opposite of these factors, that is, low socio-economic status and poor early parental supervision (Farrington, 2005).

Corporate Psychopaths and Corporate Recruitment

Corporations are reported to want to recruit employees who are energetic, charming and fast-moving. Psychopaths can appear to be like this and can present themselves in a good light because of their ability to tell interesting stories about themselves and to present themselves as interesting and attractive people. Corporate Psychopaths are thus readily recruited into organisations because they make a distinctly positive impression when first met (Cleckley, 1988). They appear to be alert, friendly, and easy to get along with, and they look and dress like everybody else. They can be persuasive and fun to be around. They appear emotionally well adjusted and of good ability, and these traits make them attractive to those in charge of hiring staff within organisations (Walker, 2005; Hare, 1999). Corporate Psychopaths make those who interact with them think that the feelings of friendship and loyalty they evoke in others are reciprocated, and can present themselves as both likeable and personally attractive (Mahaffey and Marcus, 2006). Corporate Psychopaths also present the traits of intelligence and success that many people aspire to, and thus come across as accomplished and desirable employees (Ray and Ray, 1982).

Corporate Promotions and Corporate Psychopaths

Corporate Psychopaths are reportedly good at ingratiating themselves with people by telling them what they want to hear (Clarke, 2007). This facilitates their rise within corporations. Researchers have also found that the psychopathy traits of manipulativeness and cold-heartedness are the least discernible to others. This eases their rise through the ranks of management, giving them opportunities to exploit their positions for their own ends (Mahaffey and Marcus, 2006). As already mentioned, the personal charm of Corporate Psychopaths means that they come across well at interview and can inspire senior managers to have confidence in them (Ray and Ray, 1982). Being accomplished liars (Kirkman, 2005) can also help them in obtaining the jobs they want. Once inside an organisation Corporate Psychopaths can reportedly survive for a long time (Loizos, 2005) before being discovered, during which time they can establish defences for themselves to protect their positions. Babiak and others have argued that psychopaths tend to rise quickly through the ranks because of their manipulative charisma and their sheer, single-minded dedication to attaining senior levels of management. Once embedded in an organisation, the psychopath identifies a potential support network of patrons to help them get on, as well as identifying pawns they can sacrifice on the way (Babiak and Hare, 2006). Their polish and unemotional decisiveness can make them look like they may be ideal leaders (McCormick and Burch, 2005) who react coolly under pressure, and they use their intelligence and social skills to present a veneer of normalcy which enables them to get what they want (Selamat, 2004; Gettler, 2003). Thus it is evident that once they are in organisations, Corporate Psychopaths have the personal and social abilities to facilitate their rise within them to positions of senior management and leadership (Babiak and Hare, 2006).

Corporate Psychopaths and Bad Leadership

Leadership is often written about as if it were always admirable, positive, ethical, and good, but some commentators have pointed out that this ignores the dark side of leadership, where narcissistic self-aggrandisement and the pursuit of power for personal gain is evident. The results of this type of dark leadership are reported to be wasted resources, ruined careers, and organisational collapse (Clements and Washbrush, 1999). The dark side of business is said to include environmental degradation, corruption, fraud, financial misrepresentation, and harmful work practices, and to be driven by greed, impatience, and lust for power (Batra, 2007). It is interesting to note that these are all evident in the current global financial crisis.

Goldman points out that it only takes one bad leader to bring an organisation down. The mimicking and mirroring of organisational leaders' behaviour has been found in research into the toxic leadership of organisations (Goldman, 2006) and this means that the presence of Corporate Psychopaths within an organisation will have an insidious effect on the ethical decision-making of the whole organisation. Researchers have further found that the social and peer or leadership pressures within dishonest organisations push employees to fit in and to become dishonest themselves (Zyglidopoulous, 2008). Indeed, researchers working with neuroscientists looking at the functioning of the brain have found that some neurons mimic or mirror the same neurons in other people's brains, triggering empathetic actions and feelings (Goleman and Boyatzis, 2008). In this way followers can come to mirror the emotions and actions of their leaders at a subconscious level.

Corporate Psychopaths and Corporate Leadership

Given that Corporate Psychopaths seek leadership positions because of their desire to access prestige, power, control, and financial reward, they are inevitably attracted by senior corporate positions (Babiak and Hare, 2006; Clarke, 2007). Researchers have identified various organisational mechanisms that allow psychopaths to rise relatively unchallenged and unopposed within organisations (Pech and Slade, 2007). Although psychopaths only represent about 1 per cent of the general population, various commentators have speculated that because of their skills at manipulation they may be much more prevalent at more senior levels of organisational leadership (Ferrari, 2006; Hare, 1994; Hare, 1999; Pech and Slade, 2007). Empirical evidence for this is rare, but some evidence for this view comes from research at Surrey University in the United Kingdom by psychologists Board and Fritzon (2005). In a small study of senior British executives, researched via interviews and personality tests, the researchers found that these high-level British executives were as likely or even more likely to display Hare's psychopathic personality traits as were criminals (Board and Fritzon, 2005).

The hypothesis that the higher within an organisation one goes the more likely one is to find Corporate Psychopaths appears true from research conducted so far (Boddy, 2010b). For example, Hare and Babiak found that in a study of nearly 200 senior executives, 3.5 per cent of these were Corporate Psychopaths as measured by the Psychopathy Checklist – Screening Version (PCL-SV) (Babiak and Hare, 2006). One aim of the research reported on in this chapter was to build on the scant evidence currently available and to investigate whether Corporate Psychopaths are more likely to be found at senior levels of organisations than at junior levels.

Research Undertaken

A sample of 346 white-collar workers was drawn from a variety of professional and managerial associations. Respondents included members of chambers of commerce, members of charitable organisations, postgraduate business alumni, postgraduate business students, and members of other commercial organisations in Australia, in 2008. The sample was managerial or professional, of working age (aged 21–60) with 60.5 per cent aged over 40, and 53.8 per cent male. The majority (65 per cent) were from companies of over 100 employees from a variety of manufacturing, mining, cultural, financial services, and governmental sectors, and the majority (75.7 per cent) had more than 12 years of work experience. They were well educated, with 86 per cent holding at least a Bachelor's degree.

Because research demonstrates that lay people can recognise psychopathic behaviour in others, respondents answered questions concerning the behaviour of their managerial colleagues in a self-completion questionnaire. The use of a measure of psychopathic behaviours, the Psychopathy Measure – Management Research Version (PM-MRV) enabled the anonymous identification of managers within organisations as being Corporate Psychopaths or not, based on their score on the measure. This measure is a list of eight behaviours scored in terms of the behaviour being not displayed (scored as a 0), somewhat displayed (scored as a 1), or displayed (scored as a 2). In line with the usual scoring procedure, a total score of 13 or more was taken to indicate the presence of psychopathy. Of all respondents, according to the psychopathy definition used in this research, 32.1 per cent had worked with a manager who could be classed as a Corporate Psychopath and 5.75 per cent were currently working with such a manager. In the self-completion questionnaire, respondents could answer questions about more than one manager, and 572 responses were thus gathered from 346 respondents. Statistical tests were used to ensure the reliability of the instrument. The inter-item correlations for the construct of Corporate Psychopathy were all positive, meaning that the individual items relate well to each other, and that the construct of Corporate Psychopathy has good internal consistency and reliability. Using Cronbach's alpha as a measure of internal consistency, the figure for the Corporate Psychopathy construct looked very good. In terms of statistical reliability, alphas above 0.7 are commonly deemed acceptable (Norland, 1990). For the items in the psychopathy scale used, there was a very high alpha of 0.93 based on all responses.

Research Findings

The research found that respondents in more senior positions were more likely to have come across Corporate Psychopaths than their more junior counterparts. As shown in Table 2.1, 27.4 per cent of professional workers had come across a Corporate Psychopath, as compared with just 14.5 per cent of clerical/junior workers. Workers at both managerial and professional levels were significantly more likely to have come across Corporate Psychopaths than were clerical/junior workers.

The difference in proportions test for two proportions was applied to these percentages to test for significant difference. The percentages for

Table 2.1   Experience of Corporate Psychopaths and Seniority by Position

(Base = all responses)	Clerical/ Other Junior workers N = 54	Managerial workers N = 227	Professional workers N = 201
Have experienced Corporate Psychopaths in the workplace	14.8%	24.2%^	27.4%*

managerial workers were compared to those for clerical/junior workers, and the percentages for professional workers were compared to those for clerical/junior workers. A level of significant difference at the 90 per cent level of confidence (p<.10) is denoted by one star (*) in the accompanying tables. A level of significant difference at the 80 per cent level of confidence (p<.20) is denoted by (^) in the tables.

Respondents with more work experience were also more likely to have come across Corporate Psychopaths than those with less work experience. Of respondents with 12 or more years of work experience, 26.3 per cent identified a Corporate Psychopath in their work environment, compared to 16.4 per cent of those with only one to six years' work experience. As shown in Table 2.2, this was a statistically significant difference at a 90 per cent level of confidence.

Table 2.2 Experience of Corporate Psychopaths and Seniority by Years Worked

(Base=all responses)	1–6 years worked N=67	7–11 years worked N=49	12+years worked N=369
Have experienced Corporate Psychopaths in the workplace	16.4%	20.4%	26.3%*

While most of the sample collected was drawn from senior managers and professionals, with only a small number from lower-level employees for comparison, there was a significant difference between the levels of management measured and the presence of Corporate Psychopaths. The conclusion is therefore that Corporate Psychopaths do appear, in this research, to be more prevalent at a senior level, as has already been suggested in the literature. Further research could aim to look at this in a more robust manner by increasing the sample size of junior employees so that comparisons with senior employees can be more confidently made.

As an aside, the finding that Corporate Psychopaths are to be found at senior levels of corporate management has led to the development of the theory that the recent global financial crisis was caused by the actions of Corporate Psychopaths. This theory holds that Corporate Psychopaths in senior positions within financial corporations – able to influence the moral climate of the whole organisation and to yield considerable power – largely caused the crisis by their single-minded pursuit of their own self-enrichment and self-aggrandisement. This led to the complete abandonment of the concept of *noblesse oblige* or of any real notion of any type of social or societal responsibility. If this theory is correct, then the treatment of the symptoms of the financial crisis will have little effect because the root cause is not addressed. Indeed, the very same Corporate Psychopaths who arguably caused the crisis are now advising governments on how to get out of it, awarding themselves handsome bonuses for doing so.

The ethics of screening for corporate psychopathy

Recently, calls for the screening of immoral, dysfunctional, psychopathic, and bullying managers have been made in order to protect organisations and society from their effects (Singh, 2008; Spindel, 2008; Boddy, 2005). A management research tool for the identification of Corporate Psychopaths within organisations now exists, the Psychopathy Measure – Management Research Version (PM-MRV), as used in this research. Based on Hare's comments on the corporate aspects of the Psychopathy Checklist – Revised (the PCL-R) (Hare, 1991), the PM-MRV has been shown to have good levels of statistical reliability, internal and external validity, and face validity, for use in a managerial context (Boddy, 2010b). However, if, as has already been noted, psychopathy is neurologically caused, this has particular implications for the screening of Corporate Psychopathy.

As well as the ethics of screening, there are ethical issues in not protecting employees from Corporate Psychopaths. Clarke, in his book *Working with Monsters* (Clarke, 2005) describes the adverse effects Corporate Psychopaths can have on the people working around them, and he reminds employers that they have a duty of care to protect their workforce from harm. He argues that this should include providing protection from the effects of working with psychopaths, and this has obvious legal implications. Another writer has argued that the culprits for bad leadership are those who appoint bad leaders in the first place (Allio, 2007). In either case, there are ethical issues involved with both identifying and not identifying psychopaths in the workplace. As a precautionary note, Hare warns that even experts can be taken in by psychopaths, and that great care needs to be taken with identifying and dealing with them. Their total ruthlessness should be borne in mind at all times (Hare, 1999).

Ethical implications of corporate psychopathy

Multiple research evidence suggests that organisational members are influenced in their assessment of what is right and wrong by their leaders and superiors (Hegerty and Sims, 1978). If those superiors are incapable of moral reasoning and routinely make immoral decisions then such influence will logically be a malign one. Batory (2005) and his colleagues found that ethical practices were a positive function of top management, and if top management numbers Corporate Psychopaths in its ranks then the likelihood of it exhibiting ethical behaviour as an example to lower employees is reduced. Cui and Choudhury (2003) have recommended that companies should have a formal ethical review of business plans before they are put into place. They recommend that the review body should comprise both company executives and consumer representation. In the light of these findings, this suggestion may be considered a practical and morally desirable one.

The ethics of holding corporate psychopaths morally responsible

However, in terms of holding psychopaths morally responsible for their actions, philosophers are still debating the issue. Some say that psychopaths do not lack knowledge of what they are doing at the intellectual level and so can be held responsible, while others claim that their lack of choice in being psychopaths or not means they cannot be held responsible at a moral level (Matravers, 2008). The issue of whether psychopaths can be held wholly morally and legally responsible for their own actions is thus an issue that is yet to be fully resolved.

Currently, the consensus is that psychopaths know enough about what they are doing, particularly at a rational level, to be held responsible. They cannot therefore claim a defence of insanity for any of their actions (Glannon, 1997). Indeed, in one legal case in which the PCL-R was used to help determine a plea of insanity, a high score was used to try and show that the defendant was faking insanity rather than that he was insane (DeMatteo and Edens, 2006). However, psychologists argue that people are not as free to make moral choices as lawyers believe (Alwin et al., 2006).

There appears to be no clear evidence one way or the other in terms of whether psychopaths have lower moral reasoning skills than non-psychopaths (Blair et al., 1995), but while psychopaths may also be emotionally impaired, they do have free will (Benn, 2003), so the moral philosophers argue that psychopaths are indeed responsible for their own behaviour (Glannon, 1997).

Are corporate psychopaths a universal phenomenon?

There is little reason to believe that psychopathy is a geographically localised phenomena, although there is evidence that its manifestation is regulated by the type of culture in which the psychopath exists. A leading author on psychopaths argues that culture does influence the prevalence and behaviour of psychopaths (Stout, 2005a). She has argued that societies such as the United States that promote and idealise individualism allow the development of antisocial behaviour patterns. Further, these societies facilitate the disguising of such behaviour because it blends in with the accepted norms of society (Stout, 2005b; Stout, 2005a). Other researchers agree with this view, and claim that Western society is much more materialistic and competitive than it was in the past, which promotes psychopathic traits and Machiavellianism (Jakobwitz and Egan, 2005). Hare agrees with this view, saying that modern society values some of the traits associated with psychopathy, such as egocentricity, lack of concern for others, a manipulative approach, and superficiality. This makes it easy for psychopaths to blend in with society, and facilitates their entry into business organisations, politics, government, and other social structures (Hare, 1999).

If individualistic cultures are said to create competitiveness and a tendency to shallowness and selfishness, more collectivist cultures are said to suppress the overt expression of the antisocial aspects of psychopathy (Wernke and Huss, 2008; Cooke et al., 2005). Stout (2005) argues that cultures which promote the advancement of the group as a whole rather than individuals within it, and those which teach that all living things are interconnected, may provide stronger environmental constraints to the psychopath than more individualistic Western societies. Stout uses the example of Taiwan, a Confucian and Buddhist culture, and says that levels of antisocial personality disorder are far lower there (at up to 0.14 per cent) than they are in Western cultures. Hofstede has identified four major dimensions on which to classify country culture: individualism/collectivism, masculinity/femininity, power distance, and uncertainty avoidance (Hofstede, 1991; Hofstede, 2001; Hofstede, 1998), and researchers have called for further research into country culture and psychopathy to address the current lack of research in this area (Levenson et al., 1995).

In terms of differences in psychopathy among ethnic groups from the same culture, little has been specifically researched. However, in one meta-analysis of existing studies involving re-analysis of data that could be separated by ethnic group in 21 studies involving 8,890 people; it was found that blacks and whites in the USA do not meaningfully differ in their levels of psychopathy, as measured by the PCL-R (Skeem et al., 2004; Morana et al., 2005; Harris et al., 2007).

In Japan, researchers have found evidence that supports the generalisability of the relationship between psychopathy and hypo-arousal in reaction to an emotionally evocative stimulus (Osumi et al., 2007) indicating that the possible neurological correlates of psychopathy are common across cultures. In Singapore recent research found that there was a neuroaffective processing deficit among criminal psychopaths in a prison sample, again indicating that the possible neurological correlates of psychopathy are common across cultures (Howard and McCullagh, 2007).

Research in Sweden among sub-clinical psychopaths replicated a US study and found that aberrant self-promotion, a sub-clinical form of psychopathy, was found in Sweden as well as in the United States, but that Swedish subjects scored lower on measures of narcissism than US subjects did (Pethman and Erlandsson, 2002). While country and culture are not strictly synonymous (Lenartowicz et al., 2003), the researchers speculate that these findings arise because the Swedish ideal person is highly altruistic whereas the US ideal person is more assertive and tough, and that these cultural factors have an influence on the expression of psychopathy (Pethman and Erlandsson, 2002).

However, researchers tend to agree that there are no compelling reasons to expect psychopathy to differ widely across cultures (Hobson and Shine, 1998). Indeed Hare's PCL-R has reportedly been used successfully in Canada, the United States, the United Kingdom, New Zealand, Australia, Belgium, the Netherlands, Denmark, Sweden, Norway, China, Hong Kong, Finland, and Germany, and was recently translated for use in Brazil (Morana et al., 2005).

It therefore appears that Corporate Psychopaths are a universal phenomenon, but that behavioural manifestations of the syndrome may well be modified by cultural influences at the country or even corporate cultural level.

Conclusions

According to the empirical data collected in this survey, Corporate Psychopaths are more commonly encountered at more senior levels of an organisation than at more junior levels. This finding corresponds with the hypothetical view of leading researchers into psychopathy that Corporate Psychopaths are better equipped to rise up the hierarchy within organisations and attain senior positions there. The finding implies that Corporate Psychopaths, people without conscience, are in charge of huge corporate resources, and that they will not necessarily use those resources for the good of anyone but themselves. This has led to the development of the Corporate Psychopaths Theory of the Global Financial Crisis, which is worthy of further investigation and research.

According to Hare, who is probably the world's leading expert on psychopaths, if society cannot identify psychopaths then it is forever doomed to be their victim (Hare, 1994).

Psychopaths are able to succeed in corporations largely because their colleagues are unaware that these totally ruthless and uncaring people with no conscience actually exist (Deutschman, 2005). Creating an awareness among organisational managers that psychopaths exist is thus a good first step in attempting to stem the destruction that these people cause in organisations (Clarke, 2005). The Psychopathy Measure – Management Research Version (PM-MRV) can be used to identify when psychopathy is present in corporate management. Various ethical issues are raised by this (Boddy et al., 2010).

In terms of whether they are a global phenomenon, psychopaths do appear to be universal in occurrence but they may well be limited in their possible actions in more collectivist societies. The global spread of Western, individualistically oriented corporations, which operate without such collectivist limitations, may therefore pose a threat to countries where they operate. Further research could investigate ways in which organisations can ethically and effectively screen for such psychopathic behaviours. Qualitative research could also investigate the impact of Corporate Psychopaths on other employees, and strategies for dealing with them in the workplace.

Note

Acknowledgment, with thanks: this chapter draws upon material used in my paper in *Journal of Public Affairs*, 2010, and is published by permission of John Wiley & Sons Ltd (Leaders without ethics in global business: Corporate psychopaths; by C. R. P. Boddy, R. Ladyshewsky and P. Galvin, *Journal of Public Affairs*, 10(3), Copyright © 2010, John Wiley & Sons Ltd).

Bibliography

Allio, R.J., 'Bad leaders: How They Get That Way and What to Do about Them', *Strategy and Leadership*, 35(3) (2007) 12–17.

Alwin, N., Blackburn, R., Davidson, K., Hilton, M., Logan, C., and Shine, J., *Understanding Personality Disorder: A Report by the British Psychological Society* (Leicester: The British Psychological Society, 2006).

Assadourian, E., 'When Good Corporations Go Bad', *World Watch*, 18 (2005) 16–19.

Babiak, P. and Hare, R.D., *Snakes in Suits When Psychopaths Go To Work* (New York: HarperCollinsPublishers, 2006).

Babiak, P., 'When Psychopaths go to Work: A Case Study of an Industrial Psychopath', *Applied Psychology*, 44(2) (1995) 171–188.

Batory, S.S., Neese, W. and Heineman, A., 'Ethical Marketing Practices: An Investigation of Antecedents, Innovativeness and Business Performance', *The Journal of American Academy of Business*, 2(March) (2005), pp. 135–142.

Batra, M.M., 'The Dark Side of International Business', *Competition Forum*, 5(1) (2007) 306–314.

Benn, P., 'The Responsibility Of The Psychopathic Offender: Commentary on Ciocchetti', *Philosophy, Psychiatry and Psychology*, 10(2) (2003) 189–192.

Blair, R.J.R., Jones, L., Clark, F., and Smith, M., 'Is The Psychopath "Morally Insane"?', *Personality and Individual Differences*, 19(5) (1995) 741–752.

Board, B.J. and Fritzon, K., 'Disordered Personalities at Work', *Psychology, Crime and Law*, 11(1) (2005) 17–32.

Boddy, C.R. 'Corporate Psychopaths and Productivity', *Management Services*, Spring (2010a) 26–30.

Boddy, C.R., 'The Dark Side of Management Decisions: Organisational Psychopaths', *Management Decision*, 44(9/10) (2006) 1461–1475.

Boddy, C.R., 'The Implications of Corporate Psychopaths for Business and Society: An Initial Examination and A Call To Arms', *Australasian Journal of Business and Behavioural Sciences*, 1(2) (2005) 30–40.

Boddy, C.R., Corporate Psychopaths in Australian Workplaces: Their Influence on Organizational Outcomes (Sydney: Curtin University of Technology, 2010b).

Boddy, C.R., Galvin, P.G., and Ladyshewsky, R., 'Leaders without Ethics in Global Business: Corporate Psychopaths', *Journal of Public Affairs*, 10(3) (2010).

Boddy, C.R., Ladyshewsky, R., and Galvin, P.G., 'The Influence of Corporate Psychopaths on Corporate Social Responsibility and Organizational Commitment to Employees', *Journal of Business Ethics* (forthcoming).

Buttery, A. and Richter, E., 'Machiavellian Machinations: A Way through Crisis Management?', *Australasian Business and Behavioural Sciences Association Conference* (Cairns: Australasian Business and Behavioural Sciences Association, 2005).

Clarke, J., *The Pocket Psycho* (Sydney: Random House Australia, 2007).

Clarke, J., Working with Monsters: How to Identify and Protect Yourself from the Workplace Psychopath (Sydney: Random House, 2005).

Cleckley, H., *The Mask of Sanity*, 5th edn, Private Printing for Educational Use (Augusta Georgia: Emily Cleckley, 1988) (First published by C.V. Mosley Co., 1941).

Clements, C. and Washbrush, J.B., 'The Two Faces of Leadership: Considering the Dark Side of Leader-follower Dynamics', *Journal of Workplace Learning*, 11(5) (1999) 170–176.

Cooke, D.J., Michie, C., Hart, S.D., and Clark, D., 'Assessing Psychopathy in the UK: Concerns about Cross-cultural Generalisability', *British Journal of Psychiatry*, 186 (2005) 335–341.

Cooke, D.J., Michie, C., Hart, S.D. and Clark, D., 'Reconstructing Psychopathy: Clarifying the Significance of Antisocial Behaviour in the Diagnosis of Psychopathic Personality Disorder', *Journal of Personality Disorders*, 18 (2004) 337–357.

Cui, G. and Choudhury, P., 'Consumer Interests and the Ethical Implications of Marketing: A Contingency Theory', *The Journal of Consumer Affairs*, 37(2) (2003), pp. 364–387.

DeMatteo, D. and Edens, J.F., 'The Role and Relevance of The Psychopathy Checklist-Revised in Court: A Case Law Survey of U.S. Courts (1991–2004)', *Psychology, Public Policy, and Law*, 12(2) (2006) 214–241.

Deutschman, A., 'Is Your Boss A Psychopath?', *Fast Company*, 96 (2005) 44–51.

Edens, J.F., 'Unresolved Controversies Concerning Psychopathy: Implications for Clinical and Forensic Decision Making', *Professional Psychology: Research and Practice*, 37(1) (2006) 59–65.

Edens, J.F., Marcus, D., Lilienfeld, S.O., and Poythress, N.G., 'Psychopathic, Not Psychopath: Taxometric Evidence for the Dimensional Structure of Psychopathy', *Journal of Abnormal Psychology*, 115(1) (2006) 131–144.

Farrington, D.P., 'The Importance of Child and Adolescent Psychopathy', *Journal of Abnormal Child Psychology*, 33(4) (2005), pp. 489–497.

Ferrari, P., 'Rotten at the Top: What's Really Going on? Can you say Sociopath?: Why do Bad Leaders happen to Good Firms? Two Observers offer their Theories', *The Atlanta Journal: Constitution*, 1 October (2006) B1.

Gettler, L., *Psychopath in a Suit* (Accessed online on 13 February 2006 (2003), at 4.44pm, www.theage.com.au/articles/2003/02/20/1045638423969.html).

Glannon, V.V., 'Psychopathy and Responsibility', *Journal of Applied Philosophy*, 14(3) (1997) 263–275.

Goldman, A., 'Personality Disorders in Leaders: Implications of the DSM IV-TR in Assessing Dysfunctional Organisations', *Journal of Managerial Psychology*, 21(5) (2006) 393–414.

Goleman, D. and Boyatzis, R., 'Social Intelligence and the Biology of Leadership', *Harvard Business Review*, 86(9) (2008) 96–104.

Hare, R.D., Hart, S.D., and Harpur, T.J., 'Psychopathy and the DSM-IV Criteria for Antisocial Personality Disorder', *Journal of Abnormal Psychology*, 100(3) (1991) 391–398.

Hare, R., 'Predators: The Disturbing World of the Psychopaths Among Us', *Psychology Today*, 27(1) (1994) 54–61.

Hare, R., *The Hare Psychopathy Checklist Revised* (New York and Ontario: Multi-Health Systems Inc., 1991).

Hare, R., Without Conscience: the Disturbing Word of the Psychopaths Among Us (New York: Guildford Press, 1999).

Harris, G.T., Rice, M.E., Hilton, Z., Lalumiere, M.L., and Quinsey, V.L., 'Coercive and Precocious Sexuality as a Fundamental Aspect of Psychopathy', *Journal of Personality Disorders*, 21(1) (2007) 1–27.

Hegerty, W.H. and Sims, H.P., 'Some Determinants of Unethical Decision Behaviour: An Experiment', *Journal of Applied Psychology*, 63 (1978) 451–457.

Hobson, J. and Shine, J., 'Measurement of Psychopathy in a UK Prison Population Referred for Long Term Psychotherapy', *The British Journal of Criminology*, 38(3) (1998) 504–515.

Hofstede, G., 'A Case for Comparing Apples with Oranges: International Differences in Values' *International Journal of Comparative Sociology*, 39(1) (1998) 16–31.

Hofstede, G., *Cultural Consequences*, 2nd edn (Thousand Oaks, California: Sage, 2001).

Hofstede, G., *Cultures and Organizations: Software of the Mind* (Maidenhead: McGraw-Hill, 1991) .

Howard, R. and McCullagh, P., 'Neuroaffective Processing in Criminal Psychopaths: Brain Event-related Potentials Reveal Task-Specific Anomalies', *Journal of Personality Disorders*, 21(3) (2007) 322–339.

Jakobwitz, S. and Egan, V. 'The Dark Triad and Normal Personality Traits', *Personality and Individual Differences*, 40 (2005) 331–339.

Jones, M. and Millar, C. 'Call for Papers. Special Issue on: Global Leadership, Global Ethics.' *Journal of Business Ethics*, 85(2) (2008) 107–108.

Kirkman, C.A., 'From Soap Opera to Science: Towards Gaining Access to the Psychopaths who live Amongst Us', *Psychology and Psychotherapy*, 78 (2005) 379–396.

Klann, G., 'Character Study: Strengthening the Heart of Good Leadership', *Leadership in Action*, 23(3) (2003) 3–7.

Lenartowicz, T., Johnson, J.P., and White, C.T., 'The Neglect of Intracountry Cultural Variation in International Management Research', *Journal of Business Research*, 56 (2003) 999–1008.

Levenson, M.R., Kiehl. K.A., and Fitzpatrick, C.M., 'Assessing Psychopathic Attributes in a Noninstitutionalized Population', *Journal of Personality and Social Psychology*, 68(1) (1995) 151–158.

Loizos, C., 'Is my Partner a Sociopath or just Obnoxious?' *Venture Capital Journal*, 1 November (2005) 1.

Mahaffey, K.J. and Marcus, D.K., 'Interpersonal Perception of Psychopathy: A Social Relations Analysis', *Journal of Social and Clinical Psychology*, 25(1) (2006) 53–74.

Mahmut, M.K., Homewood, J. and Stevenson, R.J., 'The Characteristics of Non-criminals with High Psychopathy Traits: Are they Similar to Criminal Psychopaths?', *Journal of Research in Personality*, 42 (2007) 679–692.

Matravers, M., 'Holding Psychopaths Responsible', *Philosophy, Psychiatry and Psychology*, 14(2) (2008) 139–142.

McCormick, I. and Burch, G., 'Corporate Behaviour; Snakes in Suits: Fear and Loathing in Corporate Clothing; They're Glib, Charming, Deceitful and Ruthless; They've been described as "snakes in suits" – and they're in an office near you', *New Zealand Management*, November (2005) 34.

McHoskey, J.W., Worzel, W., and Szyarto, C., 'Machiavellianism and Psychopathy', *Journal of Personality and Social Psychology*, 74(1) (1998) 192–210.

Morana, H.C. P., Arboleda-Florez, J., and Camara, F.P., 'Identifying the Cutoff Score for the PCL-R Scale (Psychopathy Checklist Revised) in a Brazilian Forensic Population', *Forensic Science International*,147 (2005) 1–8.

Morse, G., 'Executive Psychopaths', *Harvard Business Review*, Oct. (2004) 20–22.

Norland, E.V.T., '*Controlling Error in Evaluation Instruments*', [www.joe.org] (1990) (11 April).

Osumi, T., Shimazaki, H., Imai, A., Sugiura, Y., and Ohira, H., 'Psychopathic Traits and Cardiovascular Responses to Emotional Stimuli', *Personality and Individual Differences*, 2 (2007) 1391–1402.

Paulhus, D.L. and Williams, K.M., 'The Dark Triad of Personality: Narcissism, Machiavellianism, and Psychopathy', *Journal of Research in Personality*, 36 (2002) 556–563.

Pech, R.J. and Slade, B.W., 'Organisational Sociopaths: Rarely Challenged, often Promoted. Why?' *Society and Business Review*, 2(3) (2007) 254–269.

Perkel, S.E., 'Book Review: Bad Leadership: What it is, How it Happens, Why it Matters (by Barbara Kellerman)', *Consulting to Management*, 16 (2005) 59–61.

Pethman, T.M. and Erlandsson, S.I., 'Aberrant Self-Promotion or Subclinical Psychopathy in A Swedish General Population', *The Psychological Record*, 52 (2002) 33–50.

Ray, J. and Ray, J., 'Some Apparent Advantages of Subclinical Psychopathy', *The Journal of Social Psychology*, 117 (1982) 135–142.

Robbins, F., 'Why Corporate Social Responsibility should be Popularised but not Imposed', *Corporate Governance*, 8(3) (2008) 330–341.

Schepers, D.H., 'Machiavellianism, Profit, and the Dimensions of Ethical Judgment: A Study of Impact', *Journal of Business Ethics*, 42 (2003) 339–352.

Selamat, F., 'He's the Office Psycho', *The New Paper*, Singapore, 30 August (2004).

Singh, J., 'Impostors Masquerading as Leaders: Can the Contagion be Contained?' *Journal of Business Ethics*, 82(3) (2008) 733–745.

Singhapakdi, A., 'Ethical Perceptions of Marketers: The Interaction Effects of Machiavellianism and Organisational Ethical Culture', *Journal of Business Ethics*, 12 (1993) 407–418.

Skeem, J.L., Edens, J.F., Camp, J., and Colwell, L.H., 'Are There Ethnic Differences in Levels of Psychopathy? A Meta-analysis', *Law and Human Behaviour*, 28(5) (2004) 505–527.

Spindel, P., 'How not to hire a Bully', *Canadian HR Reporter*, 21 (2008) 26.

Stout, M., 'The Ice People: Living Among Us Are People With No Conscience, No Emotions And No Conception of Love: Welcome To The Chilling World Of The Sociopath', *Psychology Today*, January/February (2005a) 72–76.

Stout, M., *The Sociopath Next Door* (New York: Broadway Books, 2005b).

Thomas, A.S. and Simerly, R.L., 'The Chief Executive Officer and Corporate Social Performance: An Interdisciplinary Examination', *Journal of Business Ethics*, 13(12) (1994) 959–968.

Walker, I., *Pychopaths in Suits,* Australian Broadcasting Corporation. Accessed online at: www.abc.net.au/rn/talks/bbing/stories/s1265568.htm on 11 September (2005), 7.18pm.

Weber, S., Habel, U., Amunts, K. and Schneider, F., 'Structural Brain Abnormalities in Psychopaths: a Review', *Behavioral Sciences and the Law*, 26(1) (2008) 7–28.

Wernke, M.R. and Huss, M.T., 'An Alternative Explanation for Cross-cultural Differences in the Expression of Psychopathy', *Aggression and Violent Behaviour*, 13 (2008) 229–236.

Zyglidopoulous, S.C., 'Lies, Lies and more Lies', *White Paper, Cambridge University*. Accessed online on 22 September 2008, at (2008) 4.57pm, Western Australian time, at www.jbs.cam.ac.uk/news/research_focus/whitepapers database.

3
CEOs and Corporate Social Performance

Mikko Manner

Introduction

> Profits are sought and achieved within a particular set of social norms ... If society moves toward norms of social responsibility as it is now doing, then the businessman is subtly and inevitably guided by these same norms
>
> (Davis, 1973:315).

Many authors would agree with Davis (Freeman, 1984; McWilliams and Siegel, 2000; Margolis and Walsh, 2001; Bansal, 2005; Mahoney and Thorne, 2005; Waldman and Siegel, 2008). This suggests that Friedman's (1970) famous prescription, that in simply obeying the law a company satisfies their social responsibility, is insufficient. As a result, it is becoming increasingly important to understand the causes and motivations behind different approaches to corporate social responsibility. Although corporate social responsibility and social performance are not always synonymous with ethical and moral leadership, the strong correlation between these constructs is widely recognised (Swanson, 2008:231). Indeed, Berenbeim suggests that 'most of the world does not distinguish between Corporate Ethics and Corporate Social Responsibility when it comes to determining what it means for a company to be ethical' (Berenbeim, 2006:501). Rather than focusing on an elaborate theoretical justification of this perspective, this chapter embraces this perspective in its methods and interpretation of findings.

The breadth of possible definitions for the term corporate social responsibility (CSR) requires any discussion to explicitly clarify the definition being used (McWilliams et al., 2006). For these purposes, CSR will be defined as: 'actions that appear to further some social good, beyond the interests of the firm and that which is required by law' (McWilliams and Siegel, 2001:117). The term CSR is often used to describe both the conceptual social responsibilities of companies *and* the measurement of a company's performance related to CSR. This chapter will follow Wood (1991), in referring to the measurement of CSR initiatives and outcomes as corporate social performance (CSP).

While there is a growing body of research examining the differences between strongly and poorly socially performing firms, these studies typically treat the firm itself as the agent or object of observation (Hemingway and Maclagan, 2004). However, as the opening quote by Davis suggests, it is the leaders of these firms who ultimately decide upon the strategic approach to take regarding social issues. Waldman and Siegel (2008) suggest that this omission of the leadership dimension is pervasive and problematic, because studies that ignore the role of leadership in CSR may 'yield imprecise conclusions regarding the antecedents and consequences of these activities' (Waldman and Siegel, 2008:117). This study addresses this issue by using upper echelon theory, and the KLD Research Analytics CSP ratings, to show that observable CEO characteristics predict differences in corporate social performance between firms, even when firm and industry characteristics are controlled.

This chapter presents the findings from a sample of 650 public firms from the United States. It argues that exemplary/proactive CSP, as measured by the strengths categories of KLD ratings, is positively related to the CEO having a Bachelor's degree in humanities, having a breadth of career experience and being female. It also argues that exemplary/proactive CSP is negatively related to the CEO having a Bachelor's degree in economics and to their level of short-term compensation. Preliminary tests of causality support the assertion that these effects reflect CEO discretion rather than being an artifact of reverse causality. Further, the findings do not suggest any significant relationship between CEO characteristics and poor social performance as measured by the concerns categories of KLD ratings. This suggests that CEOs may have more discretion in influencing strong and exemplary social performance than in impacting poor CSP.

Theoretical framework and existing research

The assessment or measurement of a company's efforts and outcomes around corporate social responsibility will be described here as corporate social performance (CSP). Wood (1991) defines a framework for analysing CSP that splits the construct into: 1) *principles* of corporate social responsibility that define behaviour; 2) *processes* of corporate social responsiveness that define the management of these principles; and 3) the *measurement of outcomes* in terms of social impacts of corporate behaviour, programmes and policies. Wood suggests that evaluating the principles of CSR requires analysis at the institutional, organisational, and individual level, emphasising that principles motivate human and organisational behaviour. Although not the first framework for analysing CSP (Carroll, 1979; Sethi, 1979), it is perhaps the most influential and frequently applied, and is the most directly related to this project given its focus on the role of individual decision makers.

This analysis is also grounded in stakeholder and upper echelon theory. Stakeholder theory was popularised by Freeman (1984), with a seminal book in which he began 'to construct an approach to management which takes the external environment into account in a systematic and routine way' (Freeman, 1984:247). Stakeholder theory provides a logical way to examine issues related to corporate social performance, and is extensively used to frame such issues in the strategic management literature (Davis et al., 1997; McWilliams and Siegel, 2000; Waddock and Graves, 1997). Upper echelon theory was developed by Hambrick and Mason (1984), as a framework to synthesise previous works from different disciplines concerning the characteristics of a firm's top managers (Dearborn and Simon, 1958; Cyert and March, 1963 [1992]). The theory states that organisational outcomes are viewed as 'reflections of the values and cognitive bases of powerful actors in the organisation', because their cognitive biases and personal values act as screens or filters in ways that influence their strategic choices and firm outcomes (Hambrick and Mason, 1984:193). In the context of this study, Hambrick and Mason further suggest that demographic and other observable characteristics of executives (age, functional experience, education, and so on) can often be used as indicators of their cognitive and value-based filters. The hypotheses in this study about how the CEO impacts CSP are grounded in this theoretical framework, which has since been validated by studies on a wide range of performance metrics in a wide range of business settings (Hambrick, 2007; Carpenter et al., 2004).

Hypotheses

Managerial discretion and CSP

Although many studies have focused on an aggregate measure of CSP, McGuire et al. (2003) find that the different motivations in play impact the degree to which a company engages in exemplary CSP as compared to the extent to which they avoid poor CSP. Specifically, they conclude that 'strong social performance may be primarily driven by managerial beliefs' (McGuire et al., 2003:349). This idea is incorporated in the current study as the following general hypothesis:

Hypothesis 1: The relationship between CEO characteristics and CSP will be stronger for positive or exemplary CSP than for the avoidance of poor CSP.

The idea that CEOs might have more discretion in some domains than in others is described by Lieberson and O'Connor (1972), and expanded by Hambrick and Finkelstein (1987) as the theory of managerial discretion. Hambrick and Finkelstein suggest that firm leaders are likely to have more discretion in a domain where it is less obvious what *means* should be used to accomplish superior financial *ends*. This logic seems to support the current hypothesis, as the impact of avoiding poor CSP often relates to cost avoidance, which is generally easier to estimate than would be the financial benefit to the firm of exemplary CSP. For example, the risk of violating existing government regulations (or attracting new ones), and the risk of lawsuits and consumer/media backlash, may be primary drivers for avoiding poor CSP. In contrast, it seems likely that there will be more 'room' for discretion – and thus for the cognitive biases and behavioural beliefs of the CEO – in exemplary or progressive CSP. This is because of the challenge in quantifying the benefit of such initiatives, as, for example, a work/life balance programme.

Educational field of study

Hypothesis 2: A firm's level of CSP will be negatively associated with the CEO having a Bachelor's degree in economics, and positively associated with the CEO having a Bachelor's degree in humanities or the social sciences.

Hambrick and Mason (1984:200) suggest that the amount and type of education contains 'rich but complex information' concerning an individual. The argument that education shapes values and behavioural beliefs is supported by Frank et al. (1993a). They found that, after taking just one semester of micro-economics, students responded less honestly to ethical dilemma questions, and were less likely to cooperate or to expect others to cooperate than before having taken the class. This effect was shown to be more pronounced in classes where the economics professor placed more emphasis on the self-interest model. Many other studies have similarly found that economics students in particular are less likely to cooperate than students in other fields (Boone et al., 1999; Kahneman et al., 1986; Marwell and Ames, 1981; Frank and Schultz, 2000; Selten and Ockenfels, 1998; Jones et al., 1990). The possibility that an economics education promotes a concomitant lack of emphasis on CSP is supported by Arce (2004:261). He finds that discussions of ethics and social responsibility are 'conspicuous by their absence' from most managerial economics textbooks despite the importance of these issues to managerial decision-making.

Although this experimental evidence relates to economics, it seems possible that someone majoring in either humanities or a social science other than economics will be less inclined to focus exclusively on profits and self-interest, and/or to have more 'optimistic' beliefs as to the cooperative nature of others. In support of this, Rivera and De Leon (2005) find that the participation of Costa Rican hotels in 'beyond compliance' environmental certification programmes is positively related to the CEO having a Bachelor's degree in humanities.[1] Similarly, Davis et al. (1997) argue that psychology and sociology are grounded in models of human behaviour that recognise the existence of cooperative behaviours, so studying these might be expected to enhance a desire and ability to satisfy non-shareholder, stakeholder needs. However, there seems to be conflicting evidence concerning the possible impact of an MBA on CSP preferences. Although a hypothesis is not advanced for an MBA degree (and an undergraduate degree in business), both will be included as variables in the analysis.

Functional work experience

Hypothesis 3: A firm's level of CSP will be positively associated with the breadth of stakeholder functional experience of the CEO.

Dearborn and Simon (1958) found that company executives generally identify the main issue in a business case from the perspective of the department they are in, despite being instructed to consider the case from the standpoint of the CEO. They describe this form of information simplification as 'selective perception'. March and Simon (1991) propose that ideas that don't match the decision maker's frame of reference are filtered out or reinterpreted. They note that the selective exposure that occurs within company departments creates and reinforces these biases.

To analyse functional experience, many upper echelon studies use Hambrick and Mason's (1984) classification scheme which splits work experience into output and throughput functions. However, in developing a cognitive frame that enhances the ability to recognise the business case for CSP, breadth of functional experience may be even more beneficial than experience in any one stakeholder area. The greater the scope of stakeholder functional experience an executive obtains prior to becoming CEO, the greater will be their ability *to see* the business case for a range of CSR initiatives (or, conversely, the less likely they will be to filter the business case out due to a lack of direct exposure to a particular stakeholder group). Functions are divided based on the degree to which they generally focus on shareholders, other stakeholders or both.[2] It is expected that CSP is more positively related to stakeholder experience than to either of the other functional groups. This is based on the learning and biasing that is likely to occur in stakeholder functions concerning the needs and desires of stakeholder groups (Hambrick and Finkelstein, 1987).

Gender

Hypothesis 4: Having a female CEO will be positively related to the level of CSP engaged in by the firm.

Carpenter et al. (2004) suggest that gender is a characteristic that needs more focus in upper echelon research. In addition, gender seems to be a relevant characteristic to test relative to CSP, given that many of the same studies that find economics students less cooperative also find gender differences (Frank et al., 1993a; Selten and Ockenfels, 1998).

CEO compensation

Hypothesis 5: A firm's level of CSP will be negatively associated with the CEO's level of compensation.

The hypothesis for CEO compensation is related predominantly to the notion that a relatively low versus a relatively high level of compensation (with firm size, profitability, and industry held constant) might itself represent a form of poor CSP and a lack of focus on social issues (McGuire et al., 2003). Advancing this hypothesis for compensation is complicated by the fact that, unlike the other CEO characteristics, the level and composition of CEO compensation contains motivational issues that may directly impact the CEO's decision-making concerning CSP. Although McGuire et al. (2003) found that both salary and long-term compensation were 'positively' related to KLD concerns (that is, higher salaries related to poor CSP), they found no relationship between either short or long-term compensation and proactive CSP. While this finding does not conflict with the hypothesis of a negative relationship between CSP and compensation, it does suggest that the general hypothesis that relationships between CEO characteristics and CSP will be more significant for proactive than for poor CSP may not hold for compensation.

Methodology

Sample and data sources

The sample of companies and CEOs for this study is derived from the population of roughly 3,000 firms rated by KLD in 2006 (see below), based on the availability of data concerning CEO characteristics and firm finances. The source for firm financial data is S and P's Compustat. S and P's ExecuComp database is the source for CEO gender, compensation, and CEO tenure. Hambrick and Mason (1984) suggest that there are varying 'lag times' for strategic initiatives implemented by management to manifest or become apparent. For this study, the CEO needed to have been appointed in 2004 or earlier to be eligible for sample selection. Data availability combined with this criterion resulted in a final sample of 650 CEOs and firms.

Dependent variable: CSP

Although many proxies have been used to represent CSP in academic empirical studies, none has received as much recent attention as the KLD Analytics, Inc ratings. KLD, formerly known as Kinder, Lydenberg and Domini and Company, is a research firm that rates companies on a number of CSP indicators in seven major areas: community, diversity, employee relations, natural environment, human rights, product, and corporate governance. Each major area contains a set of 'strength' and 'concern' ratings. The strength ratings are often used to represent exemplary CSP, and the concern ratings poor CSP (McGuire et al., 2003; Mahoney and Thorne, 2004; Walls, 2007). Many of the academic studies that use KLD ratings as a proxy for CSP aggregate individual scores into one net CSP measure by subtracting concerns from strengths (Thomas and Simerly, 1995; Sharfman, 1996; Graves and Waddock,

1994; Waddock and Graves, 1997; Griffin and Mahon, 1997; Waldman et Al., 2006a). To test the hypothesis that the relationship between CEO characteristics and CSP is stronger for engagement in exemplary CSP (KLD strengths), separate dependent variables for the sum of strengths and the sum of concerns will be used.

The KLD ratings are based on broad reviews of company information including annual reports, 10Ks, proxy statements, quarterly reports, CSR reports, newspapers, business press and trade magazines, academic journals, regional EPA newsletters, and annual questionnaires to company Investor Relations departments on CSP issues (Waddock and Graves, 1997). Although the KLD ratings have been criticised by some as being inappropriate for empirical academic work (Entine, 2003), many prominent CSP researchers disagree (Waddock and Graves, 1997; Sharfman, 1996), with Waddock (2003:369) arguing that the KLD ratings have become 'the de facto research standard at the moment'. The ratings cover a broad and consistent range of important CSP attributes and a large sample of companies (Waddock and Graves, 1997; Etzion, 2007).

Independent variables of interest: CEO characteristics

Educational field(s) of study and functional career experience

Sources used include the *D&B Reference Book of Corporate Management*, *Who's Who in Finance and Industry, Fortune, Business Week*, and a number of other online sources such as Hoover's Online (from Dun and Bradstreet), Standard and Poor's Net Advantage, company Web pages, SEC filings, company press releases, and major newspaper and business periodical articles. The specific degrees included in the analysis are: undergraduate majors in humanities, economics, non-economics social sciences, and business and the MBA degree. Although hypotheses for degrees in engineering and other technical areas could be developed, significant results were not found for these educational fields when included. Given this, these educational fields are now excluded to avoid the introduction of multi-collinearity issues.

To test the hypothesis that the breadth of stakeholder functional career experience is positively related to CSP, measures for both breadth and specialisation of experience are included. Breadth of experience is coded as three count variables representing the number of different: a) shareholder and general management/neutral; b) stakeholder; and c) total functions (sum of a and b) in which the CEO has spent time.[3] In defining the variables this way, one can test whether breadth of functional experience is related to CSP in general, and if the effect is different for functions focused on non-shareholder stakeholders. Variables related to

specialisation in shareholder, neutral/general management, and stakeholder functions are also defined.

Gender

An indicator variable is used for gender (1 for female and 0 for male).

CEO compensation

CEO compensation is measured as the natural log of the CEO's 2006
compensation, separated into short-term compensation and long-term
compensation. Short-term compensation represents current salary and
short-term bonus, and long-term compensation represents the value of
stock options and the value of other long-term incentives.

Control variables: firm characteristics

The control variables included in this study are: industry, firm size,
financial performance, risk (leverage), and growth. These variables have
been found to be associated with the level of CSR, the characteristics
of the executives that are appointed CEO, or both. Industry is defined
as a categorical variable using two and three-digit NAICS code, similar
to Chatterji et al. (2008). Firm size is most typically measured as the
natural log transformation of either total sales or total assets in CSP
studies. The natural log of sales is used in the current study. Financial
performance is defined as ROI from 2002 to 2006, and risk is defined
as debt to total assets. Growth in the form of percentage increase in
sales between 2004 and 2006 is included to account for the theorised
impact of rapid growth, both on managerial discretion (Hambrick and
Finkelstein, 1987), and on CEO selection (Hambrick and Mason, 1984).

Statistical estimation technique: regression

Regression analysis is the primary statistical technique used in this
study. In order to reflect the different distribution characteristics of
each dependent variable, the specific regression models used are negative binomial regression for the sum of KLD strengths, poisson regression for the sum of KLD concerns, and ordinary least squares (OLS) for
net KLD (strengths–concerns).[4]

Analysis of results

Summary statistics and correlations are presented in Table 3.1, with statistically significant correlations indicated at the 1 per cent and 5 per
cent levels. Many of the control and CEO characteristics are highly

correlated with KLD strengths (strong CSP) and concerns (poor CSP). Tables 3.2 and 3.3 contain the regression results for specifications run on KLD strengths (strong CSP) and KLD concerns (poor CSP) respectively. The functional experience variables are introduced in separate models to facilitate both the analysis of their incremental effects, and to avoid multi-collinearity problems arising from the inclusion of combinations of these related and highly correlated variables. Each of the firm controls are significantly related to positive CSP (Table 3.2), or poor CSP (Table 3.3), but size and industry are the only firm characteristics significantly associated with both.[5]

One thing that becomes evident when broadly examining the CEO characteristics results is that, while many CEO characteristics are significantly related to strong social performance (Table 3.2), none are significantly related to poor CSP (Table 3.3). This supports Hypothesis 1.[6] That the CEO having a Bachelor's degree in economics is negatively and significantly related to strong or proactive CSP supports Hypothesis 2 for economics. Hypothesis 2 is also strongly supported for a degree in humanities, which is significantly and positively related to strong CSP in each model specification. When examined together, the results support Hypothesis 3 that breadth of experience, particularly stakeholder experience, is positively related to exemplary or proactive CSP, whereas specialised experience is not. The only breadth of experience variable not to show a significant relationship with strong CSP is the breadth of shareholder and general management/neutral experience variable (model 5).

Having a female CEO is positively and significantly related to proactive CSP, which supports Hypothesis 4, although the strength of this finding needs to be tempered by the fact that a very small proportion of CEOs in the sample are female (3 per cent), and that having a female CEO increases the company's KLD diversity score. However, re-running the regressions after removing the female CEO/Board diversity category still produced positive and highly significant results for gender and strong CSP (significances between 0.001 and 0.004).

Hypothesis 5 is supported for short-term CEO compensation but not for long-term compensation. This is consistent with the notion that high compensation is indicative of a lack of focus on CSP and may itself be a form of poor CSP. It should be noted that McGuire et al. (2003) reach a different conclusion. They find compensation to be significantly and 'positively' related to poor CSP but do not find significant results between compensation and strong CSP. Differences in the samples and the KLD rating categories included may explain this divergence. Space prevents this being further explored here.

Table 3.1   Correlations and Summary Statistics

	1	2	3	4	5	6	7	8	9
1 KLD strengths	1								
2 KLD concerns	0.43**	1							
3 KLD net	0.43*	−0.43**	1						
4 Size	0.59*	0.59**	0.04	1					
5 Risk (Leverage)	−0.03	0.14*	−0.14**	0.08*	1				
6 Financial performance	0.10*	0.01	0.10**	0.18**	−0.22**	1			
7 Firm growth	−0.14*	−0.14*	0.04	−0.13**	−0.09*	0.00	1		
8 Bachelor's in Humanities[a]	0.18**	0.02	0.10*	0.04	0*−0	0.15*	−0.02	1	
9 Bachelor's in Social Science[b]	−0.02	−0.02	0_2−0	0.01	0.09*	−0.06	−0.06	−0.07	1
10 Bachelor's in Economics	−0.03	0.09*−0	−0.03	0.07	−0.01	0.05	−0.05	−0.09*	−0.04
11 Bachelor's in Business	−0.24*	−0.06	−0.04	−0.02	0.03	0.01	−0.04	−0.24**	−0.13**
12 MBA degree	0.07	0.05	0.03	0.09*	0.08	0.02	0.01	0.01	0.00
13 Gender (1 = female)	0.16*	−0.03	0.11*	−0.07	0.03	0.01	0.02−0	0.16**	−0.01
14 Short-term compenation	0.29*	0.29**	−0.06	0.44**	0.44**	0.05	−0.16*	0.01	0.05
15 Long-term compensation	0.29**	0.56*	−0.02	0.56**	0.12*	0.07	−0.08	0.06	0.06
16 Specialised: Shareholder[c]	−0.08*	−0.04	−0.04	−0.03	0.29**	−0.01	−0.02	−0.11**	0.01
17 Specialised: Neutral/General[d]	−0.09*	−0.09*	−0.02	−0.06	0.03	0.04−0	0.03	0.09*	0.06
18 Specialised: Stakeholder[e]	0.02	0.02	0.020	−0.03	−0.07	0.020	0.1	−0.04	−0.05
19 Breadth of shareholder/Neutral[f]	0.05	0.06	0.050	0.11*	−0.02	0.06	50.16*	0.03	0.03
20 Breadth of stakeholder[g]	0.19**	0.10**	0.10*	0.10*	−0.05	00.08*	0.10	0.29**	0.02
21 Breadth of all functions[h]	0.20**	0.14**	0.18*	0.10*	−0.06	−0.02	−0.09	0.09*	0.04
*p<0.05									
**p<0.01									
Mean	2.16	2.65	−0.50	22.1	23.0	6.5	0.62	0.130	0.17
Std Dev	2.62	2.26	2.63	1.7	18.2	16.8	0.77	0.30	0.25
Min	0	0	−9	17.6	0	−180	−0.43	0	0
Max	19	15	11	28.0	105	89.0	6.23	1	1

[a] Languages, literature, history, philosophy, religion, visual and performing arts

[b] Anthropology, communication studies, criminology, geography, political science, psychology, and sociology

[c] Has spent over 75 per cent of 'pre-CEO' career time in 'shareholder' functions (finance or accounting)

[d] Has spent over 75 per cent of 'pre-CEO' career time in 'general/neutral' functions (CEO/ president, general manager, law)

10	11	12	13	14	15	16	17	18	19	20	21
1											
−0.26**	1										
0.09*	0.00	1									
0.05	−0.02	−0.08*	1								
0.08*	−0.05	0.08*	−0.06	1							
0.030	−0.04	0.12*	−0.03	0.56**	1						
−0.01	0.29**	0.07	−0.06	−0.05	−0.05	1					
0.03	−0.05	−0.06	−0.05	0.04	−0.03	−0.17**	1				
−0.10*	−0.20*	−0.02	0.11	−0.05	−0.04	−0.20**	−0.23**	1			
0.05	0.11**	0.04	−0.03	0.03	0.11**	0.11*	0.05	−0.47**	1		
−0.11**	−0.22**	0.03	0.29**	0.06	0.05	−0.29**	−0.41**	0.37**	−0.29**	1	
70.5	−0.06	0.06	0.05	0.07	0.14**	70.14**	70.14**	−0.07	0.14**	0.62**	1
3.814	0.4	0.21	0.03	13.8	14.7	0.13	0.17	0.21	1.67	1.04	2.72
0.35	0.48	0.49	0.16	0.7	1.7	0.34	0.37	0.41	0.84	0.88	1.03
0	0	0	0	7.5	6.7	0	0	0	0	0	1
1	1	1	1	17.3	18.7	1	1	1	5	5	6

[e] Has spent over 75 per cent 'pre-CEO' career time in 'stakeholder' functions (marketing/sales, operations, R and D, HR, public relations, medical/education/govt service)
[f] Total number of different shareholder or general/neutral functions where any time was spent
[g] Total number of different stakeholder functions where any time was spent
[h] Total number of different functions (any: shareholder, stakeholder, neutral/general) where any time was spent

Table 3.2 Full Sample Regressions on Strong CSP
Method: Negative Binomial

Firm control variables	Model 1	Model 2	Model 3	Model 4	Model 5	Model 6	Model 7
Firm size	0.416***	0.459***	0.458***	0.459***	0.457***	0.452***	0.457***
	(0.000)	(0.000)	(0.000)	(0.000)	(0.000)	(0.000)	(0.000)
Risk (Leverage)	-0.006*	-0.007**	-0.007**	-0.007**	-0.007**	-0.007**	-0.007*
	(0.019)	(0.005)	(0.006)	(0.005)	(0.005)	(0.005)	(0.005)
Financial performance	0.002	0.001	0.001	0.001	0.001	0.001	0.001
	(0.503)	(0.828)	(0.818)	(0.818)	(0.666)	(0.683)	(0.666)
Firm growth	-0.025	-0.045	-0.044	-0.045	-0.045-0	-0.044	-0.036
	(0.595)	(0.347)	(0.357)	(0.344)	(0.396)	(0.352)	(0.344)
Industry	included	included	included	included	included	included	included
CEO characteristics							
Bachelor's in Humanities[a]		0.265*	0.273*	0.257*	0.252*	0.251*	0.225+
		(0.034)	(0.028)	(0.041)	(0.046)	(0.046)	(0.077)
Bachelor's in Non-Eco Social Sciences[b]		-0.020	-0.015	-0.029	-0.036	-0.018	-0.042
		(0.893)	(0.921)	(0.844)	(0.844)	(0.844)	(0.770)
Bachelor's in Economics		-0.300**	-0.292**	-0.313**	-0.315**	-0.266*	-0.292**
		(0.004)	(0.004)	(0.003)	(0.003)	(0.012)	(0.005)
Bachelor's in Business		-0.106	-0.110	-0.119	-0.124	-0.079	-0.105
		(0.221)	(0.198)	(0.165)	(0.143)	(0.352)	(0.198)
MBA		0.103	0.099	0.103	0.102	0.087	0.088
		(0.156)	(0.172)	(0.154)	(0.172)	(0.226)	(0.218)
Gender (female = 1)		0.968***	0.962***	0.992***	0.974***	0.974***	0.936***
		(0.000)	(0.000)	(0.000)	(0.000)	(0.000)	(0.000)
Short-term compensation		-0.092*	-0.090*	-0.093*	-0.089*	-0.097*	-0.091*
		(0.041)	(0.047)	(0.039)	(0.047)	(0.029)	(0.039)

	Model 1						
Long-term compensation		−0.028 (0.356)	−0.028 (0.366)	−0.028 (0.366)	−0.030 (0.316)	−0.025 (0.408)	−0.030 (0.408)
Functional specialisation: Shareholder[c]		−0.025 (0.857)					
Functional specialisation: General/Neutral[c]			−0.051 (0.648)				
Functional specialisation: Stakeholder[c]				−0.063 (0.481)			
Functional breadth: Shareholder/Neutral[d]					0.049 (0.253)		
Functional breadth: Stakeholder[e]						0.091* (0.033)	
Functional breadth: All functions[f]							0.090** (0.009)
N		650	650	650	650	650	650
OLS adjusted R-squared	0.365	0.414	0.415	0.415	0.415	0.420	0.421
g Improvement in adj. R-sq over model 1		0.049	0.050	0.050	0.050	0.055	0.056

p-values in parentheses   + p<0.10   * p<0.05   ** p<0.01   *** p<0.001

*Dependent variable: KLD strengths

a Languages, literature, history, philosophy, religion, visual and performing arts

b Anthropology, communication studies, criminology, geography, political science, psychology, and sociology

c Has spent over 75 per cent of 'pre-CEO' career in the respective shareholder, general management/neutral or stakeholder functions

d Total number of different shareholder or neutral/general functions where any time was spent

e Total number of different stakeholder functions where any time was spent

f Total number of different functions (any: shareholder, stakeholder, neutral/general where any time was spent

g Adjusted R-squared results taken from comparable model specifications run using OLS regression

Table 3.3 Full Sample Regressions on Poor CSP
Method: Poisson

Firm Control Variables	Model 1	Model 2	Model 3	Model 4	Model 5	Model 6	Model 7
Firm size	0.315***	0.298***	0.294***	0.297***	0.297***	0.297***	0.295***
	(0.000)	(0.000)	(0.000)	(0.000)	(0.000)	(0.000)	(0.000)
Risk (Leverage)	0.002	0.002	0.002	0.002	0.002	0.002	0.002
	(0.179)	(0.255)	(0.239)	(0.246)	(0.239)	(0.246)	(0.239)
Financial performance	-0.005*	-0.005*	-0.005*	-0.005*	-0.005*	-0.005*	-0.005*
	(0.019)	(0.009)	(0.012)	(0.008)	(0.008)	(0.012)	(0.009)
Firm growth	-0.124***	-0.126***	-0.125***	-0.127***	-0.124***	-0.125***	-0.126***
	(0.001)	(0.001)	(0.001)	(0.001)	(0.001)	(0.001)	(0.001)
Industry	included	included	included	included	included	included	included
CEO characteristics							
Bachelor's in Humanities[a]		-0.080	-0.068	-0.071	-0.081	-0.081	-0.087
		(0.350)	(0.433)	(0.404)	(0.342)	(0.342)	(0.312)
Bachelor's in Non-Eco Social Sciences[b]		-0.126	-0.129	-0.124	-0.129	-0.125	-0.129
		(0.181)	(0.231)	(0.188)	(0.168)	(0.168)	(0.168)
Bachelor's in Economics		-0.077	-0.068	-0.070	-0.082	-0.068	-0.075
		(0.270)	(0.327)	(0.319)	(0.248)	(0.336)	(0.248)
Bachelor's in Business		-0.059	-0.062	-0.058	-0.06	-0.055	-0.062
		(0.299)	(0.252)	(0.291)	(0.230)	(0.315)	(0.291)
MBA		0.000	-0.009	-0.002	-0.001	-0.005	-0.005
		(0.996)	(0.848)	(0.969)	(0.975)	(0.915)	(0.921)
Gender (female = 1)		0.130	0.114	0.115	0.133	0.120	0.126
		(0.427)	(0.498)	(0.480)	(0.418)	(0.418)	(0.454)

	Model 1						
Short-term compensation		0.028 (0.429)	0.034 (0.341)	0.031 (0.392)	0.029 (0.412)	0.028 (0.429)	0.029 (0.392)
Long-term compensation		0.024 (0.190)	0.026 (0.160)	0.025 (0.172)	0.024 (0.189)	0.025 (0.174)	0.024 (0.195)
Functional specialisation: Shareholder[c]		−0.028 (0.707)					
Functional specialisation: General/Neutral[c]			−0.099 (0.131)				
Functional specialisation: Stakeholder[c]				0.041 (0.476)			
Functional breadth: Shareholder/Neutral[d]					0.008 (0.801)		
Functional breadth: Stakeholder[e]						0.022 (0.407)	
Functional breadth: All functions[f]							0.020 (0.366)
N		650	650	650	650	650	650
OLS adjusted R-squared [g] Improvement in adj. R-sq over model 1	0.411	0.407–0.004	0.409–0.002	0.407–0.004	0.407–0.004	0.407–0.004	0.407–0.004
p-values in parentheses		+ $p<0.10$	* $p<0.05$	** $p<0.01$	*** $p<0.001$		

*Dependent variable: KLD concerns

[a] Languages, literature, history, philosophy, religion, visual and performing arts

[b] Anthropology, communication studies, criminology, geography, political science, psychology, and sociology

[c] Has spent over 75 per cent of 'pre-CEO' career in the respective shareholder, general management/neutral or stakeholder functions

[d] Total number of different shareholder or neutral/general functions where any time was spent

[e] Total number of different stakeholder functions where any time was spent

[f] Total number of different functions (any: shareholder, stakeholder, neutral/genera l) where any time was spent

[g] Adjusted R-squared results taken from comparable model specifications run using OLS regression

Robustness Analysis: Causality and R and D Intensity

Hambrick (2007) suggests that issues related to causality are rarely examined but that they are critical, given that the testing of CEO characteristics is often directly related to the selection of the CEO, thus creating the possibility of positive results caused by reverse causality. Barker and Mueller (2002), based on theories from Hambrick and Fukutomi (1991) and results from Miller et al. (1982), use sub-sample analysis based on CEO tenure in an attempt to draw some 'tentative' conclusions on the issue of causality. They conclude that, where these relationships became stronger with increasing CEO tenure, it provided tentative evidence that CEO personality was influencing strategy-related variables over time (Barker and Mueller, 2002:795).

For the current study, the regressions were redone with three sub-samples of CEOs split evenly into three groups based on their tenure as CEO. The results showed that adding the CEO characteristics to the regressions produce incremental increases in adjusted R-squared over four times larger for CEOs in the medium and high-tenure groups (7.3 and 7.7 points respectively) than those in the low-tenured groups (1.7 points). This provides tentative support for the conclusion that CEO discretion and cognitive filters, signalled by these characteristics, contribute to the significant results in the full sample. The lack of significant, incremental predictive power of CEO characteristics beyond the medium-tenure group may relate to research showing that CEOs often make fewer changes as their tenures increase beyond a certain point (Barker and Mueller, 2002; Hambrick and Fukutomi, 1991; Hambrick, 2007).

McWilliams and Siegel (2000:605) suggest that, since research and development (R and D) has been theoretically and empirically shown to be positively related to firm financial performance, and that 'many aspects of CSR create either a product innovation, a process innovation or both', omitted variable bias may result if R and D is not included in CSP studies. They go on to find that the positive, significant relationship found by Graves and Waddock (1997) between CSP and corporate financial performance disappeared when R and D intensity was included in a similar model specification.[7] Although the theoretical relationship between R and D and financial performance highlighted by McWilliams and Siegel (2000) does not relate to the relationship between CSP and CEO characteristics being tested in the current study, the robustness of the results was confirmed using the sub-sample of firms that report R and D expense in Compustat.[8] Despite the smaller sample size, the inclusion of R and D intensity does not reduce the size of the significant results for CEO characteristics found for the full sample. While the significance of the education, gender, and compensation variables stay about the same, breadth of functional experience becomes an even stronger predictor of strong CSP in the sub-sample when R and D intensity is included. It can therefore be concluded that the significant results for CEO characteristics and strong CSP in this study do not appear to be the result of omitted variable bias from the exclusion of R and D intensity.

Discussion

The results from this study suggest that CSP is one of those strategic issues where the characteristics of the CEO can be used to predict organisational outcomes. In determining the power of those characteristics, support is also found for the theory of managerial discretion as a key moderating factor, both with respect to tenure and to strong versus poor CSP. Tentative support is also found for the notion that discretion increases with a CEO's tenure. The decision to engage in proactive and exemplary CSP is found to be much more strongly influenced by the characteristics of the CEO than the decision to avoid poor CSP. The implications of these results seem far-reaching. Hambrick and Mason (1984) suggest that executive characteristics should be used to influence management selection and development. Similarly, Datta and Guthrie (1994) suggest that HR executives should be more involved in CEO selection to make sure issues of 'fit' between the individual and position are sufficiently considered. The results here suggest that a company wanting to appoint a CEO who is adept at envisioning the business case for CSR should find a candidate with a greater breadth of functional career experience, particularly in those functional areas that focus extensively on stakeholders. As discussed above, the significant positive relationship between exemplary/proactive CSP and gender must be tempered because of sampling issues. Similarly, the significant negative relationship between short-term compensation and exemplary/proactive CSP must be reconciled with prior findings before definitive conclusions are drawn.

Although tests of causality using sub-sample analysis were performed, the incorporation of longitudinal data could be used elsewhere to address this issue more directly. Even if the conclusions from the preliminary tests of causality are accepted, this study has not tested whether the negative relationship between exemplary/proactive CSP and the CEO having a Bachelor's degree in economics is related to an 'indoctrination effect' from exposure to the self-interest model from traditional economic theory (Frank et al., 1993a), a 'self-selection effect' for those choosing to study economics (Frey et al., 1993), or a combination of both of these effects. Prior empirical research is split on this issue, and any causality inferences from these results do not reach far enough back in time. The positive relationship between CSP and a CEO having a Bachelor's degree in humanities similarly does not shed light on the indoctrination vs self-selection question. However, if an educational indoctrination effect is at work, then the implications seem profound, particularly for the teaching of economics in a world increasingly embracing CSR and expecting CSP. Although research into behavioural and experimental economics is doing much to moderate the model of human behaviour away from the *Homo economicus* caricature, results such as those from Arce (2004:261) that find discussions of ethics and CSR 'conspicuous by their absence' in economics textbooks demonstrate that the frontier of theory is slow to reach the classroom.

Given the US nature of this sample, the conclusions cannot be assumed to hold for CEOs with an economics degree in other parts of the world. While there may be geographical differences in the extent to which an economics education focuses on self-regarding models of human behaviour, the results from Frank et al. (1993a) support the hypothesis that a lack of focus on *Homo economicus* and the neoclassical model might reduce or eliminate the negative relationship between CSP and an education in economics. Thus, while there are many seemingly fruitful directions for future research, conducting similar studies in other countries may be among the most beneficial.

One key challenge to conducting similar studies in other countries is the identification of an appropriate proxy measure for CSP. Although Mahoney and Thorne (2005) use a set of multi-dimensional ratings similar to KLD to analyse compensation impacts in Canada, similar ratings do not appear to be available in most parts of the world, particularly ratings that reach across many countries. In a preliminary analysis, a positive relationship was found between strong CSP, as rated by KLD, and 2006 membership of the UN Global Compact and the World Business Council for Sustainable Development. Other possibilities include the Global Reporting Initiative (GRI), which provides guidance and standards for sustainability reporting now used by over 1,200 companies throughout the world.[9] As regards environmental performance specifically, the work of Bracke et al. (2007) in testing which firm characteristics are related to the EU Eco-Management and Audit Scheme could be extended to include leader characteristics, including CEO education and whether they have a degree in economics.

Some authors have suggested that an MBA and an undergraduate degree in business reinforce the same types of self-regarding preferences and behavioural beliefs (Pfeffer, 2005; Kuhn, 1998). Ghoshal et al. (1999:10) argue that the main reason corporate managers often rank at the bottom of polls on professional ethical standards is because of 'the deeply unrealistic, pessimistic assumptions about the nature of individuals and corporations that underlie current management doctrine'. The current study suggests that economics may be at least somewhat more extreme in this regard, as neither an MBA nor an undergraduate business degree is significantly related to CSP at a conventional level. Indeed, the possession of an MBA degree shows a positive relationship to proactive CSP that comes close to the significance threshold. One possible reason for this difference is highlighted by Jones (1995) who suggests that many MBA degree programmes have begun to embrace the propositions of instrumental stakeholder theory. Even while suggesting that more effective ethics education approaches are needed, Kuhn (1998) notes that ethics courses have become much more commonplace in MBA programmes. It seems reasonable to suggest that a management curriculum might adjust more quickly to the CSR trend than might economics, which often seems invested in holding on to the models of equilibrium which require the rigid assumptions of *Homo economicus* for their tractability (Gowdy, 2005; Bromley, 1990).

Conclusion

While the implications of these results are far-reaching, this conclusion will focus most heavily upon the implications for economics education. This study suggests that the negative relationship between proactive CSP and an education in economics may at least partially relate to the self-regarding assumptions of standard economic theory and the general lack of discussion of ethics and CSR in economics texts (Arce, 2004).

McPhail (2001:282) calls for more ethics education for accounting students to help 'engender a sense of moral commitment toward other individuals'. He suggests that the existing 'ethics-neutral' accounting practices are strongly influenced by neo-classical market economics, highlighting the fact that an economics education, at least in the United States, is likely even more removed from any such moral commitment.

In parallel with this call to ground accounting in an emotional commitment to others through the inclusion of ethics in the curriculum, the findings in this study suggest that the incorporation of ethical content into an economics education would ultimately facilitate more proactive CSP. While this study has used only US data, further research would demonstrate the extent to which this argument holds true more generally across the globe.

Many economists might view encouraging students and future firm leaders to develop a moral commitment to others as a purely normative argument that promotes the sacrificing of profits for social performance. However, an article by Waldman and Siegel (2008) highlights that the issue might be strategic as well. The article is organised as a sequence of four letters written back and forth between the two authors. The question debated is whether it is appropriate or inappropriate for top-level managers within companies to incorporate their personal moral values into decisions concerning CSR. Siegel is 'nervous' (Waldman and Siegel, 2008:118) when leaders make decisions partially directed by their moral beliefs, due to his being 'a purist when it comes to the fiduciary responsibilities of top-level managers'. He believes that decisions are more likely to be profit maximising if they are made in the 'cold and calculating' way described by *Homo economicus*. Waldman responds that there should be more concern with leaders who 'lack a strong moral compass' (Waldman and Siegel 2008:121). In defense of this position, he suggests that the Sarbanes-Oxley legislation was 'necessitated by a system in which firms are remiss (or potentially remiss) in policing themselves in terms of social responsibility and ethical behaviour' (Waldman and Siegel, 2008:122). Waldman's argument in favour of morally grounded leadership seems to be based less on the normative belief that it is the right thing to do (although this belief also seems evident), and more on the belief that being authentically responsible may often produce better results in the long run (Waldman and Siegel, 2008:123). The empirical study in the current paper does not measure the use, or lack of use, of a moral compass in the CSP decisions of the CEO. However, the results are consistent with the conclusion that the possibility of a profitability advantage of such a perspective is not likely to be taught in most US economics classes.[10]

Notes

1. Although they do not find significant results for Hotel CEOs with social science degrees, economics is not treated separately in that study.

2. Shareholder functions: Groups whose focus is generally directed toward financial returns to the shareholders of the company. This is defined to include the Finance and Accounting functions. Stakeholder functions: Groups whose focus is more directly related to meeting the needs of non-shareholder stakeholders. These functions include human resources (employees), public relations (community), marketing and sales (customer), operations and R and D ('product'/customer). In addition to these functions that are identifiable to a specific stakeholder group, military experience and 'other' experience (medicine, education, and government service) are also classified as stakeholder functions. This is due to the general lack of focus on financial performance and shareholder type groups in favour of service to other constituencies while employed in these roles. General management/'neutral' functions: Groups that generally split their focus more evenly between shareholder and stakeholder groups such that they may be expected to have a more neutral perspective on CSP. These functions often direct both stakeholder and shareholder functions, and often also have responsibility for overall financial performance of the area under their supervision. This category includes prior experience as a CEO, president and lower-level general management positions. Legal functional experience is also included in this category, as someone in this role will likely need to address risks related to both stakeholder and shareholder groups.

3. For example, if an executive's career included assignments in marketing, finance, human resources and CEO of another company, the breadth variables would be coded as: a) shareholder/general: 2 (finance and CEO); b) stakeholder: 2 (marketing and human resources); and c) total functions: 4.

4. CSP studies using a net KLD score (that can be a positive or negative value) typically use ordinary least squares (OLS) regression. However, the sum of KLD strengths and sum of KLD concerns only take on non-negative integer values. Although Stock and Watson (2007:420) suggest that OLS can also be used for such non-negative count data, they note that other methods, such as negative binomial regression and poisson regression, are specifically designed for this type of distribution and can overcome the shortcoming of nonsense (e.g. negative) predicted values that are possible when using OLS. Cameron and Travedi (1998) suggest that negative binomial regression is appropriate where there is significant over-dispersion (variance greater than the mean) in a count dependent variable whereas poisson regression is appropriate where not. Walls et al. (2008:18) use negative binomial regression for their measure of environmental performance that is also a count variable with properties very similar to the KLD data (range: 0 to 12, mean: 4.83, and standard deviation: 3.81). Chatterji et al. (2008) used both poisson regression and negative binomial regression for various specifications when using KLD count-dependent variables. The methods here are selected based on Cameron and Travedi's (1998) and STATA's tests for over-dispersion. Although the negative binomial and poisson regression models better reflect the distributional characteristics of the strength and concern scores, they have the shortcoming of not including an accurate 'goodness of fit' measure comparable to R-square. As the results are often qualitatively similar, many published studies use OLS, presumably to take advantage of this post-estimation measure and for easier interpretation of

regression coefficients. The regressions on strong CSP (KLD strengths) and poor CSP (KLD concerns) are also re-run for the current study using OLS, producing the same signs on all coefficients and very similar levels of statistical significance. As a result, the R-squared results from the OLS regressions are added to the bottom of the main regression tables for post-estimation analysis purposes.

5. Although industry in aggregate is highly significant in each specification, the results for the 24 included industry indicator variables is suppressed for readability given the lack of focus on the individual industry effects in this study.

6. Regressions for each KLD strength and KLD concern model from Tables 3.2 and 3.3 were also run using ordinary least squares (OLS) regression with similar results. The OLS adjusted R-squares from these regressions are included at the bottom of Tables 3.2 and 3.3 to assess the incremental predictive power of the CEO characteristics over the model with only firm controls (Barker and Mueller, 2002; Waldman et al., 2006a). While the adjusted R-squared for strong social performance improves by 4.9 to 5.6 points when CEO characteristics were added, it actually decreases slightly for poor CSP. These results again support the hypothesis that CEO characteristics are generally more strongly related to proactive than to poor social performance.

7. Despite the significant results found by McWilliams and Siegel (2000), most subsequent studies examining the impact of CSP on financial performance have not included R and D expense. This omission is likely due to data availability issues. A large percentage of the firms with financial information in the S and P Compustat database do not report a separate line item for R and D expense. Of the 650 firms in the current sample almost half (43 per cent) did not report R and D expense in 2006. In addition to dramatically reducing the size of the sample, including these variables also significantly alters the industry composition of the sample biasing it toward manufacturing companies and other firms for which R and D is a significant expense. This reduces the extent to which the results may be generalised and virtually eliminates many sectors of the economy from the analysis.

8. Due to space constraints and a desire to avoid confusion from including too much data, detailed output from the sub-sample of firms reporting R and D expense is not reported.

9. GRI: Sustainability Reporting Guidelines 2000–2006. Version 3. Amsterdam, The Netherlands.

10. It is interesting to note that the educational backgrounds of the authors seem consistent with the educational differences suggested here. While Siegel's PhD is in Economics, Waldman's is in Industrial and Organisational Psychology.

Bibliography

Arce, M.D.G., 'Conspicuous by Its Absence: Ethics and Managerial Economics', *Journal of Business Ethics*, 54 (2004) 261–277.

Bansal, P., 'Evolving Sustainably: A Longitudinal Study of Corporate Sustainable Development', *Strategic Management Journal*, 26 (2005) 197–218.

Barker II, V.L. and Mueller, G.C., 'CEO Characteristics and Firm RandD Spending', *Management Science*, 48(6) (2002) 782–801.

Berenbeim, R.E., 'Business Ethics and Corporate Social Responsibility', *Vital Speeches of theDay*, 72 (16/17) (2006) 501–503.

Berman, S.L., Wicks, A.C., Kotha, S. and Jones, T.M., 'Does Stakeholder Orientation Matter? The Relationship between Stakeholder Management Models and Firm Financial Performance', *Academy of Management Journal*, 42(5) (1999) 488–506.

Boone, C., de Brabander, B. and van Witteloostuijin, A., 'The Impact of Personality on Behavior in Five Prisoner's Dilemma Games', *Journal of Economic Psychology*, 20 (1999) 343–377.

Bracke, R., Verbeke, T. and Dejonckheere, V. 'What Distinguishes EMAS Participants? An Exploration of Company Characteristics', Working Paper No. 37 presented at FEEM (2007). Available at SSRN: http://ssrn.com/abstract=981131.

Bromley, D., 'The Ideology of Efficiency: Searching for a Theory of Policy Analysis', *Journal of Environmental Economic Management*, 19 (1990) 86–107.

Cameron, A.C. and Travedi, P.K., *Regression Analysis of Count Data* (Cambridge, UK: Cambridge University Press, 1998).

Carpenter, M. A., Geletkanycz, M. A. and Sanders, Wm. G., 'Upper Echelons Research Revisited: Antecedents, Elements and Consequences of Top Management Team Composition', *Journal of Management*, 30(6) (2004) 749–778.

Carroll, A.B., 'A Three-dimensional Conceptual Model of Corporate Social Performance', *Academy of Management Review*, 4 (1979) 497–505.

Carter, J.R. and Irons, M.D., 'Are Economists Different, and If So, Why?', *Journal of Economic Perspectives*, 5(2) (1991) 171–177.

Chatterji, A.K., Levine, D.I. and Toffel, M.W., 'How Well Do Social Ratings Actually Measure Corporate Social Responsibility?', *Journal of Economics & Management Strategy*, 18(1) (2009) 125–169.

Cyert, R.M. and March, J.G., *A Behavioral Theory of the Firm* (Cambridge, MA: Blackwell Publishers, 1963 (1992)).

Datta, D.K. and Guthrie, J.P., 'Executive Succession: Organizational Antecedents of CEO Characteristics', *Strategic Management Journal*, 15(7) (1994) 569–577.

Davis, J.H., Schoorman, F.D., and Donaldson, L., 'Toward A Stewardship Theory of Management', *Academy of Management Review*, 22(1) (1997) pp. 20–47.

Davis, K., 'The Case for and against Business Assumption of Social Responsibilities', *Academy of Management Journal*, 16 (1973) 312–322.

Dearborn, D.C. and Simon, H.A., 'Selective Perception: A Note on the Departmental Identification of Executives', *Sociometry*, 21(2) (1958) 140–144.

Etzion, D., 'Research on Organizations and the Natural Environment, 1992 – Present: A Review', *Journal of Management*, 33(4) (2007) 637–664.

Frank, B. and Schultz, G.G., 'Does Economics Make Citizens Corrupt?', *Journal of Economic Behavior and Organization*, 43 (2000) 101–113.

Frank, R.H., Gilovich, T. and Regan, D.T., 'Does Studying Economics Inhibit Cooperation', *The Journal of Economic Perspectives*, 7(2) (1993a) 159–171.

Frank, R., Robert, H., Gilovich, T. and Regan, D.T., 'The Evolution of One-shot Cooperation', *Ethology and Sociobiology*, 14 (1993b) 247–256.

Freeman, E.R., *Strategic Management: A Stakeholder Perspective* (Massachusetts and London: Pitman Publishing Inc., 1984).

Frey, B.S., Pommerehne W.W. and Gygi, B., 'Economics Indoctrination or Selection? Some Empirical Results', *Journal of Economics Education*, (1993) 271–279.

Friedman, M., 'The Social Responsibility of Business is to Increase its Profits', *New York Times Magazine*, September 13 (1970) 122–126.

Ghoshal, S., Bartlett, C.A. and Moran, P., 'A New Manifesto for Management', *Sloan Management Review*, 40 (1999) 9–20.

Gowdy, J., 'Corporate Responsibility and Economic Theory: an Anthropological Perspective', *International Journal of Sustainable Development*, 8(4) (2005) 302–314.

Graves, S.B. and Waddock, S.A., 'Institutional Owners and Corporate Social Performance', *Academy of Management Journal*, 37(4) (1994) 1034–1046.

Graves, S.B. and Waddock, S.A., 'Quality of management and quality of stakeholders' relations', *Business & Society*, 36(3) (September 1997), pp. 250–80.

Griffin, J.J. and Mahon, J.F., 'The Corporate Social Performance and Corporate Financial Performance Debate: Twenty-Five Years of Incomparable Research', *Business and Society*, 36(1) (1997) 5–31.

Hambrick, D.C. and Finkelstein, S., 'Managerial Discretion: A Bridge Between Polar Views of Organizational Outcomes', *Research in Organizational Behavior*, 9 (1987) 369–406.

Hambrick, D.C. and Fukutomi, G.D.S., 'The Seasons of a CEO's Tenure', *Academy of Management Review*, 16 (1991) 719–942.

Hambrick, D.C. and Mason, P.A., 'Upper Echelons: The Organization as a Reflection of Its Top Managers', *Academy of Management Review*, 9 (1984) 193–206.

Hambrick, D.C., 'Upper Echelons Theory: An Update', *Academy of Management Review*, 32(2) (2007) 334–343.

Hemingway, C.A. and Maclagan, P.W., 'Managers' Personal Values as Drivers of Corporate Social Responsibility', *Journal of Business Ethics*, 50 (2004) 33–44.

Jones, T.M., Thomas, T.E., Agle, B.R. and Ehreth, J., 'Graduate Business Education and the Moral Development of MBA Students: Theory and Preliminary Results', *Paper presented at the annual meeting to the International Association of Business and Society* (San Diego, CA) (1990).

Jones, T.M., 'Instrumental Stakeholder Theory: A Synthesis of Ethics and Economics', *Academy of Management Review*, 20(2) (1995) 404–437.

Kahneman, D., Knetsch, J.L. and Thaler, R., 'Fairness as a Constraint on profit Seeking: Entitlements in the Market', *The American Economic Review*, 76(4) (1986) 728–741.

Kuhn, J.W., 'Emotion As Well As Reason: Getting Students Beyond "Interpersonal Accountability" ', *Journal of Business Ethics*, 17 (1998) 295–308.

Langtry, B., 'Stakeholders and the Moral Responsibilities of Business', *Business Ethics Quarterly*, 4(4) (1994) 431–443.

Lieberson, S. and O'Connor, J.F., 'Leadership and Organizational Performance: A Study of Large Corporations', *American Sociological Review*, 37(2) (1972) 117–130.

Mahoney, L.S. and Thorne, L., 'Corporate Social Responsibility and Long-Term Compensation: Evidence from Canada', *Journal of Business Ethics*, 57 (2005) 241–253.

March, J.G. and Simon, H.A., *Organizations* (New York: John Wiley and Sons, Inc., 1991).

Margolis, J.D. and Walsh, J.P., *People and Profits? The Search for a Link between a Company's Social and Financial Performance* (New Jersey and London: Lawrence Erlbaum Associates, 2001).

Marwell, G. and Ames, R., 'Economists Free Ride, Does Anyone Else?: Experiments on the Provision of Public Goods', *Journal of Public Economics*, 15(3) (1981) 295–310.

McGuire, J., Dow, S. and Argheyd, K., 'CEO Incentives and Corporate Social Performance', *Journal of Business Ethics*, 45(4) (2003) 341–359.

McPhail, K., 'The Other Objective of Ethics Education: Re-humanising the Accounting Profession: A Study of Ethics Education in Law, Engineering, Medicine and Accountancy', *Journal of Business Ethics*, 34(3/4) (2001) 279–298.

McWilliams, A. and Siegel, D., 'Corporate Social Responsibility and Financial Performance: Correlation or Misspecification?', *Strategic Management Journal* 21(5) (2000) 603–609.

McWilliams, A. and Siegel, D., 'Corporate Social Responsibility: A Theory of the Firm Perspective', *The Academy of Management Review*, 26(1) (2001) 117–127.

McWilliams, A., Siegel, D.S. and Wright, P.M., 'Corporate Social Responsibility: Strategic Implications', *Journal of Management Studies*, 43(1) (2006) 1–18.

Miller, D., Kets de Vries, M. and Toulouse, J., 'Top Executive Locus of Control and its Relationship to Strategy Making, Structure and Environment', *Academy of Management Journal*, 25 (1982) 237–253.

Pfeffer, J., 'Why Do Bad Management Theories Persist? A Comment on Ghoshal', *Academy of Management Learning and Education*, 4(1) (2005) 96–100.

Rivera, J. and De Leon, P., 'Chief Executive Officers and Voluntary Environmental Performance: Costa Rica's Certification for Sustainable Tourism', *Policy Science*, 38 (2005) 107–127.

Selten, R. and Ockenfels, A., 'An Experimental Solidarity Game', *Journal of Economic Behavior and Organization*, 34 (1998) 517–539.

Sethi, S.P., 'A Conceptual Framework for Environmental Analysis of Social Issues and Evaluation of Business Response Patterns', *Academy of Management Review*, 4 (1979) 63–74.

Sharfman, M., 'The Construct Validity of the Kinder, Lydenberg and Domini Social Performance Ratings Data', *Journal of Business Ethics*, 15(3) (1996) 287–296.

Simon, H.A., 'Rational Decision Making in Business Organizations', *The American Economic Review*, 69(4) (1979) 493–513.

Stock, J.H. and Watson, M.W., *Introduction to Econometrics*, 2nd edn (Boston, MA: Pearson Addison-Wesley, 2007).

Swanson, D.L., 'Top Managers As Drivers For Corporate Social Responsibility',*The Oxford Handbook of Corporate Social Responsibility* (Oxford: Oxford University Press, 2008), pp. 227–248.

Thomas, A.S. and Simerly, R.L., 'Internal Determinants of Corporate Social Performance: The Role of Top Managers', *Academy of Management Proceedings*, (1995) 411–415.

Vogel, D., *The Market for Virtue: The Potential and Limits of Corporate Social Responsibility* (Harrisonburg, VA: R. R. Donnelley, 2005).

Waddock, S.A. and Graves, S.B., 'The Corporate Social Performance: Financial Performance Link', *Strategic Management Journal*, 18(4) (1997) 303–319.

Waddock, S., 'Myths and Realities of Social Investing', *Organization and Environment*, 16(3) (2003) 369–380.

Waldman, D.A., David, A.S., Donald S., and Javidan, M., 'Components of CEO Transformational Leadership and Corporate Social Responsibility', *Journal of Management Studies*, 43(8) (2006a) 1703–1725.

Waldman, D.A., Sully de Luque, M., Washburn, N. and House, R.J., 'Cultural and Leadership Predictors of CSR values of Top management. A Global Study of 15 Countries', *Journal of International Business Studies*, 37 (2006b) 823–837.

Waldman, D.A. and Siegel, D.S., 'Defining the Socially Responsible Leader', *The Leadership Quarterly*, 19 (2008) 117–131.

Walls, J.L., Phan, P.H. and Berrone, P., 'Assessment of the Construct Validity of Environmental Strategy Measures', Paper series 1105 presented at Ross School of Business, May (2008).

Walls, J.L., 'The Impact of Corporate Governance on Environmental Strategy', Doctoral Dissertation, Rensselaer Polytechnic Institute, Troy, NY, (2007).

Wood, D.J., 'Corporate Social Performance Revisited', *Academy of Management Review*, 16(4) (1991) 691–718.

4
CEOs and Financial Misreporting
Stephen Chen

Introduction

> O what a tangled web we weave/ when first we practise to deceive
>
> (Sir Walter Scott, *Marmion*, 1808).

Recent high-profile accounting scandals involving major companies like Enron, WorldCom, Parmalat and Satyam, along with recent outcries over excessive CEO remuneration, have raised questions about the relationship between ethical leadership, financial incentives, and financial misreporting (Perel, 2003). One view is based on the assumption that the problem lies with the character and integrity of those CEOs who have been motivated by personal financial gain resulting from performance bonuses. According to this view, these scandals have occurred because the individual leaders concerned have lacked integrity, and have deliberately misled investors in order to protect high bonuses linked to company share price performance. Proponents of this view argue that this shows a need to reform the morals of CEOs in order to prevent such scandals in future (Bragues, 2008).

However, on closer inspection, the claim that much of the blame for these financial scandals can be explained simply by the unethical character of the CEOs seems to lack strong evidential support. A review of the profiles of many of the CEOs cited as examples of unethical leaders shows that in most cases there is no history of prior fraud; most of the offending CEOs have been exemplary citizens in other aspects of their life. In many cases, they have made significant contributions to charitable causes, and other people have testified to their otherwise good character. For example, Bernard Ebbers, former CEO of WorldCom, gave $100 million to charity over 10 years, including leading a multimillion-dollar fundraising effort to renovate his alma mater, Mississippi College, and a gift of $50,000 to rebuild a children's playground after a fire. Similarly Kenneth Lay, the former CEO of Enron, gave almost $10 million to good causes between 2001 and 2005. Ramalinga Raju, the former CEO of Satyam, was a major contributor to non-profit foundations such as the Byrraju Foundation and the Emergency Management and Research Institute. If they are giving it away, these accounts would suggest that these CEOs are not entirely motivated by personal financial gain, and that they did not have a wholly 'bad' character. What then led these otherwise upstanding executives to perpetrate massive fraud?

This chapter argues that in order to answer this question it is necessary to look beyond the ethical character of individual CEOs and to examine other factors that may have led the CEOs to take such actions. Research in a number of disciplines including accounting, economics, sociology, criminology and psychology suggests that there are significant international differences in the institutional environment which may affect financial misreporting, such as legal penalties (Leuz et al., 2003; Bushman and Pitrioski, 2006), whistle-blowing (Tavakoli et al., 2003), cultural constraints (Koopman et al., 1999; Aycan et al., 2000) and relationships between the CEO, shareholders and subordinates (Aguilera and Jackson, 2003). Much of this research has been ignored in previous discussions, which have focused largely on the ethical character of the CEO.

Secondly, this study seeks to make a methodological contribution to business ethics. In common with other researchers who have adopted a social science approach to questions of business ethics (for example, Harman, 2003), I believe it is important to test the validity of explanations and recommendations against real-world data in order to make robust recommendations for managerial practice (Robertson, 1993). This chapter introduces the use of computer simulations as a way to explore and test some of the arguments presented by other researchers, and to test the possible role of other factors. Computer simulation has become an increasingly popular methodological approach in the management literature but has not been much used in the business ethics literature, apart from in a handful of studies (for example, Miller and Engemann, 2004). This study is designed to demonstrate how simulations can be a powerful tool to examine questions in business ethics, particularly in the absence of data from real life, and that simulations can provide support for studies based on real-life cases.

The chapter is structured as follows. First, we review previous research on ethical leadership and financial misreporting, referring to relevant research in psychology, criminology, sociology and accounting, as well as business ethics. Then we describe the simulation method and discuss some key results obtained from the simulations, before concluding with some general lessons gleaned from the simulations.

Previous research

Financial fraud comes in many forms, ranging from the simple misappropriation of company funds to complex money laundering and fraudulent investment schemes (Interpol, www.interpol.int). This paper focuses specifically on misreporting of financial accounts as highlighted in high-profile cases such as Enron, Parmalat and WorldCom. Many explanations for these frauds have been offered by scholars across the disciplines of accounting, management, economics, and psychology, as well as in business ethics. In the business ethics literature, most research on financial fraud has focused on the character and integrity of individual CEOs (Bragues, 2008; Morrison, 2001). This research has sought to answer the question of what ethical leaders should do from a philosophical perspective, often based on deontological principles such as those of Kant (1724–1804) or on virtue ethics drawn from Greek philosophers such as Aristotle and Plato (Knights and O'Leary, 2006). According to this view, CEOs bear primary responsibility for financial misreporting not only because they are the ones who sign off financial reports to shareholders, but also because they have the power to shape the ethical climate of the organisation, both through their own behaviour and through changes in organisational management systems and procedures (Sims and Brinkmann, 2003).

In contrast, Brown, Trevino and Harrison (2005) and Brown and Trevino (2006) have adopted a social scientific approach. Drawing on theories from social psychology such as social learning theory (Bandura, 1977), and on management theory about leadership (Burns, 1978), this approach involves a consideration of situational influences, like the ethical context, outcomes, like follower satisfaction, and individual leader characteristics, like moral reasoning and Machiavellianism. A key area of contention between these two schools of thought is the role of moral agency versus determinism. As discussed by Solomon (2003), if there is strict determinism, there can be no agency, and thus no moral responsibility. Two kinds of determinism can be distinguished. The first is determination by external circumstances; the second is determination within the individual, by his or her character. Most commentators are willing to admit a problem in ascribing moral responsibility in the former case, but not in the latter. Harman (2003) and Doris (2002) go further and, based on empirical studies in social psychology, they deny the existence of individual character, by which they mean an individual's established disposition. For instance, they cite the well-known 'electric shock' experiments by Milgram (1974) which demonstrated that ordinary people can be induced to carry out brutal acts under orders from an authority figure. Several lines of research from other disciplines also highlight the importance of external factors.

The significance of external factors is most strongly supported by research examining the effect of the institutional environment on corporate behaviour. First, two related lines of research highlight the importance of the institutional environment in determining responsible and irresponsible behaviour by organisational leaders. The first comes from research on the causes of corruption in different societies (Treisman, 2000; Getz and Volkema, 2001). Several studies have shown that the level of individual and corporate corruption in a country, including the level of financial misreporting, is related to the presence or lack of institutions in that country (Li et al., 2008). The second line of research comes from research on corporate social responsibility (CSR). While CSR reporting is often voluntary and so the findings may not be strictly comparable to mandatory financial reporting, a number of studies suggest that corporate social activities and reporting behaviour differ by country (Chen and Bouvain, 2009) as predicted by comparative institutional theorists (Aguilera and Jackson, 2003).

Institutional theorists argue that organisational actions are both enabled and constrained by regulative, normative, and cognitive institutional factors (Scott, 1995). Regulative aspects of the institutional environment include those regulations and laws that guide organisational actions through coercion or sanctions. For instance, factors that have been cited as contributors to variable corruption between countries are differences in the development of legal institutions, the legal penalties for financial fraud (Hodgson and Jiang, 2007; Mocan, 2008), and the general level of corruption in a given country (Davis and Ruhe, 2003). Normative factors take the form of generally accepted standards and expectations, as most clearly delineated in legitimacy theory, which argues that the continued existence of any institution depends on its social legitimacy (Suchman, 1995). In this view, acts such as charitable contributions and CSR reporting may be conducted purely in order to secure legitimacy in the eyes of key stakeholders (Chen et al., 2008). Other studies have shown the importance of cultural norms in determining the ethical behaviour of leaders. For instance, the GLOBE study (Waldman et al., 2006; Resick et al., 2006) which compared perceptions of leadership across a number of countries found that character/integrity was endorsed to a lesser extent among Middle Eastern societies compared with Nordic societies. On the other hand, altruism was endorsed most in South East Asian societies, and least among Nordic societies. These cultural norms can act to restrain the occurrence of financial misreporting as well as to promote the likelihood of whistle-blowing without the need for formal governance mechanisms (Tavakoli et al., 2003).

The institutional perspective provides an overarching framework which encompasses a variety of internal and external constraints on firm behaviour, some of which have been examined in more detail by researchers from other disciplines. Three in particular are discussed below: financial incentives for CEOs, CEO career concerns, and CEO narcissism.

Financial incentives

Accounting and economics researchers have focused on the financial incentives for CEOs to misreport financial performance (Burns and Kedia, 2006). As discussed by Carson (2003), one of the greatest lessons from recent accounting scandals concerns the role of financial incentive schemes in encouraging unethical CEO behaviour. Several recent papers investigate the potential costs and benefits of actions taken by managers to misreport financial performance, including legal liability, a decline in stock price, and management turnover (Reinstein et al., 2006). Most rely on agency theory (Jensen and Meckling, 1976), which focuses on the role of the CEO as a self-interested agent. In accordance with Becker's (1968) theory of crime, this view assumes that the decision to misreport financial performance is influenced by the CEO's personal assessment of the expected benefits versus the possible penalties, especially when the CEO owns stock options in the company, or when the CEO's bonus payments are linked to the performance of the company (Efendi et al., 2007; Zhang et al., 2008).

This problem is accentuated because CEOs are increasingly assessed on the 'bottom line' of achieving expectations set by financial analysts and investors. For example, as Sims and Brinkmann argue, in Enron: 'a negative earnings outlook would have been a red flag to investors, indicating Enron was not as successful as it appeared. If investors' concerns drove down the stock price due to excessive selling, credit agencies would be forced to downgrade Enron's credit rating. Trading partners would lose faith in the company and trade elsewhere while Enron's ability to generate quality earnings and cash flows would suffer' (Sims and Brinkmann, 2003:245).

However, financial incentives for CEOs vary considerably by country. For example, while Kaplan (2008) notes that differences are diminishing, Conyon and Murphy (2000) found that, after controlling for firm size, sector and other firm and executive characteristics, CEOs in the United States earned 45 per cent higher cash compensation and 190 per cent higher total compensation compared with CEOs in the United Kingdom, a difference they attribute to political and cultural differences between the two countries.

CEO career concerns

Longer-term career concerns have also been found to encourage misreporting by CEOs. Although accusations of financial fraud by CEOs carry a stigma (Pozner, 2008), there is also evidence that the failure to achieve financial targets is also a cause of stigma for executives (Semadeni et al., 2008), affecting their future employability. The career concerns literature (Boyer and Ortiz-Molina, 2008) argues that, while career concerns can potentially mitigate agency problems between managers and shareholders (Fama, 1980), they can also induce CEOs to take risky actions to improve their chances of appointment in the future. Such concerns arise from both the external labour market, which provides managers with outside opportunities, and the internal labour market, which determines how a manager is promoted within his own organisation. Managers realise that, if they perform poorly, their employability will decline.

Once again there may be differences depending on the institutional environment. Aycan et al. (2000) in a comparison of 10 countries found that socio-cultural factors influenced HRM practices, including the use of performance-based rewards as well as job design and supervisory practices in companies. Other differences between countries in career pathing may also influence management career concerns. For instance, although it is now changing, the traditional lifetime employment policy that is typical of Japanese companies is quite different from that in US firms (Ono, 2007).

CEO narcissism

In contrast, psychological research on financial misreporting has focused on the non-financial motivations of offending CEOs. One body of work points to the overconfidence of CEOs who believe they can achieve the mis-stated targets. Overconfidence refers to an inflated subjective probability of a particular outcome occurring. According to this perspective, financial misreporting may result not simply from a desire of CEOs to inflate earnings for self-benefit, but from misjudgement of true performance. In reporting firm performance, CEOs may initially form a tentative estimate of performance and, with this answer in mind, search for more evidence to support that initial estimate, using it in turn to colour the interpretation of subsequent evidence. This misjudgement can also arise from the incorrect assessment of information (Erev et al., 1994), and the predictive value of different sources of information (Soll, 1996). Some studies suggest that the greatest overestimation comes from poor performers. Kruger and Dunning (1999) argue that this happens because people who perform poorly at a task also lack the meta-cognitive skill to realise that they have performed poorly. On the other hand, people who are more skilled have both the ability to perform well and the ability to accurately assess the superiority of their performance. In many situations, motivational factors can exacerbate the bias. Many studies have shown that people like to think that they are more intelligent and knowledgeable than they may actually be (Larrick, 1993).

One group of individuals which has been shown to be particularly prone to overconfidence are those who exhibit a high degree of narcissism. Ellis (1898) introduced narcissism to the psychology literature, drawing the term from the young man in Greek mythology, Narcissus, who fell in love with his own reflection in a pool and ultimately perished as a result of his self-preoccupation. The concept had a major influence on Freud (1957), who described various manifestations of narcissism, including self-love, self-admiration, self-aggrandisement, and a tendency to see others as an extension of one's self. Narcissists rate themselves more highly than is objectively warranted on an array of dimensions, including intelligence, creativity, competence, and leadership ability (Farwell and Wohlwend-Lloyd, 1998). Narcissists also have an intense need to have their superiority reaffirmed and, though self-admiring, crave further admiration in the forms of affirmation, applause, and adulation (Emmons, 1981; Wallace and Baumeister, 2002). Schwartz (1991) has gone as far as to argue that some organisations, suffering from what he terms 'organisational totalitarianism', foster and encourage corporate narcissism.

Narcissism could be expected to affect CEO judgement of the likelihood of various outcomes. Actions that would be considered by most people as being unfeasible, or unlikely to succeed, might be seen in a positive light by highly narcissistic CEOs who crave the attention that such bold actions attract (Emmons, 1981; Wallace and Baumeister, 2002). Such behaviours can be accentuated by the actions of the

financial press and others who praise those CEOs who take bold decisions (Hayward et al., 2004). Narcissists are also likely to view themselves as Nietzschean 'overmen' (*Übermensch*) to whom the ordinary
rules do not apply (Norberg, 2009). This can lead to a greater likelihood
of unethical behaviour and can provide a rationalisation for these acts
(Zyglidopoulos et al., 2009), an extreme example being the inappropriate use by the Nazis of Nietzsche's philosophy to justify unconscionable
acts of cruelty (Ascheim, 1994).

Narcissism too seems to be culturally dependent. Narcissism has been
found to be less prevalent in some societies, particularly ones where collectivism and humility are valued (Morris et al., 2005). Koopman et al.
(1999) in a comparison of 21 European countries found significant differences in a number of preferred leadership dimensions, including narcissistic leadership, while Trevor-Roberts et al. (2003) in a related study
comparing leadership styles in Australia and New Zealand again found
significant differences in a number of leadership dimensions including
narcissism.

Methodology

Institutional theory would, therefore, predict that the extent of financial misreporting should vary by country, depending on several factors in the institutional environment. However, a key methodological
problem in investigating financial misreporting, as well as many other
forms of socially undesirable behaviour, is the difficulty of obtaining
reliable data. Most researchers have thus been forced to rely on anecdotal evidence or on unreliable and incomplete survey data. Although
such studies have provided useful insights in certain cases, the idio-
syncrasies of each case often make generalisation and the testing of
hypotheses difficult. As it is not feasible to test differences in financial
misreporting between organisations in different countries owing to a
lack of reliable data, a series of computer simulations were used to test
how varying levels of CEO confidence, honesty, and shareholder expectation might influence the degree to which financial misreporting takes
place. The simulations also examined the effect of various institutional
constraints like legalistic control and whistle-blowing by subordinates
on financial misreporting by CEOs.

Simulation is defined as a method for using computer software to
model the operation of real-world processes, systems, or events, by creating a computational representation of the underlying theoretical logic
that links constructs together within these simplified worlds (Davis

et al., 2007). These representations are coded into software that is run repeatedly under varying experimental conditions, such as alternative assumptions and different values of key variables, in order to test the effects and the validity of certain hypotheses. Simulation has become an increasingly significant methodological approach to theory development in the organisational science literature (Harrison et al., 2007) and several influential research papers in organisational science have resulted from the use of simulations (e.g. Cohen et al., 1972; March, 1991).

Simulation has several advantages over other methods. It provides an analytically precise means of specifying assumptions and theoretical logic, especially when there are empirical data limitations, or when the complexity of interactions in the system precludes simple analytical methods. In particular, simulations have been useful to show how complex, seemingly chaotic behaviours can result from simple processes (Anderson, 1999). Several simulation approaches have been used for theory development in the organisational literature, including system dynamics (Rudolph and Repenning, 2002), NK fitness landscapes (Levinthal, 1997), genetic algorithms (Bruderer and Singh, 1996), and cellular automata (Lomi and Larsen, 1996). This simulation uses the well-known system dynamics approach (Forrester, 1961; Sterman, 2000), which focuses on how causal relationships among constructs can influence the behaviour of a system. The approach typically models a system (for example, an organisation) as a series of simple processes with circular causality: variable A influences variable B, which influences variable A, and so on. These causal loops can be positive, such that feedback is self-reinforcing and amplifying, or negative, such that feedback is dampening. While each process may be well understood, their interactions are often difficult to predict.

System dynamics simulations are particularly useful for understanding the initial conditions that lead to abrupt, non-linear changes, such as tipping points, catastrophes, and the emergence of vicious or virtuous cycles. For example, Rudolf and Repenning (2002) used system dynamics to examine why minor interruptions sometimes trigger sudden catastrophes within organisations. This approach employs system dynamics to examine the cycle of increasing financial misreporting that has been noted in many high-profile cases.

In this approach, the visual modelling tool Vensim is used to allow the construction of simulation models from causal loop or stock and flow diagrams. By connecting words with arrows, relationships among system variables are entered and recorded as causal connections. This diagram can then be used as the basis for constructing a series of equations linking the variables in the model. When all the variables and their relationships have been specified, the behaviour of the model can be explored with different values of the variables.

In creating and testing simulation models, a balance needs to be struck between realism and the purpose of the model (Burton and Obel, 1995). While complex models that include many variables may be more realistic, their outcomes are often difficult to analyse, so they may not achieve the purpose of the modelling exercise. The purpose of this model was to serve as an instrument for Socratic dialogue (Morrell, 2004) rather than to forecast or predict, so simple but plausible modelling was preferred to complex but possibly more realistic models. The aim is to expose inconsistencies and contradictions in accepted beliefs (Morrell, 2004:386). Socrates would have done it through philosophical dialogue and argumentation, but here the validity of propositions is examined by testing them in computer simulation models of various hypothetical but plausible scenarios. By isolating certain key variables, and excluding other variables which may lead to noisy results, this approach permits controlled experiments, something which cannot be done in the real world.

Model-building is an iterative process, so many models were tried and discarded before nine were eventually selected which, though fairly simple, capture succinctly the variables and relationships highlighted as significant in the research. These nine also demonstrate the observed behaviours described in well-publicised cases of financial misreporting. The variables and their relationships examined are listed in Table 4.1, and the results are summarised in Table 4.2.

Control model

Figure 4.1 shows the baseline model with stable shareholder expectations. This models growth and expected growth in firm assets as two processes that need to be aligned. Variables are shown as text, stocks are shown as boxes, and causal relationships are shown as arrows. Thus, reading from left to right, shareholder expected assets are determined by the average industry growth, which increases or decreases the expected value of the firm each year. At the same time, the real value of the firm's assets is determined by actual firm performance each year. The difference between the expected and actual values gives rise to the shortfall which must be corrected by the CEO. One way is to improve the firm performance. The alternative is to mis-state the value of the firm assets in the financial report to shareholders.

In the baseline model (Model 4.1) it is assumed that:

1. Shareholders expect at least average industry performance (10 per cent).
2. Initial firm assets are $100 million.
3. Firm assets increase steadily at a rate of $4, 8, 12, 16 and 20 million from years 1 to 5, then at a constant $20 million per year.
4. If the real assets are less than the expected value, the CEO re-states real assets to meet shareholder expectations by an amount depending on his/her dishonesty and confidence.
5. The CEO is completely honest.

Table 4.1   Modelling Variables and their Relationships

Variable	Description
Average industry growth	10% p.a.
CEO confidence	CEO's confidence set initially at 10% and increasing as 1% of annual growth in firm assets
CEO dishonesty	CEO dishonesty set initially at 50% and increasing as 1% of misreporting
Chances of discovery	Chances of fraud being discovered, which increases with the level of misreporting
Misreporting	The difference between the real and stated asset values
Penalty	Penalty for misreporting, calculated as penalty rate x misreporting x chances of discovery
Real assets	The real value of the firm's assets
Real growth	The real growth achieved by the firm (0 in year 0 and increasing by 4% p.a. each year to 20% p.a. in year 5 and thereafter)
Reported assets	The value of the firm's assets reported by the CEO, calculated as maximum of shortfall*CEO overconfidence or real growth in assets (minus penalty for misreporting where present)
Previous assets	The value of the firm's assets that is stated in accounts for the previous year
Shareholder expected assets	The value of the firm's assets expected by shareholders
Shortfall	The difference between the real and expected asset values
Whistle-blowing	Constant initially set at 10%

Table 4.2 Modelling Results

Model	Settings of variables in model	Misreporting pattern	Maximum misreporting ($)
4.1: Base model	Average industry growth 10%; initial values of actual and reported assets 100; CEO dishonesty 0	No misreporting	0
4.2: Dishonest CEO	CEO dishonesty 50%; Reported growth calculated as maximum of shortfall*CEO dishonesty or real growth in assets	Increases steadily from 0 in year 1 to 550 in year 6 and thereafter	550
4.3: Narcissistic CEO	Initial CEO confidence 10%; Reported growth calculated as maximum of shortfall*CEO confidence or real growth in assets	Slow then increasingly rapid growth in misreporting from 0 in year 1 to 2,300 in year 6 and thereafter	2,300
4.4: Narcissistic and dishonest CEO	Initial CEO confidence 10%; CEO dishonesty 50%; Reported growth calculated as maximum of shortfall*CEO confidence*CEO dishonesty or real growth in assets	Slow then increasingly rapid growth in misreporting from 0 in year 1 to 3,000 in year 6 and thereafter	3,000
4.5: Narcissistic and dishonest CEO with rising shareholder expectations	As Model 4.4 and shareholder expectation set to maximum of industry average or last year's performance	Relatively insignificant growth in misreporting, then explosive growth in year 6	43 billion
4.6: Legal control	(a) As Model 4.5 and penalty calculated as penalty rate*misreporting*chance of discovery; penalty rate 10%; CEO dishonesty 30%	Slow increase to 2,500 in years 6 and 7 then rapid increase to 12,000 in year 8 and thereafter	12,000

Model	Description	Pattern	Value
	(b) As above and CEO dishonesty increased to 50%	Slow increase in years 1–4, increase to 2,500 in years 5 and 6 then rapid increase to 10,000 in year 7 and thereafter	10,000
	(c) As above and CEO dishonesty increased at 70%	Slow increase to year 4 then rapid increase to 12,000 in year 5 and thereafter	12,000
4.7: Legal control and whistle-blowing	(a) As Model 4.6 (b) and chance of discovery increased by whistle-blowing, set at 10%	Increase to 2,400 in years 6 and 7 then rapid increase to 7,000 in year 8 and thereafter	8,500
	(b) As above and chance of discovery increased by whistle-blowing, set at 50%	Increase to 2,500 in years 5 and 6 then rapid increase to 3,750 in year 7 and thereafter	3,750
	(c) As above and chance of discovery increased by whistle-blowing, set at 90%	Slow increase to year 4 then rapid increase to 2,500 in year 5 to 8 and 4,500 in year 9 and thereafter	4,500
4.8: CEO restraint	Confidence at 90% of value in Model 4.5	Negligible in years 1–5 and rapid increase in year 6	4.5 billion
4.9: Shareholder restraint	Shareholder expectation of above industry average performance expectation is 90% of value in Model 4.5	Negligible in years 1–5 and rapid increase in year 6	9.5 billion

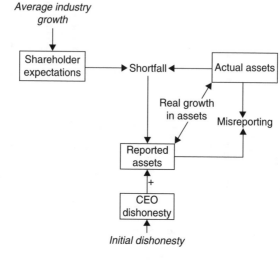

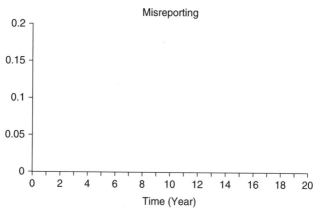

Figure 4.1   Baseline Model – Model 4.1

As expected, the baseline model shows that with steady shareholder expectations and a completely honest CEO there is no misreporting.

Unrestrained growth models

The next four models examine the effects of CEO dishonesty, narcissism and shareholder expectations on the level of financial misreporting.

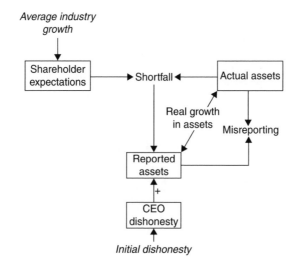

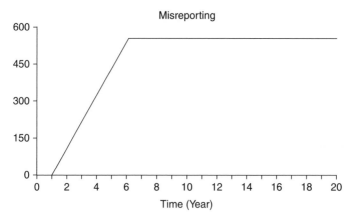

Figure 4.2 Dishonest CEO – Model 4.2

In Model 4.2 we examine the effect of CEO dishonesty. Based on research in criminology which suggests that many repeat offenders go on to commit more serious crimes, especially when they get away with it (Blumstein et al., 2006), it is assumed that misreporting CEOs who get away with it tend to misreport more over time. The model shows that the result is a steady increase in misreporting to $550 in year 6, with misreporting remaining at that level thereafter.

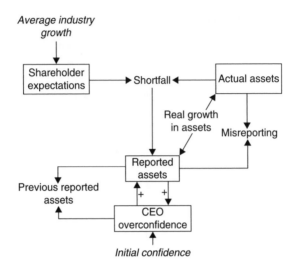

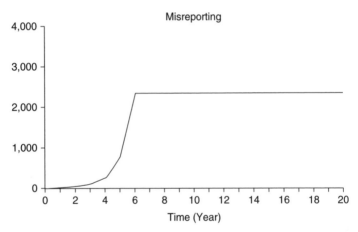

Figure 4.3　Narcissistic CEO – Model 4.3

In Model 4.3 we include the effect of including a feedback loop between CEO confidence and reported assets. CEO confidence is measured as a percentage of the firm's asset growth. This is based on the assumption that a CEO's ego will be bolstered by a significant increase in the firm's value. This corresponds to the scenario postulated by Hayward et al. (2004) that CEOs who believe their own press start believing that they can accomplish more than they can, and so have an even greater tendency to misreport firm performance. This in turn leads to overconfidence, which further increases their tendency to misreport. The effect will be particularly strong in narcissistic CEOs who will tend to misreport assets due to overconfidence (Kruger and Dunning, 1999), rationalisation of wrongdoing (Zyglidopoulos et al., 2009), and craving for the attention it creates (Wallace and Baumeister, 2002). The model shows an exponential increase in misreporting to $2,300 in year 6, remaining steady thereafter.

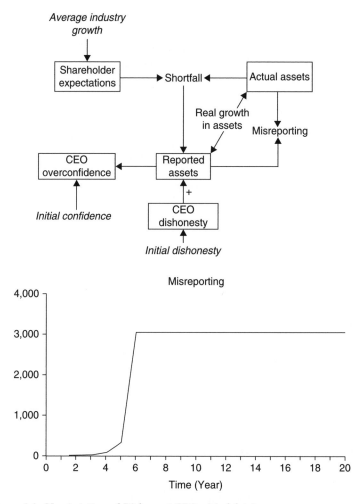

Figure 4.4 Narcissistic and Dishonest CEO – Model 4.4

In Model 4.4 we include the joint effects of CEO dishonesty and CEO narcissism. The result is an exponential growth pattern for misreporting as in Model 4.3 but increasing to a higher level of $3,000 in year 6 and remaining steady thereafter.

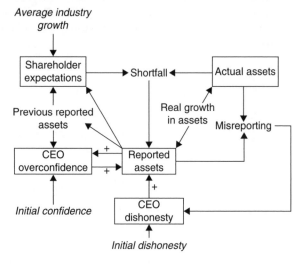

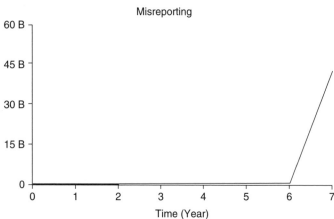

Figure 4.5   Narcissistic, Dishonest CEO and Rising Shareholder Expectations – Model 4.5

In Model 4.5 we add the additional assumption that shareholders have a minimum expectation of industry-average increase in assets year on year, but if the firm performs better than the industry average in one year then this becomes the new expected performance. As demonstrated in recent cases, such a scenario is well within the realms of reality. In the Enron case, share prices quadrupled in the four years from 1997 to 2000. Few shareholders raised any concerns and many expected such growth to continue. As the model shows, including this assumption creates a positive feedback loop that results in increasing shareholder expectations and an exponential increase in misreporting, which now reaches $43 billion in year 7. It is also noteworthy that this increase occurs even when the firm is outperforming the industry average (from year 3 onwards) since the firm gets trapped in a vicious cycle of better firm performance leading to an ever-increasing shareholder expectation which it cannot meet.

Models with restraints

Models 4.6 to 4.9 examine the effects of introducing various explicit and implicit institutional constraints on CEO behaviour (Scott, 1995; Matten and Moon, 2008): formal legalistic controls, whistle-blowing by subordinates, social constraints on CEO behaviour, and social norms for shareholder behaviour.

Model 4.6 tests the effect of formal controls such as legal penalties on misreporting. This corresponds to those countries with strong legal institutions that deter financial misreporting. The penalty is determined by the degree of misreporting, the chances of discovery, and the penalty rate. As depicted in the graphs, and as might be expected, the effect of introducing penalties for misreporting is a general reduction in the level of misreporting. However, what is also interesting is that increasing CEO dishonesty does not always lead to an increase in misreporting. Increasing CEO dishonesty from 30 per cent to 50 per cent results in an increase in misreporting in years 1 to 7 but results in a decrease in misreporting in year 8 and onwards, as increasing financial penalties start to reduce the level of misreporting.

Model 4.7 tests the scenario where subordinates actively engage in whistle-blowing (Taylor and Curtis, 2010). This models the effect in societies such as Scandinavia and the United States where there is relatively low power distance (Hofstede, 1980) and subordinates are freer to criticise their leaders, as compared with societies with high power distance such as Korea (Park et al., 2005) or Croatia (Tavakoli et al., 2003), where subordinates are culturally constrained from criticising their leaders. Now it is assumed that subordinate whistle-blowing increases the chances of discovery of wrongdoing. As expected, this results in a substantial decrease in the amount of misreporting to a maximum of $8,500 with 10 per cent whistle-blowing. However, what is also shown

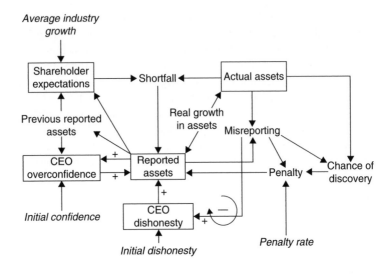

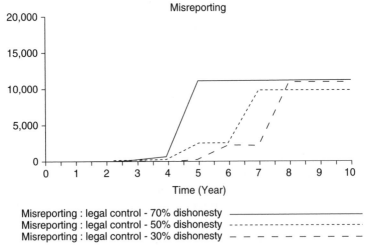

Figure 4.6   Legalistic Control – Model 4.6

is that, like the relationship between CEO dishonesty and misreporting in Model 4.6, the relationship between whistle-blowing and misreporting is not always downward-sloping. Increasing whistle-blowing does not always lead to a decrease in misreporting. While increasing whistle-blowing from 10 per cent to 50 per cent results in a decrease in misreporting in years 7 to 10 and onwards, increasing whistle-blowing

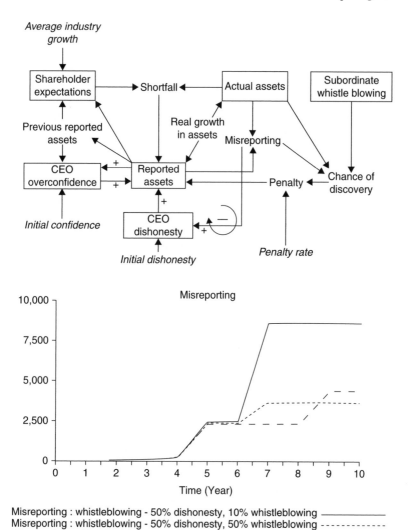

Figure 4.7 Whistle-blowing Subordinates – Model 4.7

from 50 per cent to 90 per cent results in a decrease in years 6 to 8 but
an increase in misreporting in years 9 to 10. This is because a high level
of whistle-blowing increases the chance of discovery which increases
the penalty and decreases the level of misreporting, but this in turn has
the opposite effect of reducing the chance of discovery.

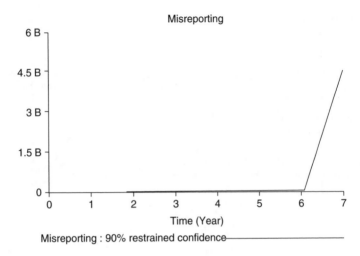

Figure 4.8 Social Constraints on CEOs – Model 4.8

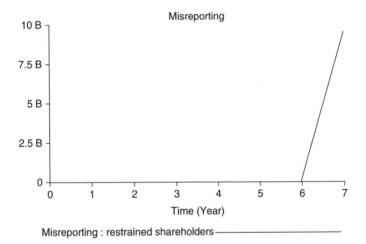

Figure 4.9 Social Constraints on Shareholders – Model 4.9

Model 4.8 tests the effect of reducing CEO overconfidence. This corresponds to countries where there are social constraints on self-aggrandisement (Morris et al., 2005). The results show that even a small change in CEO overconfidence can have a dramatic effect on misreporting. Reducing the CEO confidence values in Model 4.5 by 10 per cent results in a 90 per cent drop in the value of misreporting in year 7 which now reaches $4.5 billion compared with $43 billion in Model 4.5.

Model 4.9 tests the effect of restraining shareholder expectations. This models the case in many Continental European countries where shareholders have less power compared with stakeholders like workers and government, and have lower expectations. The results show that even a small change in shareholder expectations results in a massive decrease in misreporting. A 10 per cent reduction in shareholder expectations of above-average industry performance leads to a 78 per cent drop in the value of misreporting in year 7 to $9.5 billion compared with $43 billion in Model 4.5.

Discussion

One of the clearest findings from this exercise is the significant effect of positive feedback loops in the models in determining the level of financial misreporting by firms. This supports those theoretical models and empirical studies which have suggested the importance of various self-sustaining cycles in corruption at the societal level (Andvig and Moene, 1990), and shows how this can extend to corruption at the firm level.

The most significant feedback loop is that between firm performance and shareholder expectations. This finding is consistent with the anecdotal reports by CEOs and others who report that increasing expectations from shareholders and the market have been influential motives in some key financial accounting scandals such as Enron (Sims and Brinkmann, 2003). It is also consistent with accounts from CEOs of how they got trapped in cycles of misreporting, which echo Sir Walter Scott's quote at the beginning of this chapter. For instance, in his resignation statement, Satyam's CEO, Ramalinga Raju, described it as follows:

> What started as a marginal gap between actual operating profit and the one reflected in the book of accounts continued to grow over the years ... The differential in the real profits and the one reflected in the books was further accentuated by the fact that the company had to carry additional resources and assets to justify higher level of operations – thereby significantly increasing the costs ... It was like riding a tiger, not knowing how to get off without being eaten.

This finding is also consistent with theoretical models of self-fulfilling cycles of corruption proposed elsewhere (e.g. Andvig and Moene, 1990), as well as with findings in other real-life cases. Similar vicious cycles of decline have been identified in Enron (Sims and Brinkmann, 2003) and Nortel (Fogarty et al., 2009). It also provides support for theoretical explanations of escalating cycles of corruption in organisations (Zyglidopoulos et al., 2009; den Nieuwenboer and Kaptein, 2007; Street et al., 1997). One implication of this analysis is that more attention needs to be paid to the responsibilities of shareholders, financial analysts, and the financial press in setting realistic expectations for companies. Simply focusing on improving the ethical behaviour of individual CEOs without removing this root cause is unlikely to have much effect on the level and frequency of misreporting.

The findings should not be taken as an apologetic for financial misreporting by CEOs. The majority of CEOs do not engage in such behaviour, despite extreme pressures. However, the simulations suggest that even well-meaning CEOs who make small mis-statements in the belief that it will lead to no long-term harm may get caught up in cycles of increasing misreporting from which they find it difficult to extricate themselves. This can occur even if the performance of the firm is above the industry average. In some cases, such as the one modelled, whether the CEO is honest or dishonest makes little difference compared with other factors.

A second significant feedback loop is that between firm performance and CEO confidence. When CEOs and others believe that they alone are responsible for the firm's high performance (and are rewarded financially or psychologically based on that belief) there is a strong tendency to exaggerate firm performance in order to bolster the CEO's ever-increasing ego. This tendency can be fuelled by commentary from the press and by others who foster that belief. As shown in Model 4.5, adding in this relationship results in an acceleration of the level of mis-statement of performance, as another vicious cycle is created in which higher reported assets increase the CEO's confidence, which in turn increases the need to misreport performance in order to feed an ever-increasing ego.

As expected, Model 4.6 shows that misreporting can be reduced to a low level or eliminated completely by increasing penalties and the risk of detection. This is consistent with findings in other areas of legal enforcement such as tax fraud that even a small change in penalties and detection can have a significant deterrent effect (Feld and Frey, 2007). However, the fact that the relationship between CEO dishonesty and misreporting is not always upwards sloping also highlights the importance of examining the outcomes of interactions between CEO dishonesty and legal constraints, which can sometimes lead to unexpected results.

As shown in Model 4.7, in societies where there is a higher level of whistle-blowing, generally the effect is to reduce the level of misreporting compared to societies where there is no whistle-blowing. However, the models also show that the effect depends critically on the level of whistle-blowing relative to penalties and misreporting. In some circumstances, contrary to expectations, an increase in whistle-blowing can actually lead to an increase in financial misreporting. As with legal penalties it highlights the importance of considering interactions with other variables.

What is also interesting is that the simulations show that the same effect can be achieved by removing the feedback loops between reported firm assets and CEO confidence as in Model 4.8 or between reported firm assets and shareholder expectations as in Model 4.9. These simulations suggest that informal social constraints on CEO and shareholder behaviour can be just as effective at reducing the extent of financial misreporting as can legalistic controls.

Limitations and future research

There are clearly limitations in the models and much more work could be done. First, in order to simplify the analysis this study does not examine the role of other stakeholders such as suppliers, customers, and competitors, nor other potentially significant factors such as firm ownership structures, tax compliance systems, culture, and so on. These other factors could be included in more complex models, although it is unlikely that the conclusions presented here about the key effects of feedback loops between CEOs, subordinates, and shareholders would be changed.

Secondly, these models have not been tested against real-world data. It has proven surprisingly difficult to obtain reliable figures, for example, on the percentage of CEO pay that is linked to company performance, or how the level of penalty affects financial misreporting. One reason to use computer simulations is precisely to overcome the difficulty of obtaining such data. However, if real-world data is available, further studies could test the simulations using this data, or else test the propositions derived from the simulations using other methods. In particular, it would be useful to examine data on financial misreporting in different countries to see if the effects vary by country as predicted.

Conclusion

There are many factors that have been identified as contributing to financial misreporting by CEOs. However, most previous studies have focused on only one or two key factors, and from a single disciplinary perspective. There are few studies that have taken a more comprehensive view, incorporating findings from different disciplines. One aim of this research, therefore, was to examine how these findings might be integrated into a single simulation. Given the large number of possible factors that have been suggested, another aim was to test the relative significance of ethical leadership in different institutional settings as well as to examine the possible interactions between variables. Given the widespread public interest in the issue, a further aim of this research was to test the efficacy of various solutions to the problem of financial misreporting. In particular, the exercise tests the importance of the ethical character of the leader, given how often this is cited as a general cure for the problem.

This chapter has argued for the need to integrate findings from research across the disciplines in examining questions of ethical leadership. Questions about the ethics of corporate leaders are inevitably bound up with questions of personal motives, responsibility to shareholders and other stakeholders, and organisational incentive structures. While it does not entirely resolve the question about the individual moral responsibility of corporate leaders in financial misreporting cases, it does demonstrate that, based on empirical findings in psychology, criminology, and other fields, it is perfectly plausible that in certain circumstances the ethical character of leaders is of less consequence than many have argued. In some cases, CEO dishonesty can hypothetically lead to reduced misreporting, contrary to expectations.

The models also show clearly the need to take into account the institutional environment in which firms operate. In particular, while not completely absolving CEOs of blame for corporate malfeasance, they also suggest that other individuals and groups – subordinates, shareholders, financial analysts and the financial press – can significantly affect the level of misreporting, and should therefore bear some of the blame. This lends weight to recent theoretical arguments for 'connected moral agency' rather than individual moral agency (Watson et al., 2007), and the importance of considering moral agency in the context of different institutional environments (Wagner-Tsukumoto, 2005).

This study also raises questions about the 'dark side' of leadership (Conger, 1990). The leadership qualities much admired in many CEOs, such as drive, confidence, charisma, and good impression management, while sometimes capable of producing exceptional results for the organisation, can also in the wrong set of circumstances lead to its downfall. The models show how a combination of a narcissistic and dishonest

CEO in conjunction with increasing shareholder expectations and acquiescent subordinates can easily lead to self-propelling increasing cycles of financial misreporting.

This simulation has suggested some ways in which the extent of financial misreporting may be reduced. One key to reducing financial misreporting is to break the feedback loops that sustain a cycle of misreporting. The models also provide further support for the argument that informal social constraints, such as social and individual restraints on behaviour, can be more effective in reducing corporate fraud and encouraging responsible behaviour than are formal control mechanisms (Tavakoli et al., 2003; Matten and Moon, 2008). This may also explain why financial misreporting appears to be less prevalent in certain countries or cultures. In contrast to praising and emulating those celebrity leaders who are often the focus of attention but who often are also prone to excesses, we may do well to learn from cultures and religions across the world which advocate humility as a virtue (Morris et al., 2005).

Finally, this chapter provides an example of how simulation methods can be used in business ethics to investigate hypothetical relationships between factors, particularly where there is a lack of real-world empirical data and it is difficult to use conventional methods. This has applications beyond financial misreporting to the investigation of other forms of unethical behaviour.

Bibliography

Aguilera, R.V. and Jackson, G., 'The Cross-National Diversity of Corporate Governance: Dimensions and Determinants', *Academy of Management Review*, 28(3) (2003) 447–465.

Anderson, P., 'Complexity Theory and Organization Science', *Organization Science*, 10(3) (1999) 216–232.

Andvig, J.C. and Moene, K.O., 'How Corruption May Corrupt', *Journal of Economic Behaviour and Organization*, 13 (1990) 63–76.

Aschheim, S.E., *The Nietzsche Legacy in Germany 1890–1990* (Berkeley: University of California Press, 1994).

Aycan, Z., Kanungo, R.N., Mendonca, M., Yu, K., Deller, J., Stahl, G., and Kurshid, A., 'Impact of Culture on Human Resource Management Practices: A 10-country Comparison', *Applied Psychology: An International Review*, 49(1) (2000) 192–221.

Bandura, A., *Social Learning Theory* (Englewood Cliffs, NJ: Prentice Hall, 1977).

Becker, G.S., 'Crime and Punishment: an Economic Approach', *Journal of Political Economy*, 76 (1968) 169–217.

Blumstein, A., Cohen, J., and Farrington, D.P., 'Criminal Career Research: Its Value for Criminology', *Criminology*, 26(1) (2006) 1–35.

Boyer, M.M. and Ortiz-Molina, H., 'Career Concerns of Top Executives, Managerial Ownership and CEO Succession', *Corporate Governance*, 16(3) (2008) 178–193.

Bragues, G., 'The Ancients against the Moderns: Focusing on the Character of Corporate Leaders', *Journal of Business Ethics*, 78 (2008) 373–387.

Brown, M.E., Treviño, L.K., and Harrison, D., 'Ethical Leadership: A Social Learning Perspective for Construct Development and Testing', *Organizational Behaviour and Human Decision Processes*, 97 (2005) 117–134.

Brown, M.E. and Treviño, L.K., 'Ethical Leadership: A Review and Future Directions', *The Leadership Quarterly*, 17 (2006) 595–616.

Bruderer, E. and Singh, J.S., 'Organizational Evolution, Learning, and Selection: A Genetic-Algorithm-based Model', *Academy of Management Journal*, 39 (1996) 1322–1349.

Burns, J.M., *Leadership* (New York: Harper and Row, 1978).

Burns, N. and Kedia, S., 'The Impact of Performance-based Compensation on Misreporting', *Journal of Financial Economics*, 79 (2006) 35–67.

Burton, R.M. and Obel, B., 'The Validity of Computational Models in Organization Science: From Model Realism to Purpose of the Model', *Computational and Mathematical Organization Theory*, 1(1) (1995) 57–71.

Bushman, R.M. and Piotroski, J.D., 'Financial Reporting Incentives for Conservative Accounting: The Influence of Legal and Political Institutions', *Journal of Accounting and Economics*, 42 (2006) 107–148.

Carson, T.L., 'Self-interest and Business Ethics: Some Lessons of the Recent Corporate Scandals', *Journal of Business Ethics*, 43(4) (2003) 389–394.

Chen, J.C., Patten, D.and Roberts, R.W., 'Corporate Charitable Contributions: A Corporate Social Performance or Legitimacy Strategy', *Journal of Business Ethics*, 82 (2008) 131–144.

Chen, S. and Bouvain, P., 'Is Corporate Responsibility Converging? A Comparison of Corporate Responsibility Reporting in the USA, UK, Australia, and Germany', *Journal of Business Ethics*, 87 (2009) 299–317.

Cohen, M.D., March, J.G.and Olsen, J.P., 'A Garbage Can Model of Organizational Choice', *Administrative Science Quarterly*, 17 (1972) 1–25.

Conger, J., 'The Dark Side of Leadership', *Organizational Dynamics*, 19 (1990) 44–55.

Conyon, M.J. and Murphy, K.J., 'The Prince and the Pauper: CEO Pay in the United States and United Kingdom', *Economic Journal*, 110 (2000) 640–671.

Davis, J.P., Eisenhardt, K.M., and Bingham, C.B., 'Developing Theory Through Simulation Methods', *Academy of Management Review*, 32(2) (2007) 480–499.

Davis, J.H. and Ruhe, J.A., 'Perceptions of Country Corruption: Antecedents and Outcomes', *Journal of Business Ethics*, 43 (2003) 275–288.

Den Nieuwenboer, N.A. and Kaptein, M., 'Spiraling Down into Corruption: A Dynamic Analysis of the Social Identity Processes that Cause Corruption in Organizations to Grow', *Journal of Business Ethics*, 83 (2007) 133–146.

Doris, J., *Lack of Character: Personality and Moral Behaviour* (New York: Cambridge University Press, 2002).

Efendi, J., Srivastava, A., and Swanson, E.P., 'Why Do Corporate Managers Misstate Financial Statements? The Role of Option Compensation and Other Factors', *Journal of Financial Economics*, 85 (2007) 667–708.

Ellis, H., 'Auto-eroticism: A Psychological Study', *Alienist and Neurologist*, 19, 1898, 260–299.

Emmons, R., 'Relationship between Narcissism and Sensation Seeking', *Psychological Report*, 48(1) (1981) 247–250.

Erev, I., Wallsten, T.S., and Budescu, D.V., 'Simultaneous over- and Underconfidence: The Role of Error in Judgment Processes', *Psychological Review*, 101 (1994) 519–528.

Fama, E., 'Agency Problems and the Theory of the Firm', *Journal of Political Economy*, 88 (1980) 288–307.

Farwell, L. and Wohlwend-Lloyd, R., 'Narcissistic Processes: Optimistic Expectations, Favorable Self-evaluations, and Self-enhancing Attribution', *Journal of Personality*, 66 (1998) 65–83.

Feld, L.P. and Frey, B.S., 'Tax Compliance as the Result of a Psychological Tax Contract: The Role of Incentives and Responsive Regulation', *Law and Policy*, 29(1) (2007) 102–120.

Fogarty, T., Magnan, M.I., Markarian, G., and Bohdjalian, S., 'Inside Agency: The Rise and Fall of Nortel', *Journal of Business Ethics*, 84 (2009) 165–187.

Forrester, J., *Industrial Dynamics* (Cambridge, MA: MIT Press, 1961).

Freud, S., 'On Narcissism: An Introduction', In J. Strachey (ed. and trans.), *The Standard Edition of the Complete Psychological Works of Sigmund Freud* (London: Hogarth Press, 1957) 14, pp. 67–104

Getz, K.A. and Volkema, R.J., 'Culture, Perceived Corruption and Economics: A Model of Predictors and Outcomes', *Business and Society*, 40 (2001) 7–30.

Harman, G., 'No Character or Personality', *Business Ethics Quarterly*, 13(1) (2003) 87–94.

Harrison, J.R., Lin, Z., Carroll, G.R., and Carley, K.M., 'Simulation Modeling in Organizational and Management Research', *Academy Of Management Review*, 32(4) (2007) 1229–1245.

Hayward, M.L.A., Rindova, V.P., and Pollock, T.G., 'Believing One's Own Press: The Causes and Consequences of CEO ego', *Strategic Management Journal*, 25 (2004) 637–653.

Hodgson, G.M. and Jiang, S., 'The Economics of Corruption and the Corruption of Economics: An Institutionalist Perspective', *Journal of Economic Issues*, 61(4) (2007) 1043–1061.

Hofstede, G., *Culture's Consequences: International Differences in Work Related Values* (Beverly Hills, CA: Sage, 1980).

Jensen, M. and Meckling, W., 'Theory of Firm: Managerial Behaviour, Agency Costs and Ownership Structure', *Journal of Financial Economics*, 3 (1976) 305–360.

Kaplan, S.N., 'Are U.S. CEOs overpaid?', *Academy of Management Perspectives*, 22(2) (2008) 5–20.

Knights, D. and O'Leary, M., 'Leadership, Ethics and Responsibility to the Other', *Journal of Business Ethics*, 67 (2006) 125–137.

Koopman, P.L., Den Hartog, D.N., and Konrad, E., 'National Culture and Leadership Profiles in Europe: Some Results From the GLOBE Study', *European Journal of Work and Organizational Psychology*, 8(4) (1999) 503–520.

Kruger, J. and Dunning, D., 'Unskilled and Unaware of it: How Difficulties in Recognizing One's Own Incompetence Lead to Inflated Self-assessments', *Journal of Personality and Social Psychology*, 77 (1999) 1121–1134.

Larrick, R.P., 'Motivational Factors in Decision Theories: The Role of Self-protection', *Psychological Bulletin*, 113 (1993) 440–450.

Leuz, C., Nanda, D., and Wysocki, P.D., 'Investor Protection and Earnings Management: An International Comparison', *Journal of Financial Economics*, 69 (2003) 505–527.

Levinthal, D.A., Adaptation on Rugged Landscapes, *Management Science*, 43(7) (1997), 934–950.

Li, J., Moy, J., Lam, K., and Chu, W.L.C., 'Institutional Pillars and Corruption at the Societal Level', *Journal of Business Ethics*, 83 (2008) 327–339.

Lomi, A. and Larsen, E.R., 'Interacting Locally and Evolving Globally: A Computational Approach to the Dynamics of Organizational Populations', *Academy of Management Journal*, 39 (1996) 1287–1321.

March, J.G., 'Exploration and Exploitation in Organizational Learning', *Organization Science*, 2 (1991) 71–87.

Matten, D. and Moon, J., '"Implicit" And "Explicit" CSR: a Conceptual Framework for a Comparative Understanding of Corporate Social Responsibility', *Academy of Management Review*, 33(2) (2008) 404–424.

Milgram, S., *Obedience to Authority* (New York: Harper Collins, 1974).

Miller, H. and Engemann, K.J., 'A Simulation Model of Intergroup Conflict', *Journal of Business Ethics*, 50 (2004) 355–367.

Mocan, N., 'What Determines Corruption? International Evidence from Microdata', *Economic Inquiry*, 46(4) (2008) 493–510.

Morrell, K., 'Socratic Dialogue as a Tool for Teaching Business Ethics', *Journal of Business Ethics*, 53 (2004) 383–392.

Morris, J.A., Brotheridge, C.M. and Urbanski, J.C., 'Bringing Humility to Leadership: Antecedents and Consequences of Leader Humility', *Human Relation*, 58 (2005) 1323–1350.

Morrison, A., 'Integrity and Global Leadership', *Journal of Business Ethics*, 31 (2001) 65–76.

Norberg, P., 'I Don't Care that People Don't Like What I Do – Business Codes Viewed as Invisible or Visible Restrictions', *Journal of Business Ethics*, 86 (2009) 211–225.

Ono, H., 'Careers in Foreign-owned Firms in Japan', *American Sociological Review*, 72 (2007) 267–290.

Park, H., Rehg, M.T. and Lee, D., 'The Influence of Confucian Ethics and Collectivism on Whistle-blowing Intentions: A Study of South Korean Public Employees', *Journal of Business Ethics*, 58(4) (2005) 387–403.

Perel, M., 'An Ethical Perspective on CEO Compensation', *Journal of Business Ethics*, 48 (2003) 381–391.

Pozner, J.E., 'Stigma and Settling Up: An Integrated Approach to the Consequences of Organizational Misconduct for Organizational Elites', *Journal of Business Ethics*, 80 (2008) 141–150.

Reinstein, A., Moehrle, S.R., and Reynolds-Moehrle, J., 'Crime and Punishment in the Marketplace: Accountants and Business Executives Repeating History', *Managerial Auditing Journal*, 21(4) (2006) 420–435.

Resick, C.J., Hanges, P.J., Dickson, M.W., and Mitchelson, J.K., 'A Cross-cultural Examination of the Endorsement of Ethical Leadership', *Journal of Business Ethics*, 63 (2006) 345–359.

Robertson, D.C., 'Empiricism in Business Ethics: Suggested Research Directions', *Journal of Business Ethics*, 12(8) (1993) 585–599.

Rudolph, J. and Repenning, N., 'Disaster Dynamics: Understanding the Role of Quantity in Organizational Collapse', *Administrative Science Quarterly*, 47 (2002) 1–30.

Schwartz, H.S., 'Narcissism Project and Corporate Decay: The Case of General Motors', *Business Ethics Quarterly*, 1(3) (1991) 249–268.

Scott, W.R., *Institutions and Organizations: Foundations for Organizational Science* (Thousand Oaks, CA: Sage, 1995)

Semadeni, M., Cannella, A.A., Fraser, D.R., and Lee, D.S., 'Fight or Flight: Managing Stigma in Executive Careers', *Strategic Management Journal*, 29 (2008) 557–567.

Sims, R.R. and Brinkmann, J., 'Enron Ethics (Or: Culture Matters More than Codes)', *Journal of Business Ethics*, 45 (2003) 243–256.

Soll, J.B., 'Determinants of Overconfidence and Miscalibration: The Roles of Random Error and Ecological Structure', *Organizational Behaviour and Human Decision Processes*, 65 (1996) 117–137.

Solomon, R.C., 'Victims of Circumstances? A Defense of Virtue Ethics in Business', *Business Ethics Quarterly*, 13(1) (2003) 43–62.

Sterman, J., *Business Dynamics: Systems Thinking and Modeling for a Complex World* (New York: Irwin McGraw-Hill, 2000).

Street, M.D., Robertson, C., and Geiger, S.W., 'Ethical Decision Making: The Effects of Escalating Commitment', *Journal of Business Ethics*, 16 (1997) 1153–1161.

Suchman, M.C., 'Managing Legitimacy: Strategic and Institutional Approaches', *Academy of Management Review*, 20(3) (1995) 571–610.

Tavakoli, A.A., Keenan, J.P., and Crnjak-Karanovic, B., 'Culture and Whistle-blowing: An Empirical Study of Croatian and United States Managers Utilizing Hofstede's Cultural Dimensions', *Journal of Business Ethics*, 43 (2003) 49–64.

Taylor, E.Z. and Curtis, M.B., 'An Examination of the Layers of Workplace Influences in Ethical Judgments: Whistle-blowing Likelihood and Perseverance in Public Accounting', *Journal of Business Ethics*, 93(1) (2010) 21–37.

Treisman, D., 'The Causes of Corruption: a Cross-national Study', *Journal of Public Economics*, 76 (2000) 399–457.

Trevor-Roberts, E., Ashkanasy, N.M., Kennedy, J.C., 'The Egalitarian Leader: a Comparison of Leadership in Australia and New Zealand', *Asia Pacific Journal of Management*, 20 (2003) 517–540.

Wagner-Tsukumoto, S., 'An Economic Approach to Business Ethics: Moral Agency of the Firm and the Enabling and Constraining Effects of Economic Institutions and Interactions in a Market Economy', *Journal of Business Ethics*, 60 (2005) 75–89.

Waldman, D.A., de Luque, M.S., Washburn, N., and House, R.J., 'Cultural and Leadership Predictors of Corporate Social Responsibility Values of Top Management: a GLOBE Study of 15 Countries', *Journal of International Business Studies*, 37 (2006) 823–837

Wallace, H.M. and Baumeister, R.F., 'The Performance of Narcissists Rises and Falls with Perceived Opportunity for Glory', *Journal of Personality and Social Psychology*, 82 (2002) 819–834.

Watson, G.W., Freeman, R.E., and Parmar, B., 'Connected Moral Agency in Organizational Ethics', *Journal of Business Ethics*, 81 (2007) 323–341.

Zhang, X., Bartol, K.M., Smith, K.G., Pfarrer, M.D., and Khanin, D.M., 'CEOs on the Edge: Earnings Manipulation and Stock-Based Incentive Misalignment', *Academy of Management Journal*, 51(2) (2008) 241–258.

Zyglidopoulos, S.C., Fleming, P.J., and Rothenberg, S., 'Rationalization, Overcompensation and the Escalation of Corruption in Organizations', *Journal of Business Ethics*, 84 (2009) 65–73.

5
Life at the Sharp End

Keith T. Thomas and Allan D. Walker

Introduction

As is argued elsewhere in this collection, among the many consequences of the recent financial crisis is a growing mistrust of corporate leaders and the public regulatory agencies charged with watching them. In many discussions, the crisis has been linked to a general failure of leadership and, more specifically, to the absence of appropriate ethics. Indeed Zakaria (2009) labels the near collapse of the financial system a 'moral crisis'. A perceived failure of self-regulation is central to the call for more ethics and greater formal accountability. But not everything can be written down, and not everything that is legally permissible is ethical. Instead, in this chapter we suggest that it may be more productive to look below the surface of dramatic and seemingly unethical action to ask *why* leaders make the decisions they make. This chapter argues that there are particular tensions when the rhetoric of policy meets the reality of organisational leadership. These contextual tensions are inherent in most activity, but are most evident at the operational end of leadership, the 'sharp end' where policies are implemented, values enacted, and practices evidenced. The sharp end leaves little room for intellectual introspection or the detailed post-hoc analysis favoured by the critics.

The chapter falls into five sections, each illustrated with examples. The first section teases out the debate around individual leader ethics, and leadership and organisational misfortune. The second section describes leadership realities and explains further what is meant by 'the sharp end'. In the third section, leadership reality is organised through a multi-stage framework to illustrate the interconnected activity space in terms of individual and organisational dynamics. In the fourth section, two cases are used to illustrate this activity space, flagging some of the challenges and tensions encountered at the sharp end. The fifth section draws on this analysis to identify some countervailing forces that could be used to support leadership practice at the sharp end.

When things go wrong

With the benefit of hindsight, there appears to be universal agreement that in the recent financial crisis the banks got things badly wrong (Tett, 2009), as did public watchdogs and regulators. Given the complexity of the situation, agreement on why may never be reached (Faiola et al., 2009; Zakaria, 2009). In any case, our argument is that when things go wrong a simple lack of ethics is an insufficient explanation, and that public policy must look wider at the other factors at play if we are to obviate future failures.

Failure, regardless of its level of impact, is often attributed to a lack of leadership. This assumes that the leader – as an individual – is ultimately responsible for whatever happens on 'their patch'. This may be an overly simplistic notion, but it is consistent with one of two broad ways of viewing failure: a person-based approach or a systems approach (Reason, 2000). Each approach has important practical implications for understanding leader behaviour. The most commonly applied approach is person-based, which focuses on errors and procedural violations as a result of inattention, poor motivation, negligence, or recklessness. A variation of the person-based approach is to apportion a darker side to leadership – of greed, ethical misconduct, even criminality. This perspective invites a focus on the disposition, character, and/or personality type of leaders themselves and ends up in judgements that these leaders are corrupt or unethical.

Blaming individuals is easy and emotionally satisfying, and the target is more readily discernible than a complex, non-human system (Reason, 2000). It is, however, unproductive, and if we are to learn and prevent future mistakes we must dig more deeply. We suggest that the proper task is to focus on how systems work and how this affects the decisions leaders make. A systems approach operates on the premise that humans are fallible in both benign and sinister ways, so errors and intentional deviations are to be expected, even in the best organisations. These errors and deviations may be 'consequences rather than causes' (Reason, 2000:768), and the origin of failure may be linked to upstream systemic factors. In such cases, countermeasures should target the changing of the conditions in which they work rather than just focusing on changing the person involved.

Leadership realities

Because it is a key driver of organisational performance, leadership has attracted huge interest from researchers and practitioners alike (Mumford et al., 2003; Murray and Chapman, 2003; Dexter and Prince, 2007). One of the many definitions of leadership describes it as a contextually sensitive social process that facilitates collective action towards a common goal (Rost and Baker, 2000). Central to this definition is the importance of context, though some studies of leadership privilege the view of leaders as heroic figures and reduce critical inspection of structural-contextual factors (Sinclair, 2005). Others note that the environment has become more complex (Senge, 1995; Castells, 2000) and that this has in turn encouraged distributed forms of leadership (Gronn, 2003). Much of what has been written about leadership has emphasised the positive, of leaders effecting change for the good of their organisation and society, while the darker effects of context are often downplayed. However, in stark contrast to the hope vested in leadership, the past decades have witnessed a series of high-profile failures and associated scandals, with the roll-call including Enron, Hollinger, Tyco, Parmalat, and the National Australia Bank. The problem with leadership is not limited to the corporate sector, with similar issues emerging in the military, the police, in education, the church, the health-care industry, and in politics, but what seems to be new is the scale and visibility of apparent leadership failure. Coupled with an apparently increased sensitivity to unethical behaviour, these concerns collectively suggest the need for a critical examination of behaviour, and particularly behaviour at the sharp end.

The term 'sharp end' refers to the front line of institutional activity. At the sharp end, time to think is short, and decisions, perhaps involving life and death, must be made under pressure, with little opportunity to properly consider options or seek advice. There is no safety net. At the sharp end, failures are usually active failures – the result of some action. These failures have immediate and usually short-lived effects, in contrast to latent – usually system – failures that can lie dormant for a long while until they interact with local conditions to great effect. Given this immediacy and unpredictability of leading at the sharp end, it is no surprise that when things go wrong decisions taken can easily look irrational, inhuman, or even unethical. But the clarity this lends the situation affords the commentator an unambiguous opportunity to understand the interaction between person and situation.

Based on a categorisation of activity by type (many or few novel cases) and the complexity of finding solutions (hard to solve or easy), four broad types can be defined (Perrow, 1967):

1. those involving *many* non-routine, poorly structured and unpredictable organisational activities that by the nature of the problem are *hard* to solve, such as military operations, investment banking, politics, and crisis management
2. those involving *many* non-routine activities, but the nature of problem solutions is mostly relatively *easy*, such as police work and project management
3. those involving *few* exceptional cases and mostly *easy* problem solutions such as manufacturing and traditional banking
4. those involving *few* exceptional cases, but usually *hard* problem solutions, such as the operation of nuclear plants and geriatric medicine.

We turn now to examine some representative cases that illustrate aspects of the realities of leadership at the sharp end. The aim is to briefly present the conflicting internal and external demands and the potential unintended consequences that can accompany decision-making at the sharp end, using two examples. Both examples have as a context operational military activity, where, as in a medical context, the 'sharp end' is particularly poignant, tending to involve decisions about life and death.

Case: children overboard

This incident in late October 2001 emerged out of the Australian Defence Force's expanded role under a new border protection regime. It involved a naval vessel the HMAS *Adelaide* and a vessel carrying refugees, known as SIEV 4 (Senate, 2002). Politically, the 'children overboard' controversy involved a claim by the government, based on an oral and uncorroborated report made by a ship's commander during a telephone conversation in the midst of a complex tactical operation, that 'boat people' (refugees and asylum seekers) had throw their children overboard (Forbes et al., 2002). The particular sensitivity of the claim was that it was made at the beginning of and sustained throughout a Federal election campaign. Importantly, during this campaign, 'border protection' and national security were key issues. The claim that asylum seekers were the kinds of people who would throw their children overboard was used by the government to demonise them as part of the argument for the need for a 'tough' stand against external threats (Senate, 2002).

Overall, the 'children overboard' incident embroiled junior and senior leaders of the Australian Defence fraternity in a professionally and personally damaging debate over conflicting evidence. The subsequent Senate Select Committee investigation reported genuine miscommunication or misunderstanding, inattention, avoidance of responsibility, a public service culture of responsiveness and perhaps over-responsiveness to the needs of ministers, and deliberate deception motivated by political expedience. Noting also the 'sequence of unusual features surrounding the treatment of SIEV 4', the committee pointed to the likelihood that the government had decided early to make an example of SIEV 4 (Senate, 2002:xxv). Nor was there any correction, retraction, or communication about the existence of doubts in connection with the alleged incident itself, or the photographs as evidence for it, made by any member of the Federal government prior to the November 2001 election. Worse, the Defence Minister was reported as having made a number of misleading statements and of having deceived the Australian people – in short, of being intentionally 'unethical'.

Case: The USS Vincennes

Unlike the complex, political manipulation behind the 'children overboard' incident, this tragic incident, which involved the accidental shooting down of an Iranian civilian aircraft (Flight 655) by USS Vincennes in July 1988, is an example of an intentional action by a military leader under considerable duress. Like the previous case, this incident needs to be seen against the backdrop of powerful external political considerations. In the case of the USS Vincennes, competing national interests and a collusive in-group ethos shaped the unfortunate event.

The official story surrounding this incident was of an American warship minding its own business. However, the real story involved an undeclared war in which the United States was the de facto ally of Saddam Hussein and Iraq in its war against Iran. The subsequent chain of events was set in motion by decoy distress transmissions from a phantom merchant vessel, organised by US forces to lure out Iranian gunboats from the islands in the Strait of Hormuz (Koppel, 1992). Compounding the tension, the Vincennes had minutes earlier been under fire from an Iranian gunboat and, as the ship's commander states, when the approaching aircraft reached minimum weapons range a decision had to be made. Regardless of the immediate operational decision, the reason the USS Vincennes was in location was the political imperative to ensure free use of the vital Persian Gulf sea-lanes. The subsequent response by the government to the accident, in the midst of a presidential campaign, was described as 'a tissue of lies, fabrications, half-truths and omissions' (Koppel, 1992).

Both of these cases illustrate complex and unpredictable workplace realities that are by nature *hard* to solve. The specific realities play out at two levels: the immediate and pressing concerns at the sharp end, and the wider contextual pressures. In the aftermath of the recent financial crisis, the then US Treasury Secretary Robert Rubin was asked why he had not previously suggested stricter capital requirements. He is reported to have said, 'There was no political reality of getting it done...We had a lot going on' (Faiola et al., 2009). In the two cases outlined, it is similarly possible to argue that, like in the financial crisis, there was a lot going on. In the 'children overboard' incident, external actors and considerations primarily caused the attendant difficulties. Contributing forces included local 'noise', coupled with moral ambiguity and a shifting of responsibility at the tactical level. Further up the chain, there was the dehumanisation of refugees and intentional, politically inspired deception. In the incident involving the USS Vincennes, there was again a lot of 'noise', coupled with dehumanisation and moral ambiguity, and a clear attempt to shift responsibility at several levels. Viewed in the wider context of the Iran–Iraq War, the intensive operational context invites aggressive norms. These norms collectively may have led to incremental degradation in the rules of engagement, which in this case resulted in tragedy.

Towards a multidimensional contextual framework

Reflecting on unpredictable workplace realities, we might also consider the effect of what Reason (1997) called 'countervailing forces'. These can either increase resistance (through factors like commitment, competence, awareness, and adequate resources) or increase vulnerability (through factors such as the likelihood of detection, personal benefit, and unfamiliar tasks). To better understand them, it is useful to examine possible countervailing forces and their related challenges in a contextualised framework. Figure 5.1 describes a multidimensional activity space. In this space, nominal challenges in terms of routine or exceptional errors and intentional violations are described at two levels, the individual and the organisational, and in terms of low-level and/or episodic issues, or major and/or systemic ones.

Figure 5.1   Activity Space and Nominal Challenges

As Reason points out, people involved in incidents are mostly not reckless, stupid, or blind to the consequences of their actions. And it may be the best people who make the worst mistakes (Reason, 1990:201; Reason, 2000). Consequently, we need to understand the tensions that result in fallible decision-making, whether through failure or lack of expertise, or intentional violation. Two broad considerations involve irrational psychological impulses (including cognitive bias), and collective behaviour.

First, irrational psychological impulses: systemic factors aside, psychological precursors challenge the idea of man as a purely rational animal. These concepts, drawn from behavioural psychology, highlight the power of context and the impact of irrational impulses that result from cognitive bias. Intuitive judgements are especially important at the sharp end, and the defining property of these judgements is that they are snap judgements because, in most cases, only a single option comes to mind (Kahneman, 2003). These intuitive judgements are not always clean, because short-cutting logical cognitive processing can produce errors. These biases include: *confirmation bias*, where people seek out and give disproportionate weight to information that confirms their viewpoint; and *availability bias*, where decisions are based on the most recent and readily available information. In instances such as stock market movements, this relates to the *herding* effect, the tendency to follow the crowd. A further bias arises from the clarity of retrospection. Called *hindsight bias*, there are two difficulties. First, hindsight tends to exaggerate what others should have been able to anticipate, or what they saw if involved. Secondly, it causes uncertainty over how much knowledge of the outcome influences the perception of events (Reason, 1990). Two further influences can bear down on individual decision-makers. First, the tendency to discount outcomes that are merely prob-able in comparison with outcomes that are certain, the *certainty effect*, which in turn contributes to *loss aversion*, where possible losses are seen as far more significant than any potential gain (Kahneman, 2003; Teece, 2007). Secondly, there is the psychological tendency to overestimate the importance of character traits. This *fundamental attribution error* can lead people to underestimate situational or contextual factors.

As well as the distortion arising from irrational psychological impulses and cognitive bias, there is the danger posed by collective behaviour (Quick and Kets de Vries, 2000; McNary, 2004). This concerns the recip-rocal relationship between individual and group, and the consequent group norms and established ways of doing things. Key influences driv-ing collective behaviour include blind loyalty to the group leader, the tendency towards group-think, and an escalation of commitment, all of which can blind people to the realities of the situation (Reiter-Palmon and Illies, 2004). There can, however, be more sinister influences. For example, a study that modelled escape behaviour in emergency situa-tions offers insight into the collective norms that can emerge in groups, particularly at the sharp end. This study noted that when group mem-bers had an option of aggressive behaviour, the salience of the aggres-sive norm in a larger group was stronger than its salience in a smaller group. Conversely, once competitive and aggressive norms had formed in a small group, competitive and aggressive behaviours could become more severe than those in a larger group (Kugihara, 2001). Reinforcing the effect of aggressive norms, an earlier study of soldiers in Vietnam highlights the liberating effect of the use of dehumanising slang to describe the enemy and his homes (gooks, hooches), and the 'love of destruction and the thrill of killing' by otherwise thoughtful men. This propensity was encouraged not by any political cause or hatred of the enemy, but by the forces of comradeship, the freedom and escape from everyday bonds, the chance to test one's physical and emotional limits, and the seeming power over life and death (Mack, 1986).

Illustrating the activity space framework

These types of interconnections and complexities can be illustrated using the activity space framework. For example, one response to the financial crash has been to blame it on credit default swaps (Tett, 2009). The essence of this story is how a financial instrument that once seemed good turned bad over a period of two decades. These instruments, created in a situation of moral ambiguity (Quadrant 3) diffused around the global economy through social influence (Quadrant 4). Aided by herding and a shift in responsibility (Quadrant 1) they spawned a credit bubble and created a 'wicked' problem (Quadrant 2). The financial crisis story is also compelling for what people did not do. The shift of responsibility effected by a culture of silence (Quadrant 1), as bankers initially associated with these instruments failed to declare their concern and to link 'bundled risk' to mortgage debt (Tett, 2009:81). It is also possible to point to incremental degradation over time (across both Quadrants 4 and 1), as capital adequacy rules and rules about leverage were progressively dismantled or not updated over time (Zakaria, 2009).

The framework can also be used to illustrate the two cases of the 'children overboard' incident and the USS Vincennes. Complex military operations require an individual to have considerable discretion. This is enshrined in 'mission control', an approach that delineates broad actions by a commander and allows flexibility and discretionary authority with downward delegation of decision-making (Defence, 2005). What this approach does not preclude is the potential for interference from above, such as was evident in the 'children overboard' case. This effect, long recognised in military and other politicised working environments, is referred to as the 'long screwdriver' (Coll, 2008).

In the 'children overboard' incident (Figure 5.2), the events central to the drama occur a long way from the actual ship and its personnel. The trigger provided by the asylum seeker boat set in play complex tensions in a politically inspired drama. In effect, public policy and related management actions at the political level played a large part in exacerbating the pressure on the leader at the sharp end. Situational factors in

Figure 5.2 Children Overboard

Figure 5.3   USS Vincennes

Canberra, and the associated mishandling and manipulation of events as they unfolded, embroiled both junior and more senior military staff in a professionally and personally damaging debate over conflicting evidence.

In the case of the USS Vincennes (Figure 5.3), we have another complex competitive context that risked depersonalisation and other blurred issues. In this stress-filled time-sensitive situation, there was great potential for unethical or otherwise aberrant actions (such as excess force) and unintended consequences, as was borne out by subsequent events. The immediate trigger for the unfortunate event was a commercial airliner departing innocently from a well-known airport being mistaken for a hostile aircraft. This local trigger, however, intersected with pressure for mission achievement. It appears that this tension created the conditions for imperfect rationality and cognitive bias, including confirmation bias and loss aversion, as well as the distortion created by the presence of strong emotion.

Supporting leaders at the sharp end

Any call for better leader accountability and control must therefore be seen in terms of 'workplace realities' (Collins, 2004:125). This is not to let leaders off the hook, but to acknowledge the particular complexities of life at the sharp end. In determining how to support leaders at the sharp end, one needs to first understand the special challenges that they face in time-pressured and stress-loaded contexts. These contexts are ripe for emotional distortion, human fallibility and cognitive bias, as well as the often-unintended consequences that accompany many seemingly innocent actions. Based on these considerations, two broad strategies are recommended to build resistance against and to reduce vulnerability to failure.

First, there is a need to describe and understand the ethical landscape. This landscape, as we have described it, comprises a spectrum that ranges from low-level and sporadic issues to high-level and endemic ones. In describing this landscape, it is important to discriminate between the spectrum of risk at both the individual and the organisational levels. These risks can be categorised in terms of cognitive bias and collective behaviour. However, there is also an interconnection between the individual and organisational levels, as demonstrated by the cases discussed through the lens of the activity space framework.

Secondly, drawing on insights from studies in the use of hazardous technologies and safety practice, greater efforts might be directed towards the conditions under which leaders at the sharp end are expected to perform. Particular focus might be given to promoting those countervailing forces that can increase institutional resistance to failure. These forces include reducing the contextual complexity caused by external political machinations, and moderating the effect of psychological precursors and context.

Conclusion

This chapter has offered a systems perspective that goes beyond the means–ends instrumentalism of leadership ethics. When viewed as a system, most incidents show many interconnections and an inherent complexity that together offer a richer account about why things can sometimes spiral out of control. A systems perspective requires us to understand and take into account the interdependency of conflicting goals, and to recognise the inevitability of unintended consequences. In terms of leadership, there are no easy answers. This is not new. But recognising that leadership is a symbiotic relationship between leader and followers, in a specific context, emphasises the role that cognitive biases and group dynamics can play in a complex and interconnected activity space. These influences can help to explain the anxiety and faulty rationality at play at the sharp end, as illustrated in the case of the USS Vincennes. Group and organisational dynamics similarly generate their own tensions, and unintended consequences, as illustrated in the 'children overboard' case.

In conclusion, no amount of regulatory intervention would be sufficient to insulate the wider community from the pressure of competition and the need to perform, whether in financial services or elsewhere. At the sharp end, where many problems are grey, the leader is also not likely to have the luxury of flexibility and time to think. At the sharp end, there is rarely a single cause of error, and we need to acknowledge that (accidental) failures or (intentional) deviations are multidimensional and multi-causal phenomena. This discussion has clear implications for the content and method of public policy, which is one obvious area for future research. But, based on this argument, one urgent issue is the need for strategies that decouple activity at the sharp end from policy responses to emerging challenges.

Note

Acknowledgment, with thanks: this chapter is an edited version of our original paper in *Journal of Public Affairs*, 2010, and is published by permission of John Wiley & Sons Ltd (The sharp end: Real life challenges in a complex activity space; by K. T. Thomas and A. D. Walker, *Journal of Public Affairs*, 10(3) Issue 3, Copyright © 2010, John Wiley & Sons Ltd).

Bibliography

Castells, M., The Information Age: Economy, Society and Culture Volume 1 – The Rise of the Network Society (Malden, MA: Blackwell Publishers Inc., 2000).

Coll, S., 'The General's Dilemma', *The New Yorker*, retrieved 3 September (2008) www.newyorker.com/reporting/2008/09/08/080908fa_fact_coll?printable=true.

Collins, J., *Good to Great* (London: Random House Business Books, 2004).

Defence, *Command, Strategic Leadership and Management*, Australian Defence Staff College, Defence Strategic Studies Course (Canberra: University of Canberra, 2005).

Dexter, B. and Prince, C., 'Turning Managers into Leaders: Assessing the Organisational Impact of Leadership Development', *Strategic Change*, 16(5) (2007) 217–226.

Faiola, A., Nakashima, E., and Drew, J., 'The Crash: What Went Wrong', *Solutions to the Economic Crisis*, (2009) (accessed 18 August 2009).

Forbes, M., Gordon, M., and Taylor, K., 'Children Overboard', *The Age*, (1) 21 February (2002).

Gronn, P. *The New Work of Educational Leaders* (London: Sage Publications, 2003).

Kahneman, D., 'Maps of Bounded Rationality: Psychology for Behavioural Economics [dagger]', *The American Economic Review*, 93(5) (2003) 1449.

Koppel, T., The USS Vincennes: Public War, Secret War, USA, ABC News (1992).

Kugihara, N., 'Effects of Aggressive Behaviour and Group Size on Collective Behaviour in an Emergency: A Test between a Social Identity Model and Deindividuation Theory', *The British Journal of Social Psychology*, 40(24) (2001) 575.

Mack, J.E., 'Nuclear Weapons and the Dark Side of Humankind', *Political Psychology*, 7(2) (1986) 223–233.

McNary, L.D., 'Organisational Misbehaviour', *The Journal of Business Communication*, 41(2) (2004) 212–217.

Mumford, M.D., Connelly, S., and Gaddis, B., 'How Creative Leaders Think: Experimental Findings and Cases', *Leadership Quarterly*, 14 (2003) 411–432.

Murray, P. and Chapman, R., 'From Continuous Improvement to Organisational Learning: Developmental Theory', *The Learning Organisation*, 10(4/5) (2003) 272.

Perrow, C., 'A Framework for the Comparative Analysis of Organisations', *American Sociological Review*, 32 (1967) 194–208.

Quick, J.C. and Kets de Vries, M.F., 'The Next Frontier: Edgar Schein on Organisational Therapy', *The Academy of Management Executive*, 14(1) (2000) 31–48.

Reason, J., 'Human Error: Models and Management', *British Management Journal*, 320 (2000) 768–770.

Reason, J., *Human Error* (Cambridge, UK: Cambridge University Press, 1990).

Reason, J., Managing the Risks of Organisational Accidents (Aldershot, UK: Ashgate, 1997).

Reiter-Palmon, R. and Illies, J., 'Leadership and Creativity: Understanding Leadership from a Creative Problem-solving Perspective', *The Leadership Quarterly*, 15 (2004) 55–77.

Rost, J.C. and Baker, R.A., 'Leadership Education in Colleges: Toward a 21st Century Paradigm', *The Journal of Leadership Studies*, 7(1) (2000) 3–12.

Senate, *Select Committee for an inquiry into a certain maritime incident*. S.S. Committee. Canberra, Department of the Senate, Australian Commonwealth Government (2002) www.aph.gov.au/senate/committee/maritime_incident_ctte/report/report.pdf (accessed on 13 February 2010).

Senge, P., *The Fifth Discipline: The Art and Practice of a Learning Organisation* (Sydney: Random House, 1995).

Sinclair, A., 'Body Possibilities', *Leadership*, 1(4) (2005) 387–406.

Teece, D., 'Explicating Dynamic Capabilities: The Nature and Microfoundations of (Sustainable) Enterprise Performance', *Strategic Management Journal*, 28(13) (2007) 1319–1350.

Tett, G., *Fool's Gold: How Unrestrained Greed Corrupted a Dream, Shattered Global Markets and Unleashed a Catastrophe* (London: Little, Brown Book Group, 2009).

Zakaria, F. 'The Capitalist Manifesto: Greed is Good (to a point)', *Newsweek* (2009) 37–41.

Part II

Perspectives from Around the World

6
Inclusive Leadership in Nicaragua and the DRC

Josep F. Mària and Josep M. Lozano

Introduction

The conference at which this chapter was originally introduced started with the question: What is the meaning and role of ethics in effective leadership and corporate social responsibility in an age of globalisation? (Jones and Millar, 2009). Globalisation has had controversial effects (Beck, 2000; Castells, 2000). Recent outcomes of this process are ambivalent: while there has been substantial growth in the GDP of certain countries, we have also witnessed new forms of social exclusion (Mària, 2007:71f.). The mechanisms of this social exclusion are multifaceted: individuals are excluded for economic, political, social, or cultural reasons. Therefore, the struggle for a more inclusive form of globalisation is equally multifaceted (Mària, 2008:214f.).

In this struggle, inter-organisational relationships play a crucial role. Examples of experiments where groups of organisations have succeeded in addressing social exclusion are microfinance and social enterprise (Yunus, 2006; Wille and Barham, 2009). These initiatives include the development of relationships between NGOs, local communities, public administrations, SMEs, and large private enterprises (Austin, 2000). The literature relating to such experiments can be classified around three main concepts: 'partnerships for development' (Business Partners for Development, 2002; Casado, 2008; Reed and Reed, 2009); certain working models at the 'bottom of the pyramid', or BOP (Prahalad and Hammond, 2002; Karnani, 2007; Hahn, 2009; Wille and Barham, 2009); and the more general domain of 'networks' (Inkpen and Tsang, 2005; Biggs and Shah, 2006; Mesquita and Lazzarini, 2008). In this literature the question of leadership is not always explicit, although it is considered important (Wille and Barham, 2009:4). Therefore, this chapter addresses explicitly the question of leadership in groups of organisations that are oriented towards the creation of economic and social value in developing countries. It presents the special traits and challenges of leadership in these contexts by comparing two conceptual approaches and illustrating this comparison with two practical cases.

The chapter starts by presenting and comparing the theories of Responsible Leadership (Thomas Maak and Nicola Pless) and of the Work of Translation (Boaventura S. Santos), selected because of their orientation towards inter-organisational relationships directed at social inclusion. This comparison is then illustrated with the two cases of FENACOOP and CADICEC (economic development organisations in Nicaragua and in the Democratic Republic of Congo, respectively), with special emphasis on the leadership characteristics displayed by their leaders, S. Cáceres and M. Ekwa. We then discuss leadership traits derived from both the theories and the cases, and conclude by proposing the extension of these leadership traits to business leaders wishing to work towards a more inclusive form of globalisation.

Responsible leadership

Thomas Maak and Nicola Pless understand responsible leadership as 'a relational and ethical phenomenon, which occurs in social processes of interaction with those who affect or are affected by leadership and have a stake in the purpose and vision of the leadership relationship' (Maak and Pless, 2006:103). Their understanding of leadership can be summarised as 'the art of building and sustaining good relationships to all relevant stakeholders' (Maak and Pless, 2006:104). They argue that, in a globalised world, this is becoming more of a requirement than an option, because good and ethical relationships with stakeholders are increasingly necessary for firms to secure both long-term profits and their short-term license to operate (Maak, 2007:330).

These stakeholder relationships are built through a process which is not merely instrumental. It is more than just give and take, more than generalised 'norms of reciprocity': 'In other words, the way an organisation conducts its business, how it interacts with stakeholders, which stakeholders it considers relevant and what stakeholders perceive as a responsible business (and business leader), depends considerably on how both business leaders and stakeholders *think* about it. If they think alike, tapping into common social resources may be easier. If they think differently, some "bridging" needs to be done to align the cognitions' (Maak, 2007:335). A responsible leader, therefore, is asked to 'think alike' or to 'align cognitions' with both internal and external stakeholders in order to ensure value creation for them.

This need to align with both internal and external stakeholders is not easy and may again require 'bridging'. The external front, in particular, may be more problematic, since the business leader must connect stakeholders who have different mindsets and organisational cultures (for instance, managers, NGO activists and community leaders). This special sort of connection with external stakeholders is approached through the image of the responsible leader as a 'bridge-builder' (Maak, 2007:337). Connected to the idea of being a bridge-builder, Maak and Pless explore the role of the leader as 'weaver', weaving webs of sustainable relationships to create trust and value for all stakeholders, building a more inclusive society through relationships of equality (Maak, 2007:330 and 337; Maak and Pless, 2006:104).

The Responsible Leadership approach contrasts with the conceptualisation of the leader as a 'great man', focused only on organisational goals, and possessing a certain moral superiority over his subordinates/followers (Maak and Pless, 2006:102f.). While the 'great man' style might have been appropriate for hierarchically structured firms, it is certainly not suited to today's 'flattened hierarchies and networked structures' (Maak and Pless, 2006:102–106). In fact, attending to external stakeholders requires business leaders to move from a 'hierarchical' position to a 'central' position in the network of stakeholders (Maak, 2007:336). The business leader should accept and assume the role of broker, enabler, facilitator or bridge-builder in order to engage in a dialogue among equals (Maak, 2007:340). Consequently, the authority of a responsible leader does not come from her status and position of power, but from her task as 'a weaver of different kinds of people into the fabric of society' (Maak and Pless, 2006:103f.).

By conceptualising a theory of Responsible Leadership, Maak and Pless have earned a position in the emergent debate on business leadership, in particular on the creation of a 'culture of inclusion' (Pless and Maak, 2004:136) and on the role of business leaders as agents of social justice in globalisation (Pless and Maak, 2009; Maak and Pless, 2009a).

Work of translation

According to the Portuguese Sociologist Boaventura de Sousa Santos, present-day society is defined by capitalism, which has constructed the concepts of the 'West' and 'globalisation' as we know them. Santos contends that the West has taken only those elements that favour the expansion of capitalism from a broader vision that would otherwise include a multiplicity of worlds (earthly and ultra-earthly) and a multiplicity of times (past, present, future, cyclical, linear, and simultaneous) (Santos, 2005:157). As a result, the multiplicity of worlds is reduced to the earthly world, through the process of secularisation; and the multiplicity of times is reduced to linear time, through the substitution of the idea of salvation by those of progress and revolution (Santos, 2005:157). He argues that this operation imposes a reasoning style which invades the analysis of societies and shapes actions in them, reducing the broader vision to a world shaped by dichotomies such as scientific/literary culture, scientific/traditional knowledge, man/woman, culture/nature, civilised/primitive, capital/work, black/white, North/South, West/East (Santos, 2005:156). According to Santos, the Western style of reasoning subordinates each pole in a dichotomy to the other one. One of the most relevant dichotomies is the global/local duality, where global is understood as superior, and local realities are inferior alternatives to what 'exists' globally (Santos, 2005:161f.).

However, Santos contends that this 'hegemonic globalisation' imposed by the West has not fulfilled the modern promises by which it was originally inspired: equality, liberty, peace, progress, and dominion over nature (Santos, 2005:97f.). In light of this, Santos advocates an *oppositional postmodernism*: an approach to the social debate which offers alternatives to both Western modernity and hegemonic globalisation. He argues that the approach is 'oppositional' because the construction of these alternatives should begin 'from below' and 'in a multicultural and participatory manner' (Santos, 2005:112). As such, it *opposes* the dominance of 'global realities' which have acquired a status of superiority over 'local realities', a superiority which triggers top-down, monocultural and non-participatory strategies, disguised under the label of 'global'. As for 'postmodernism', Santos argues that alternatives to hegemonic globalisation cannot only be carried out by the supposedly almighty actors that modern sociological theories have worshiped: the market or the state. Rather, these alternatives correspond to diverse actors working in a coordinated fashion (Santos, 2005:101).

The Work of Translation is a task that allows leaders to recognise and connect projects and organisations that create social and economic value beyond hegemonic globalisation. Thus, 'the objective of the Work of Translation is to create constellations of knowledge and practices which are strong enough to offer credible alternatives to what is defined today as neo-liberal globalisation and which is nothing more than a new step of global capitalism to tie the inexhaustible totality of the world to merchant logic' (Santos, 2005:186). This Work of Translation demands dialogue between 'alternative' organisations and causes (the 'wandering fragments') which promote diverse rights: those of future generations, indigenous peoples, workers, women, children, and the right to development. This dialogue, freed from preconceived ideas regarding the articulation of organisations or interests, respects local identities and leads to the slow emergence of a counter-hegemonic globalisation (Santos, 2005:153). Santos also sees the Work of Translation as being one way to facilitate discourse between hegemonic and non-hegemonic practices and organisations (Santos, 2005:177). This would mean that negotiations and partnerships were possible between organisations belonging to hegemonic globalisation (typically, private firms) and organisations involved in the counter-hegemonic globalisation (social movements, social enterprises, local communities, NGOs, and so on). Successful examples of recent partnerships between companies and NGOs or social enterprises have generated both profits for firms and social value for their partners (Maak, 2007:337f. and Plana, 2008:35f.).

Comparison

A comparison between the contrasting approaches of Santos and Maak and Pless is possible because each permits or promotes dialogue among organisations on both sides of the globalisation fence. Santos admits the possibility of 'translating' social experiences between organisations from the counter-hegemonic globalisation realm and private firms. Maak and Pless similarly invite business leaders to pay attention to the firm's stakeholders – particularly to stakeholders in need – in order to contribute to the creation of a more inclusive society (Maak and Pless, 2009a). A comparison of these two approaches is fruitful because it can reveal the leadership characteristics needed to create economic and social value at both ends of the globalisation spectrum, that is, global leadership 'from the top', and 'from the bottom'. The concepts of Responsible Leadership and Work of Translation can therefore be compared using a structure of five dimensions: perspective (What is the point of view adopted in these approaches?); diagnosis (What do they argue are the causes of social exclusion?); main task (What do they see as the leader's role in fighting social exclusion?); style of action (What ethical conditions/inspiring guidelines do they suggest?); and leadership outcome (What is the desired outcome of the leadership action?).

Perspective

While Maak and Pless, who are management scholars, take the perspective of leaders at the heart of hegemonic globalisation, Santos, a sociologist, looks at globalisation through the eyes of social movements striving to articulate counter-hegemonic globalisation. Contrasting the author and actor perspectives sheds light on the responsible leader's visions and interests: while the leader must decide on stakeholder engagement (Maak, 2007:337), financial constraints might prevent this by marginalising certain social actors who, at first glance, may not seem to contribute in profit-related ways to the firm's core activity. This is an important limit to the task of inclusion. Therefore, a sociological perspective is needed to balance a managerial one, especially if it focuses attention on the 'wandering fragments' that hegemonic capitalism/globalisation has tended to exclude.

Diagnosis

By taking a business perspective, Maak and Pless do not provide a philosophical or sociological explanation of the present globalisation process. However, they acknowledge that a change in business practice can promote social inclusion. Santos, in turn, explains the present situation both philosophically and sociologically in terms of Western reductionism/modernity, a broader vision which has expelled 'wandering fragments'. As a postmodern scholar, he criticises the existence of single-principle social transformation: no organisation (like the modern nation state) or principle (like the free market) can in isolation guarantee a positive transformation of society. The contrast of diagnoses challenges those who wish to solve social problems with preconceived formulas: the competitive market, the modern state or an almighty hierarchical company with a great-man-style leader at the top.

Main task

Maak and Pless's theory of leadership describes the main task of a responsible leader as being the 'bridge-builder', building connections between stakeholders who are otherwise disconnected in the social structure, and as the 'weaver', weaving webs of inclusion among stakeholders and the excluded to create a just and inclusive society. Santos doesn't offer an explicit theory of leadership, but the Work of Translation metaphor assumes that, in the global dialogue, actors 'speak different languages', having different values, aspirations, goals, ideas, styles of working, and styles of living together. Since there is no one actor who speaks the universal/global meta-language, this translation task is inevitable and compulsory for every single actor. In this multilingual dialogue, possibilities exist for the articulation of the excluded's particular interests in order to contribute to counter-hegemonic globalisation. Private companies can and should also enter this stage and, thus, the dialogue. The exercise of translation is notably easier if leaders serve as bridge-builders and weavers of webs of inclusion.

Style of action

According to Maak and Pless, the equal treatment of stakeholders includes the leader inviting each stakeholder 'to share her experiences', to communicate how she is trying to attain her particular interests, and what vision is implicit in this task. For Santos, the idea that there is no meta-language or 'lingua franca' implies a multicultural approach to participatory interaction between organisations. This approach is the foundation for the articulation of 'global' (or supra-local) initiatives: a bottom-up articulation that starts at the local level.

Leadership outcome

Maak and Pless use different expressions to describe the outcome of a responsible leader's actions: going beyond 'just give and take', 'thinking alike with stakeholders', finding a 'common ethical ground', reaching a 'group of shared norms and values', or achieving 'a commonly desired vision' (Maak, 2007:335; Maak and Pless, 2006:104). According to Santos, the outcome of the Work of Translation is to come to a 'reciprocal intelligibility' (Santos, 200:178) or to 'create constellations of knowledge and practices' in which, however, no common vision is possible because no common language exists (Santos, 2005:186).

Synthesis

This comparison raises a central question about those leadership traits oriented to creating economic and social value. A responsible leader should be aware that the different positions sustained by stakeholders might not be reduced to a 'common vision' after a period of dialogue. Instead, the desired outcome of dialogue should be a change in the tension between irreducible positions towards a point where this tension becomes a creative source of economic and social value in a way that is acceptable for all stakeholders. In other words, the play does not have a script, but the actors may progressively discover that it is about the shared creation of economic and social value, about an attempt to accommodate particular interests, about inclusion, and about the

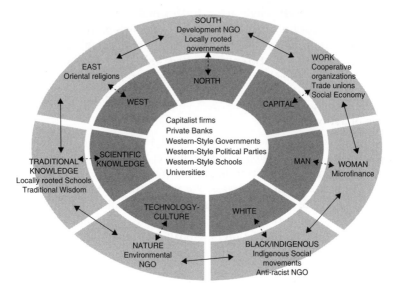

Figure 6.1 Synthesis
Source: the authors

promotion of human dignity. This common awareness will facilitate agreements and shared actions.

Figure 6.1 offers a synthesis of the two contrasting theories by way of a graphic summary to depict the complexity of the actors and their relationships. The inner circle includes the elements of the broader vision that the West and hegemonic globalisation have privileged in economic activities: the North, capital, man, the white race, technology and culture, scientific knowledge, the West. The outer circle consists of the 'wandering fragments' which, according to Santos, have been subordinated by hegemonic globalisation. Counter-hegemonic globalisation, in turn, is the result of the Work of Translation, represented by the solid arrows, which link the wandering fragments in the outer circle. The translation between hegemonic and counter-hegemonic organisations is represented by the discontinuous arrows that link organisations inside the circle with organisations outside: this corresponds to the responsible leader's role as bridge-builder or weaver of webs of inclusion. It is important to underscore that relationships between actors – signalled in the figure by both continuous and discontinuous arrows – are conflictive because of the different interests promoted (or languages spoken) by each organisation or social group. Unfortunately, these conflicts often have dramatic consequences in developing countries, and they are often addressed by violent means. The Work of Translation is designed to be a peaceful and creative way to address such conflicts.

Now that we have presented and compared the theoretical approaches, in the next section we introduce two case study organisations and their leaders (FENACOOP/Sinforiano Cáceres and CADICEC/Martin Ekwa) to illustrate the main leadership traits that foster social inclusion.

Cases in Nicaragua and in the Democratic Republic of the Congo

'So how do you teach leadership here [in Africa]?' I asked, and he shot back, 'We just show it' (Mintzberg, 2006:4).

According to the Ghanaian professor, Kwame Bediako, Henry Mintzberg's interlocutor in the quotation above, teaching leadership has to do with 'showing leadership', and, therefore, with cases of leadership (Maak, 2007:330). The two cases used here are FENACOOP, a federation of co-ops in Nicaragua led by Sinforiano Cáceres, and CADICEC, an employer organisation in the Democratic Republic of the Congo led by Martin Ekwa. The cases have been chosen, first, because they are 'located' at the border between hegemonic and counter-hegemonic organisations, a border where dialogue (Work of Translation) between these two kinds of organisations is necessary if they wish to create economic and social value; secondly, because FENACOOP and CADICEC are successfully creating economic and social value; and thirdly because, as we argue below, Sinforiano Cáceres (FENACOOP) and Martin Ekwa (CADICEC) display the leadership traits (visions, roles, and virtues) which are adequate for this value creation. In this section, each case will start with a brief presentation of the situation in each respective country. We then describe the organisations and lastly analyse their respective leaders' leadership style.

Nicaragua, FENACOOP, and Sinforiano Cáceres

Nicaragua is a small country with about 6 million inhabitants; a country that suffered a cruel succession of dictatorships by the Somoza Dynasty from 1936 to 1979. In 1979 a revolution overthrew the Dynasty's last dictator and Nicaragua became a Socialist Democratic country, strongly influenced by Cuban politics (Mària, 2009:159). Between 1982 and 1990, the country was wracked by civil war. With the victory of a right-wing party in the 1990 elections, Nicaragua implemented an economic policy in line with the Washington Consensus, and started a process of regional economic integration under the Central American Free Trade Association (CAFTA). These CAFTA negotiations were crucial for the different economic groups in Nicaragua, especially for poor farmers (Mària, 2009:155f.).

The National Federation of Co-ops (FENACOOP from its Spanish acronym) was created in 1990. By 2006, FENACOOP represented 620 agriculture and agro-industrial co-ops and approximately 40,000 families out of a total of 80,000 in the co-op sector in Nicaragua. Since its creation, FENACOOP has maintained its cooperative identity despite pressure from Nicaraguan political parties and private firms. However, this identity has not prevented FENACOOP from carrying out the Work of Translation with the Socialist Party or with private firms. For example, in 2005, the Federation participated in an operation to import 2,500 tons of Venezuelan urea, an operation in which different actors were involved, especially the Venezuelan government, the Nicaraguan Socialist Party, and a group of firms in the urea industry. The result was lower prices for the benefit of all Nicaraguan farmers, including FENACOOP members (Mària, 2009:190f.). Another illustration of the Work of Translation was the Federation's participation in the negotiations of the Central American Free Trade Agreement (CAFTA). In these multilateral talks, FENACOOP was part of the Nicaraguan Delegation, defending the position of Nicaraguan small farmers and obtaining favourable transition conditions that helped poor farmers to adapt to the new regional market.

The son of a poor farmer, with only a primary school education, Sinforiano Cáceres has developed a personal style of leadership. In 1990, he realised that the Socialist Party's rule had developed a great-man style of leadership that hindered liberalisation and economic regional integration processes. Searching for a new style of direction, Cáceres strived to keep his loyalty to cooperative members in order to articulate their interests with those of other groups. This loyalty has allowed him to resist the petitions made by political parties for him to sacrifice the cooperative principles for his own personal financial interest and to resist proposals by private companies to transform FENACOOP into a private enterprise. As a result of participation in the CAFTA negotiations, Cáceres has elaborated a set of 'negotiation rules' which can be summarised in three points. First, a leader needs to articulate the interests of both external and internal stakeholders. Internal consensus implies a process of debate with co-op members who are sometimes illiterate farmers: an adequate method of consultation and an understandable vocabulary (Work of Translation) must be found in questions with high complexity related to international trade. Secondly, at the beginning of a multilateral negotiation process like CAFTA, leaders should trust each other and technical experts in spite of their fear of 'losing identity'. This trust implies that, in certain aspects of the negotiations, one leader should be the protagonist and the others should be the followers; but in other aspects, the roles should be inverted. Third, in a negotiations process, the particular goals of each organisation should be made transparent to all parties. In fact, if a leader hides the particular interests of her organisation and pretends to 'strive for the common good', that organisation's particular objectives cannot be articulated, and an agreement will not be achieved in the end.

The Democratic Republic of the Congo, CADICEC, and Martin Ekwa

The Democratic Republic of the Congo (DRC, known as Zaire until 1997) is, with 61.2 million inhabitants (UNFPA, 2007), the fourth most populous country in Africa. It is geographically at the heart of Africa, making it vulnerable to regional conflicts. The DRC is one of the poorest countries in the world, ranked 168th out of 177 countries (UNDP, 2007). Since shortly after the country's independence from Belgium in 1960, the country has been ruled by Joseph Mobutu's long and bloody dictatorship. The transition to democracy (1996–2003) involved two terrible wars. In full conflict in 2001, Joseph Kabila became president and received the support of the international community to stop the war and start a transition to democracy. After a very difficult transition, he was elected constitutional president in 2007, although disputes continue (Obotela, 2008).

The Action Centre for Enterprise Leaders and Managers in Congo (CADICEC from the French acronym) was founded in 1956 in order to 'help managers discover all the dimensions of their social mission' (Ekwa, 2006:10). CADICEC's activities have evolved to meet the different needs of employers and managers over time and, with the country's independence in 1960, the organisation became a centre where black and white leaders could exchange opinions. It also offered training to the country's new leading class. In 1984, CADICEC began to support the key sector of small and medium enterprises (SMEs) (Ekwa, 2006:47f.). Through some of these activities, dialogues were initiated with public officials and private bankers to favour both becoming aware of the specific needs of SMEs and to improve the legislation and the financial services affecting them. This dialogue, under CADICEC's leadership, is another illustration of a Work of Translation. Another illustration is a series of activities under what is called the 'Common House' (Ekwa, 2006:108ff.), where regular meals were organised by Martin Ekwa at CADICEC headquarters to connect leaders and intellectuals from different sectors in the Congo, including the diplomatic community. The dialogue stemming from these meals has enabled trustful information-sharing and basic communication between the sectors.

The Congolese Jesuit, Martin Ekwa (Secretary General of CADICEC since 1983) has become a weaver of webs of inclusion between diverse organisations: SMEs, public administrations, banks, NGOs, and representatives of the international community. In particular, CADICEC's support for SME managers includes support for a high proportion of black, poor, and often illiterate women (Santos's 'wandering fragments') who were not previously integrated economically and socially in Congolese society (Ekwa, 2006:50). Ekwa's style of leadership and his understanding of CADICEC are inspired by a pre-colonial African institution: the palaver tree. The palaver tree is a traditional African institution: 'A key socio-political institution of pre-colonial Africa, the palaver is an assembly where a variety of issues are freely debated, and important decisions concerning the community are taken. Its purpose is to resolve latent and overt conflicts in certain highly specific situations. The participants usually gather under a "palaver tree" where everyone has the right to speak and air their grievances or those of their group' (Sopova, 1999). The African palaver is a specific form of discourse, used in combination with proverbs and narratives in educational contexts, which has a normative goal to discover and justify norms (Gichure, 2006:46). Therefore, in the palaver exercise, individuals are taught by each other and, at the same time, they articulate their particular interests (Sopova, 1999). Martin Ekwa does not pretend to lead the CADICEC palaver tree using a great-man style. Instead, he contends that the organisation must 'accompany' enterprises and NGOs: he seems to accept the role of the 'humble networker and mediator who engages herself among equals' (Maak, 2007:340).

Discussion: leadership traits

In this section, the comparison of Responsible Leadership and the Work of Translation, as illustrated by the cases in Nicaragua and the DRC, will be used to describe the characteristics of a leader oriented to the creation of economic and social value. That is, the visions, roles, and virtues of a leader focused on building a more inclusive society, and a more inclusive form of globalisation.

First, the leader should distribute his attention between two ambits or spaces: the limited space of the organisation being led, and the broader space of society, where a complex interaction among organisations occurs. Maak and Pless contend that a responsible leader should display 'dual vistas', being both reflective and active in the consideration of internal and external stakeholders. The concept of Work of Translation includes the idea that every organisation 'speaks a specific language', with its own goals and styles of action, but that each needs to broaden its vision towards other organisations and try to understand their languages in order to cooperate. The cases have shown that Cáceres and Ekwa display a capacity to be attentive to the interests and visions of internal stakeholders (FENACOOP members or SME managers) and to the problems and perceptions of other social groups in Nicaragua or the DRC, with the objective of taking joint action. However, powerful stakeholders may struggle to deal with this 'dual vista' and feel inclined to swallow up stakeholders into their own particular organisation. For instance, in Nicaragua, Sinforiano Cáceres has resisted attempts by powerful political parties and private firms to subordinate FENACOOP to their own 'languages' by incorporating them into their own systems of values, visions, and practices.

Secondly, the leader should strive to connect both spaces (the organisation and other groups) in an active attempt to capture and evaluate the diverse activities carried out by internal and external stakeholders. This includes the articulation of every actor's visions and interests in agreements that create economic and social value in mutually acceptable ways. Maak and Pless describe the leader's role here as the 'bridge-builder' or the 'weaver of webs of inclusion'. Santos's metaphor of the Work of Translation stresses the desired goal of reciprocal understanding between social groups or organisations that speak different languages.

Thirdly, in order to promote social inclusion, the leader's vision and practices must prevent processes of marginalisation among certain groups or organisations. One extreme mechanism of marginalisation is war: a 'social experiment' that Nicaragua suffered until 1990, and the Democratic Republic of the Congo between 1996 and 2003. According to Santos, however, more subtle forms of exclusion are promoted by the West and hegemonic globalisation. This type of exclusion encourages the possible melting of particular languages into a supposed universal/global language. Universal languages or general interests constitute those particular languages and interests of the powerful, who impose their will upon the weak. Following this linguistic metaphor, social inclusion involves respect towards the language spoken by each participant. Where all actors see each other as human beings, treat each other as equals, ensure that each language is respected, and value each other's experiences as worthy, then the dialogue becomes socially inclusive.

Fourthly, in order to develop the visions and roles for social inclusion, the leader must cultivate two central virtues: creativity and trust. Creativity is essential because there is no magic formula to create economic and social value. Interactions with diverse stakeholders are opportunities to identify and develop ventures for value creation. For instance, Cáceres created social value by discovering new ways of negotiating better prices for poor farmers and, in the DRC, Ekwa created economic and social value by empowering SME managers through dialogue with private banks and public officials. As for trust, this virtue is necessary for a fruitful dialogue. Trust increases the elements considered negotiable and, therefore, the range of agreement possible. It is worth noting that trust might be absent at the beginning of processes of dialogue, but it can emerge during these if the leaders believe in it. Equally, trust allows the delegation of leadership to others in certain aspects of complex negotiations. Finally, after the end of a given negotiation, trust leaves the door open for future negotiations and agreements.

Fifthly, the leader must work actively to identify and promote concrete spaces of creative interaction and trust between organisations or social groups. Sinforiano Cáceres identified the Nicaraguan Delegation in the CAFTA negotiations as one of these spaces. Inside the country's delegation, new relationships among leaders developed: trust, transparency, and reconciliation. By simultaneously being immersed in this space and working to build it, each leader was able to transform his vision and search for common and fruitful articulations of particular interests acceptable by all. In the case of Martin Ekwa, the space for creative interaction and trust is CADICEC as a palaver tree: under its branches all members are heard. They know and feel that they belong to 'the family of CADICEC', and they are encouraged to share their conflicts and trained to solve them. Also under CADICEC's branches, different leaders gather and learn to appreciate each other, as a previous and necessary step to promote 'the happiness of the Congolese people'.

Conclusion

In times of globalisation, responsible organisational leaders can contribute to the inclusion of marginalised individuals and social groups. The action of responsible leaders against exclusion involves different tasks: the common effort to reduce economic poverty; the invitation to all affected groups or organisations to 'share their experiences'; the engagement with them in dialogue as equals; the respect for the dignity and human rights of all individuals; the enhancement of different 'languages' as opposed to one universal hegemonic language; and the promotion of spaces of trust and creativity where particular interests can be openly exposed and articulated. These leadership traits have been illustrated by the two organisations studied. While the organisations used are not private firms, we contend that the leadership displayed by both Cáceres and Ekwa can be applied alike to private firms, including multinational corporations. Firstly, because such firms need to set the creation of economic *and* social value as an objective of their activity, an objective shared with organisations such as FENACOOP and CADICEC. Secondly, because this objective cannot be reached without dialogue between hegemonic and counter-hegemonic organisations, a dialogue encouraged by the leadership style described above. And thirdly, because the teachings of leadership at the local level, with Santos's participatory, bottom-up and multicultural approach, may serve as the inspiration for multinational corporations, too.

Finally, this study triggers an interesting reflection about how theories and models on business leadership can profit from examples of responsible leadership in other sectors. We could argue that if research on leadership focuses attention merely on traditional cases of business leaders, it limits possibility. We therefore believe that examples of leaders such as Cáceres and Ekwa open up new perspectives, and enrich the field of business leadership.

Note

1. An earlier version of this paper was presented at the Ashridge International Research Conference at Ashridge Business School on 15 May 2009. The authors would like to thank Deborah Poff, Lindsay Thompson, Carla Millar, and Marc Jones for their comments during this conference.

Bibliography

Austin, J.E., *The Collaboration Challenge: How Nonprofits and Business Succeed through Strategic Alliances* (San Francisco: Jossey Bass, 2000).

Beck, U., *What is Globalization?* (Cambridge: Blackwell/Polity Press, 2000).

Biggs, T. and Shah, M.K., *African Small and Medium Enterprises, Networks, and Manufacturing Performance* (Washington: World Bank, 2006), Policy Research Working Paper 3855.

Business Partners for Development: *Putting Partnering to Work*, 2002, www.bpd-web.com/docs/ngo5of5.pdf (Accessed 15 October 2009).

Casado, F., *Las alianzas para el desarrollo a través de una gestión para resultados: retos y oportunidades para la cooperación española* (Madrid: Fundación Alternativas, 2008) Documento de trabajo 22/2008.

Castells, M., *The Information Age: Economy, Society and Culture. Volume III. End of Millenium* (Oxford: Blackwell, 2000).

Ekwa bis Isal, M. (dir.), *CADICEC. 50 ans d'histoire et d'actions. Devoir de mémoire d'un peuple* (Kinshasa: Editions CADICEC, 2006).

Friedman, T.L., *The World is Flat: A Brief History of the 21st Century* (New York: Farrar, Strauss and Giroux, 2005).

Gichure, C.W., 'Teaching Business Ethics in Africa: What Ethical Orientation? The Case of East and Central Africa', *Journal of Business Ethics*, 63 (2006) 39–52.

Hahn, R., 'The Ethical Rational of Business for the Poor: Integrating the Concepts Bottom of the Pyramid, Sustainable Development and Corporate Citizenship', *Journal of Business Ethics*, 84 (2009) 313–324.

Inkpen, A. and Tsang, E., 'Social Capital, Networks and Knowledge Transfer', *Academy of Management Review*, 30(1) (2005) 146–165.

Jones, M. and Millar, C.C.J.M., 'Global Leadership, Global Ethics? Call for Papers', *Journal of Business Ethics*, 85 (2009) 107–108.

Karnani, A., 'The Mirage of Marketing at the Bottom of the Pyramid: How the Private Sector Can Help Alleviate Poverty', *California Management Review*, 49(4) (2007) 90–111.

Maak, T., 'Responsible Leadership, Stakeholder Engagement, and the Emergence of Social Capital', *Journal of Business Ethics*, 74 (2007) 329–343.

Maak, T. and Pless, N., 'Responsible Leadership in a Stakeholder Society: A Relational Perspective', *Journal of Business Ethics*, 66 (2006) 99–115.

Maak, T. and Pless, N., 'Business Leaders as Citizens of the World. Advancing Humanism on a Global Scale', *Journal of Business Ethics*, 88 (2009a) 537–550.

Maak, T. and Pless, N., 'The Leader As Responsible Change Agent: Promoting Humanism in and beyond Business', in Spitzek, H. et al. (eds) *Humanism in Business* (Cambridge: Cambridge University Press, 2009b).

Mària, J.F., 'De la guerra a la democracia: la República Democrática del Congo', *Revista de Fomento Social*, 238 (2005) 283–312.

Mària, J.F., 'The Many Faces of Globalization', in L. Bouckaert and L. Zsolnai (eds) *Spirituality as a Public Good* (Antwerpen/Apeldoom: Garant, 2007).

Mària, J.F., 'La globalización y los estados de bienestar en Europa', *Revista de Fomento Social*, 250 (2008) 207–231.

Mària, J.F., 'Ay mi Nicaragüita! The Construction of the Common Good in Nicaragua as a Work of Translation' in H.C. de Bettignies and F. Lépineux (eds), *Business, Globalization and the Common Good* (Oxford: Peter Lang, 2009).

Mesquita, L.M. and Lazzarini, S.G., 'Horizontal and Vertical Relationships in Developing Economies: Implications for SMEs' Access to Global Markets', *Academy of Management Journal*, 51(2) (2008) 359–380.

Mintzberg, H., 'Developing Leaders? Developing Countries? Learning from Another Place', *Development in Practice*, 16(1) (2006) 4–14.

Obotela, N., 'Afrique Actualités : Novembre-Décembre 2007', *Congo-Afrique*, 422 (2008) 147–158.

Plana, M., *Platforms to Social Investment: danone.communities Case* (Barcelona: ESADE Master Thesis, 2008).

Pless, N. and Maak, T., 'Building an Inclusive Diversity Culture: Principles, Processes and Practice', *Journal of Business Ethics*, 54 (2004) 129–147.

Pless, N. and Maak, T., 'Responsible Leadership As Agents of World Benefit: Learnings from "Project Ulysses"', *Journal of Business Ethics*, 85 (2009) 59–71.

Prahalad, C.K. and Hammond, A., 'Serving the World's Poor, Profitably', *Harvard Business Review*, September (2002) 4–11.

Reed, A.M., and Reed, D., 'Partnerships for Development: Four Models of Business Involvement', *Journal of Business Ethics*, 90 (2009) 3–37.

Santos, B.S., 'Towards a Multicultural Conception of Human Rights' in M. Feathersome and S. Lash (eds), *Spaces of Culture: City, Nation, World* (London: Sage, 1999).

Santos, B.S., *El milenio huérfano. Ensayos para una nueva cultura política* (Madrid: Trotta, 2005).

Sopova, J., 'In the Shade of the Palaver tree' *The UNESCO Courier*, May (1999) 42.

UNDP: 2007, *Human Development Report 2007/2008. Fighting Climate Change*, http://hdr.undp.org/en/media/hdr_20072008_en_complete.pdf (Accessed 13 March 2008),

UNFPA: 2007, *State of World Population. Unleashing the Potential of Urban Growth*, www.unfpa.org/swp/2007/english/notes/indicators/e_indicator2.pdf (Accessed 13 March 2008).

Wille, E. and Barham, K., *A Role for Business at the Bottom of the Pyramid* (Berkhamsted: Ashridge Business School, 2009).

Yunus, M., *¿Es posible acabar con la pobreza?* (Madrid: Editorial Complutense, 2006).

7
A New Ideal Leadership Profile for Romania

Nicolae Bibu, Valentin Munteanu, Elena Sărătean, and Laura Brancu

Introduction

The GLOBE project – Global Leadership and Organizational Behaviours Effectiveness – (House et al., 2004), is based at Wharton Business School in the United States. The project comprised 170 researchers in 62 societies, and ran over an 11-year period. The project's objective was to determine the extent to which the practices and values of business leadership are universal, and the extent to which they are specific to just a few societies. In this chapter, GLOBE project data is used to examine the relationship between ethical issues and the characteristics of the ideal leader as identified by Romanian middle managers. The study aims to elucidate the cross-cultural management issues that may arise for foreign companies doing business in Romania or with Romanian businesses, particularly as regards ethical behaviours. First, we discuss Romania's ideal leadership profile in practice (as it is), then at value level (as it should be). Secondly, we analyse the GLOBE results in relation to the desired profile of the ideal leader. Finally, we discuss our findings, and formulate some conclusions and recommendations for international managers working in Romania.

Romania is situated in Central/Eastern Europe and is a Latin island in a Slavic world. Romanians speak a Latin-based language, with roots going back to the Roman Empire. After the Second World War, a communist state and a centralised economy was established, backed by the Soviet Union, until the resulting communist dictatorship was overthrown in 1989. Since then, Romania has undergone dramatic social and economic change at huge social and economic cost. It has became a market economy, a democratic state, a member of NATO, and a member of the European Union.

Romania's Socio-cultural Profile

The GLOBE culture model has nine cultural variables: power distance, uncertainty avoidance, institutional collectivism, in-group collectivism, gender egalitarianism, assertiveness, humane orientation, performance orientation, and future orientation (House et al., 2004). The GLOBE Project Romania was carried out in 2006 by a consortium of 12 universities, and used the methodology recommended by Gupta et al. (2002). The analysis of the societal culture was carried out both at practice level (as it is) and at value level (as it should be), based on a representative sample of 362 questionnaires.

Romania's current socio-cultural profile (the practice level) is shown in Table 7.1. The maximum score is 7, while the minimum score is 1. Rank indicates the position of Romania among the 62 societies participating in the GLOBE study.

Romania's socio-cultural practice (life as it is) in absolute measures (mean) is rated high on power distance (5.63), in-group collectivism

Table 7.1   Romanian Socio-cultural Practice Scores

GLOBE: current situation	N	Min	Max	Mean	SD	Rank*	Band
Power distance	355	3.4	7.00	5.6263	.8079	6th	A (highest)
Uncertainty avoidance	355	1.0	6.25	3.660	.9601	46th	C (relatively low)
Institutional collectivism	355	1.5	5.75	3.748	.8481	54th	C (relatively low)
In-group collectivism	355	2.6	7.00	5.4322	.8025	31st	A (highest)
Gender egalitarianism	355	1.6	5.80	3.881	.7085	7th	A (highest)
Assertiveness	355	1.5	6.75	4.1396	.8160	32nd	B (middle)
Humane orientation	355	1.0	7.00	4.093	.9343	31st	C (relatively low)
Performance orientation	355	1.0	7.00	3.508	1.0719	56th	C (lowest)
Future orientation	355	1.0	5.60	5.560	.8755	53rd	C (relatively low)

* n=355

Source: Bibu et al., 'Characteristics of the Organizational Culture in Romanian Organizations Based on the Results of the GLOBE-Romania Project', *Review of International Comparative Management*, new issue no. 9 (2007) p. 36.

Table 7.2   Romanian Socio-cultural Values Scores

GLOBE: desired situation	N	Min	Max	Mean	SD	Rank	Band
Power distance	354	1.00	5.20	2.777	0.8835	22nd	C (medium)
Uncertainty avoidance	354	2.75	7.00	5.392	0.8390	3rd	A (highest)
Institutional collectivism	353	2.50	7.00	4.977	0.8673	23rd	B (relatively high)
In-group collectivism	353	3.25	7.00	6.122	0.8051	9th	A (highest)
Gender egalitarianism	353	2.40	6.20	4.628	0.6840	30th	B (relatively high)
Assertiveness	353	2.30	7.00	4.530	0.9000	11th	A (highest)
Humane orientation	353	3.00	7.00	5.295	0.7327	42nd	C (relatively low)
Performance orientation	353	2.50	6.33	4.924	0.6008	60th	E (lowest)
Future orientation	354	2.75	7.00	5.560	0.8904	30th	B (relatively high)

*n = 354
Source: Bibu et al., 'Characteristics of the Organizational Culture in Romanian Organizations Based on the Results of the GLOBE-Romania Project', *Review of International Comparative Management*, new issue no. 9 (2007) p. 37.

(5.43), and gender egalitarianism (3.88). It has low ratings for uncertainty avoidance (3.66), performance orientation (3.51), future orientation (3.33), institutional collectivism (3.75), and humane orientation (4.09). One cultural dimension, assertiveness (4.14), is rated mid-range. Hence, Romania can be characterised as being hierarchical, small-group oriented, and egalitarian towards gender. At the same time, it encourages societal individualism and does not particularly prioritise modesty in its leaders, as indicated by the medium score for humane orientation. It is a society that focuses more on the present than the future and which tolerates uncertainty, being somewhat relaxed about performance (Bakcsi et al., 2006:18).

Romania's socio-cultural values (life as it should be) are shown in Table 7.2 as means. Again, the maximum score is 7, while the minimum score is 1, and Rank indicates the position of Romania among the 62 societies participating in the GLOBE study.

In absolute measures these rate high on uncertainty avoidance (5.39), assertiveness (4.53), and in-group collectivism (6.12); relatively high on institutional collectivism (4.98), gender egalitarianism (4.63), and future orientation (5.56); medium on power distance (2.78); relatively low on humane orientation (5.30); and among the lowest in the GLOBE study on performance orientation (4.92) (Bakacs et al., 2006). Consequently, in terms of ideal values, Romanians would prefer less hierarchy, more institutional collectivism, more certainty, and more of a focus on the future. There is therefore somewhat of a discrepancy between the current and desired socio-cultural make-up of Romania.

Romania's ideal leader

Against this backdrop, the GLOBE research also permits the formulation of the profile of the ideal Romanian leader. In the GLOBE research, leadership has been measured by 112 leadership traits and attributes, from which 21 first-order variables have been identified by factor analysis. Conceptually, the leadership construct of GLOBE is normative, reflecting the desired behaviour, traits and attributes of leadership in different cultures, rather than the status quo. The variables identified act as indicators of the characteristics, skills, and abilities that are perceived around the world as *contributing to*, or *inhibiting*, outstanding business leadership. The Romanian GLOBE results are summarized in Table 7.3.

These characteristics therefore fall into three groups of elements that comprise the profile of the ideal leader in Romania. The first group consists of a number of highly valued variables (mean >5.85) with a relatively low standard deviation (standard deviation <0.9). This indicates that the Romanian middle managers mostly agreed that these characteristics would be ideal. The following first-order leadership variables belong to this group: performance oriented, benevolent, inspirational charismatic, team integrator, decisive, administratively competent, visionary charismatic, integrity, diplomatic, and collaborative team orientation.

In contrast, the third group in the table, of characteristics the ideal leaders should avoid, consists of only one highly rejected variable (mean < 2) with a relatively low standard deviation (standard deviation < 0.9): self-centredness. This suggests that, alongside these positive variables, the ideal leader should avoid being perceived as self-centred, which may relate to an ethical expectation.

The middle group, with a mean score of between 5.3 and 3 with a relatively high standard deviation (standard deviation > 0.9) consists

Table 7.3   Primary (First-order) Leadership Variables in Romania

First-order leadership variables	Mean	SD
Highly rated (Expected) (mean > 5.85) and agreed (st.dev. < 0.9)		
Performance oriented	6.36	0.81
Benevolent (reverse scored) – Malevolent: 1.69	6.31	0.74
Team 2 (Team integrator)	6.27	0.71
Charismatic 2 (Inspirational)	6.24	0.75
Administratively competent	6.22	0.85
Decisive	6.15	0.86
Integrity	6.1	0.86
Charismatic 1 (Visionary)	6.07	0.74
Diplomatic	5.98	0.77
Team 1 (Collaborative team orientation)	5.88	0.76
Medium score (5.3 > mean > 3) and differently viewed		
Charismatic 3 (Self-sacrificial)	5.3	1.05
Modesty	5.05	0.93
Non-autocratic (reverse scored) – Autocratic: 2.97	5.03	1.19
Status conscious	4.78	1.26
Participative (reverse scored) – Non-participative: 3.26	4.74	1.18
Humane oriented	4.71	1.3
Conflict inducer	4.37	0.94
Procedural	4.28	0.93
Autonomous	3.5	1.28
Face-saver	3.1	1.32
Rejected (mean < 2 and agreed (st.dev. < 0.9)		
Self-centred	1.8	0.89

*n=354
Source: Bakacsi et al., *Final report on the results of GLOBE – Romania project* (2006, unpublished), p. 44.

of variables that have been rated less highly than those in the first group, and on which respondents have also disagreed or reacted neutrally. Hence it consists of leadership characteristics Romanian middle managers do not generally endorse, about which they are broadly neutral, and on which they do not agree either. These are traits like being: self-sacrificial charismatic, non-autocratic, modest, status conscious, participative, humane oriented, conflict inducer, procedural, autonomous, and face-saver. The ambiguity of these variables makes them attractive for further research beyond the scope of this chapter, particularly in the context of the desired ethical profile of a leader in Romania.

The six GLOBE dimensions

A second factor analysis of the 21 first-order variables compressed these into six dimensions (the second-order variables), which can also be used to summarise these first-order findings. The six second-order variables are: being charismatic/value-based, team oriented, self-protective, participative, humane oriented, and autonomous. The GLOBE research suggests that Romanian middle managers expect their outstanding leaders to be particularly team oriented (6.13) and charismatic/value-based (6.09). They also regard the variables of being participative (4.93) and having a humane orientation (4.88) as contributing somewhat to ideal leadership. However, self-protective (3.69) and autonomous (3.56) leadership behaviour is not regarded as ideal in Romanian culture.

Taking these in numerical order, Romanian managers rated the leadership characteristic 'team oriented' most highly. In the GLOBE research, the definition of team-oriented leadership emphasises effective team-building and the implementation of a common purpose or goal among team members. It includes five primary leadership sub-scales: a collaborative team orientation, being a team integrator, being diplomatic, being benevolent (malevolency reverse scored), and being administratively competent (House et al., 2004:675). The scores for this variable put Romania at the top of the Eastern European cluster and third highest in the world. The results suggest that a Romanian leader is expected to be particularly collaborative compared with leader behaviour elsewhere in the world. This finding is corroborated by other research (Catana and Catana., 1996; Nastase, 2009:523) which indicates that working in teams is gaining greater acceptance in Romanian companies, and it resonates with the socio-cultural finding about the importance of in-group collectivism.

The definition and composition of charismatic/value-based reflects the ability to inspire, to motivate, and to expect high performance outcomes from others on the basis of firmly held core values. It includes six primary leadership sub-scales: being visionary, inspirational, self-sacrificial, having integrity, being decisive, and being performance oriented (House et al., 2004:675). In Romania, the charismatic/value-based leadership variable is the second most valued characteristic. In the GLOBE study, it again means Romania tops the league table for the Eastern European cluster and on this variable Romania is 11th highest in the world. The high ranking suggests that Romanian managers expect their ideal leader to show a high degree of integrity in their managerial activity. This particular finding resonates more widely. At a political level, Romanians voted in 2004 for a president campaigning on promises for more justice, more truth, more integrity, and less corruption. The opposing candidate, who was perceived to be corrupt and less virtuous, lost the election. However, the socio-cultural GLOBE data for Romania is ambiguous about the related indicator of humane orientation, which might otherwise throw light on this discussion.

In the GLOBE data for Romania, the third most valued ideal characteristic was participative leadership. Participative leadership reflects the degree to which managers involve others in making and implementing decisions. It includes two primary leadership sub-scales: being autocratic and being non-participative, both reverse-scored (House et al., 2004:675). While Romania's score for participative leadership was medium, both compared to other Eastern European countries and in comparison with other GLOBE data – being the eighth lowest in the world – it was relatively low. This suggests that Romanian middle managers are comparatively tolerant of non-participative leadership behaviour and relates to the low score for the first-order leadership dimension about being non-autocratic, although this finding too is rather ambiguous and would repay further investigation.

The fourth most popular leadership characteristic was 'humane oriented'. This variable reflects supportive and considerate leadership, and includes compassion and generosity. It includes two primary leadership sub-scales, modesty and humane oriented (House et al., 2004:675). On humane oriented leadership the score for Romania is medium (4.88) with somewhat moderate agreement (standard deviation = 0.97), which ranks Romania at medium when compared to other Eastern European countries, and at the 32nd position (also medium) in the world. This indicates that Romanian managers have a moderate expectation of a humane orientation from their leaders, in line with general findings across the GLOBE project. Only respondents in Southern Asia gave this variable a comparatively high ranking, yet still within the medium band.

If these four characteristics represent the four most desired ideal leadership traits, the two traits that Romanian middle managers wished to discourage were self-protective and autonomous leadership behaviours. The first of these relates specifically to ethics. Self-protective leadership focuses on ensuring the safety and security of the individual or group member. It includes five primary leadership sub-scales: being self-centred, being status-conscious, being a conflict inducer, being a face-saver, and being procedural (House et al., 2004:675). This variable has also been labelled as 'narcissism'. While in Romania this trait scores low (3.67) with moderate agreement (standard deviation = 0.70), this score reflects a medium-high expected participation compared to other Eastern European countries, being ranked 17th (medium-high) in the world. This suggests that Romanian middle managers are relatively tolerant of self-protective or narcissistic leaders, particularly when compared to cultures like the Nordic-Scandinavian or the Germanic that report a strong dislike of this type of behaviour. This may affect their expectation of ethical leadership and as such would repay further investigation, although it may be mitigated to an extent by the low score on the cultural variable relating to performance.

Conclusion

This chapter shows that there is a wide gap between what is commonly desired from the ideal leader and what is currently practised in Romania. Our findings are drawn from responses made by Romanian middle managers participating in the GLOBE Romania research project. First, we have presented Romania's socio-cultural profile at the practice level (as it is) and at the value level (as it should be). Secondly, we have presented the results of the research describing the desired profile of the ideal leader in Romania in relation to the first and second-order leadership variables as defined by the GLOBE project.

The findings on the desired culture suggested that Romanians would prefer their leaders to operate in a context that has less hierarchy, more institutional collectivism, more certainty, and more of a focus on the future. Specifically, their ideal leader should be performance oriented, benevolent, inspirational, a team integrator, decisive, administratively competent, visionary, and diplomatic, having integrity and a strong collaborative team orientation. In particular, the Romanian leader should avoid being perceived as self-centred. Of all the variables, those that were most prized were those leadership traits concerning team orientation and participation, and charisma and values, with little appetite for modesty.

The comparison between the 'as it is' and 'as it should be' culture shows that Romania is evolving away from the traditional model of the powerful man, paternalistic and almighty, towards a more modern idea of leadership. This trend is closely linked to changes in the Romanian socio-cultural environment, which are in turn driving a shift in what the Romanian people expect of those leading these changes. This study shows what kind of leadership middle managers want, offering a valuable stakeholder perspective for anyone wishing to do business in Romania.

Bibliography

Bakcsi, Gy, Catana, Al, Catana, D., *Final report on the results of GLOBE – Romania project*, unpublished (2006).

Bibu, N., Petrisor, I., Cazan, E., Ionescu, Gh., Saratean, E., Vlad, S., and Bizoi, G., 'Characteristics of the Organizational Culture in Romanian Organizations Based on the Results of the GLOBE – Romania Project', *Review of International Comparative Management*, 9 (2007) 35–52.

Catana D. and Catana, A., 'Aspects of Transformation of Corporate Cultures in Romania', *Wandel von Unternehmenskulturen in Ostdeutschland und Osteuropa*, Vergal (1996).

Gupta, V., Hanges, P.J., and Dorfman, P., 'Cultural Clusters: Methodology and Findings', *Journal of World Business*, 37(1) (2002) 11–14.

House, R.J., Hanges, P.J., Javidan, M., Dorfman, P.W., and Gupta, V. (eds), *Culture, Leadership, and Organizations: The GLOBE Study of 62 Societies, Vol. 1* (Thousand Oaks, CA: Sage, 2004).

Nastase, M., 'Importance of Trust in Knowledge-based Leadership', *Review of International Comparative Management*, 10(3) (2009) 518–526.

8
Virtue-based Leadership in the United Kingdom and Nigeria

Kola Abimbola and Temi Abimbola

Introduction

This chapter discusses the role of ethics in strategic leadership within competitive and dynamic markets. Using two case studies, The Body Shop and the Nigerian Stock Exchange, we examine the need for a better understanding of the ethical aspects of leadership within corporations. The argument is that not only is it imperative for market-based institutions to be socially responsible to their stakeholders, but that virtue is an essential component of strategic leadership. The interactive effects of the prevailing micro and macro economic factors require a correspondent alignment between strategic leadership at the self, organisation, and societal levels. Our justification for these two cases is that a theory of ethical leadership needs to be generalisable, and applicable to the different socio-cultural environments within which organisations and businesses are incorporated. These different environments create complexities for competition, leadership, and decision-making.

Scholars such as Bettis and Hitt (1995), D'Aveni (1994), Hitt (2000), and Ireland and Hitt (2005) assert that increasing complexity makes competing in a global economy particularly challenging. The hyper-competition of today's environment arises from the commingling of factors such as globalisation, deregulation, and technological advancement (Prahalad and Hamel, 1994; Hamel, 2001). An important consequence of this hyper-competitiveness is that previously successful methods may no longer be adequate in contemporary settings. Other important consequences include: idiosyncratic risks, the diminishing ability to accurately predict market outcomes, ambiguities in industry/market boundaries, and upheaval at the macro level. Thus, leadership requires flexibility and agility as the prerequisites for operating in conditions of

135

uncertainty (Sirmon et al., 2007) and dynamic environments challenge the existing micro models of leadership research (Crossan et al., 2008; Waldman et al., 2006).

Strategic leadership theory maintains that organisations reflect the decisions of their leaders, who set the course for the firm (Hambrick and Mason, 1984). These leaders are responsible for crafting strategies for survival in dynamic environments (Boal and Hooijberg, 2000; Crossan et al., 2008; House and Aditya, 1997). One emerging paradigm acknowledges the need for the integration of contextual, micro, and macro influences (Waldman, 2007; Yukl, 1999), and the need for a pluralist approach to strategising (Jarzabkowski and Fenton, 2006; Whittington et al., 2006). This is essential in developing strategic leadership studies that are capable of providing managers with guidance on the complex and dynamic globally competitive landscape, which is riddled with opportunities and threats in equal measure. This call for a multidisciplinary and a multi-level approach to the study of strategic leadership provides the impetus for this study. We provide an innovative and integrative conceptualisation of strategic leadership, an approach in which we examine leadership of self, organisation, and society. Our work conceptualises the virtues as they relate to the ethical challenges that arise from the concrete decision-making of corporate leaders.

Leadership theory

Much scholarship on leadership has focused on the relationship between the leader and the follower. The notions of servant leadership, supervisory leadership, and strategic leadership (Javidan and House, 2001) reflect some key emerging schools of thought on the study of leadership. We would argue that leadership should not be viewed only in terms of the leader as an agent of the shareholders, or the leader as an individual (Waldman and Siegel, 2008). Strategic leaders should also have the capacity to lead at a societal level, where they balance the needs of their organisations against those of society in general (Crossan et al., 2008; Waldman and Siegel, 2008).

Barnard (1938) conceives of firms as social organisations whose leaders are susceptible to social cues and pressures both within and beyond the boundaries of the organisation. In an interdependent, networked and global world, the mandate to lead requires collaborative and relational cooperation with different internal and external stakeholders. There will always be conflicts of interest among the various stakeholders like management, employees, shareholders, the public, and so on. If we factor in the dynamic roles of leaders, a new type of agency deficit ensues, because the stakeholders have to place some trust in the quality of their leaders. Leadership agency cost is the cost of monitoring the effectiveness of leaders in an effort to prevent them from prioritising their own interests above those of all other stakeholders.

Various types of stakeholders place a premium on the ethical behaviours of corporations. For instance, few stakeholders want corporations to employ child labour, damage the environment, or trade unfairly. Crucially, consumers are now willing to pay premium prices for goods and services that have been produced, manufactured, or supplied by socially responsible corporations. Increased visibility means that corporations are having to become more socially responsible, because stakeholders can evaluate their actions (and inactions), and this in turn translates into increased or reduced profits. Corporate social responsibility is increasingly associated with macro organisational theories, and it has been argued that firms need to adopt this approach in order to gain legitimacy (Meyer and Rowan, 1997; DiMaggio and Powell, 1983).

As defined by the UK Department for Business, Enterprise and Regulatory Reform (BERR), corporate responsibility is 'how companies address the social, environmental and economic impacts of their operations and so help to meet our sustainable development goals'. Further, the World Business Council for Sustainable Development defines it as 'the commitment of business to contribute to sustainable development, working with employees, their families, the local community and society at large to improve their quality of life'. These and other definitions raise concerns about the relationships between corporations and the societies they impact on, the markets they operate in, and their geographical environments. Given that corporations are artificial persons whose actions are dependent on the action of their leaders, it is therefore imperative to examine the roles and functions of these leaders in this sphere.

Strategic leadership and the ethical compass

Leader behaviour has been shown to be the best predictor of behaviour at the lower level within organisations (Greenleaf, 2002; Luthans and Slocum, 2004; Pearce et al., 2008). Leaders are able to set the tone and influence behaviour within organisations because they have the ultimate accountability for the performance of the whole organisation. Mendonca argues that the behaviour and strategies of corporate leaders influence their followers and employees, thereby impacting the behaviour of the organisation as a whole (Mendonca, 2001:268). However, Baumhart (1961) and Brenner and Molander (1977) found that there is a correlation between the behaviours of the leaders of a firm and unethical decision-making. This makes the character of the leader of particularly weighty importance in any discussion on the ethical behaviour of corporations.

Kanungo and Mendonca (1996) and Mendonca (2001) have put forward a virtues-based model for the analysis and evaluation of ethical leadership. They distinguish between the 'transactional' and 'transformational' modes of influence, and the 'cardinal virtues of character formation'. In transactional modes of influence, leaders see their subordinates as something akin to robots, primarily there just to implement decisions. Control and compliance is enforced through a wide range of mechanisms that some have argued 'offend against the dignity of the human person' (Mendonca, 2001:268). In the transformational mode, followers are regarded as autonomous individuals. Desired attitudinal, belief, and value changes in followers are therefore effected through empowerment and other cognitive strategies designed to respect the personhood of followers. Leadership itself depends on the character development of the leaders. This character development is referred to as 'self-transformation for ethical leadership' (Mendonca, 2001:269). Corporate leaders require prior self-transformation in their moral strength or backbone, that is, character. This character functions as the sense of virtue, on the basis of which decisions, strategies, and actions are taken. The development and formation of virtue enables leaders to acquire an inner compass to guide their will and their strength. This helps to ensure that their decisions are based on ethical reasoning. Mendonca (2001) explains the four cardinal virtues, as identified by Plato, as follows:

> **Prudence** requires the habitual assessment, in the light of right standards, of the situation or issue on which a decision is to be made. The leader who is in the habit of practising prudence will not abdicate his or her responsibility for unethical behaviour. The prudent person will not only not resent that others disagree with his or her views but will actively seek such information to better assess the situation and exercise sound judgement.

> **Justice** requires the individual to strive constantly to give others what is their due. The 'due' means more than the legalistic notion of the contractual rights of others. It includes whatever others might need to fulfil their duties and exercise their rights as persons.

Fortitude is the courage to take great risks for an ideal that is worthwhile. One of the underlying characteristics of fortitude is perseverance and endurance against great odds.

Temperance involves distinguishing between what is reasonable and necessary and what is indulgent (Mendonca, 2001:269f.).

Based on the transformational theory of leadership, and the research that attests to the particular influence of leaders, the adoption by leaders of these virtues would transform their organisation from the top down. Because it is our view that the virtue theory of ethical leadership applies equally to both private and public companies, in the next section we present two case studies to illustrate the application of these virtues.

The virtues of leadership

Corporate social responsibility and The Body Shop

The Body Shop International Plc (TBS) was incorporated as a limited liability company in the United Kingdom in 1976 by Anita Roddick. The corporation has over 2,000 outlets around the world. L'Oréal acquired TBS in March 2006. Prior to its acquisition by the L'Oréal Group, TBS was known for its commitment to ethical values and corporate social responsibility (CSR). As such, one of the key concerns of TBS stakeholders was that it would lose its distinctive moral fibre by becoming acquired by L'Oréal. Our study suggests that TBS managed to retain its unique ethical orientation because of the inculcation of virtues into the character of its leaders, employees, and franchisees.

The Body Shop is founded on the philosophy that strong ethical values are compatible with corporate profitability. At the heart of the company's approach are five principles:

1. Animal protection
2. The environment
3. Community trade
4. Human rights
5. Self-esteem.

In relation to each of these principles, the company distinguishes between its vision (which it regards as its 'non-operational principles') and its policies (which are the specific actions it adopts to operationalise these principles in its corporate activities). The company presents its hierarchy of values as shown in Figure 8.1. Levels 1 to 3 of this hierarchy constitute the TBS 'vision' (that is, its non-operational values). These are the foundational values that the company inculcates into the character of its leaders, directors, employees, and franchisees. One way in which this inculcation is done is through the Corporate Values Training Programme, designed to impart these values to TBS leaders and employees. The distinction between non-operational principles and operational policies is about 'character formation' and 'practical action'. Consider, for example, the company's animal protection principle. This principle is a non-operational principle in the sense that the level at which it is introduced into the corporation is at the 'internal' level of corporate character formation. TBS directors, leaders, employees, and franchisees are expected to embody the value of animal protection in their character, thereby turning it into a virtue which informs their operational activities. The belief is that any TBS person who accepts the animal protection principle will translate this principle into action by ensuring that no animals are harmed in the production of cosmetics. Character formation is enhanced through the values training, and through values-related remuneration programmes. While the values training programme instils the virtues of the five core values into the character of its people, the values remuneration programme

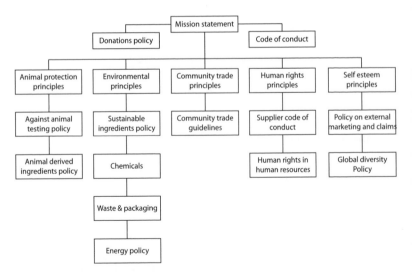

Figure 8.1   The Body Shop's Ethical Policy Hierarchy

officially includes these values as objectives in its leader, employee, and franchisee appraisal process.

Although L'Oréal has its own values and mission statement, these do not necessarily cohere with those of TBS. For example, one of the five cardinal values of TBS is that it supports the protection of animals, and this translates into its practice of not manufacturing and retailing cosmetics that have been tested on animals. L'Oréal, its parent company, does not subscribe to this principle, so how can TBS maintain its values, virtues and practices within this context? The practical solution adopted is that TBS is run and managed independently of the L'Oréal Group. It has not been folded into any of L'Oréal's business divisions; it retains its own unique brand; and it remains a separate business unit with its own separate management team. Only time will tell whether this will protect TBS, but preliminary indications show that TBS still retains its own unique virtues. As an example, since its acquisition by L'Oréal Group, TBS has moved from being mostly to 100 per cent 'vegetarian'. Prior to its acquisition, TBS sold two products that violated its animal protection values. Its men's shaving brush was made from hogs' hair, and its bath beads contained gelatin. Since its acquisition, TBS has found an alternative to hogs' hair, and has discontinued the sale of the bath beads that contain gelatin.

Corporate governance and the Nigerian Stock Exchange

The current global financial crisis began in 2007 as a result of the subprime mortgage lending crisis in the United States. The resulting collapse of a variety of financial institutions can be viewed as the result of inadequate inculcation of social responsibility in the banking and financial markets sectors. In an effort to avert financial crisis, US and European governments adopted extraordinary measures (including the provision of substantial financial bailout packages to stabilise banking systems; the cutting of interest rates by Central Banks; and market interventions such as the buying of large amounts of corporate short-term debt by governments). Nigeria was not exempt from this global turbulence, and the crisis in the Nigerian Stock Exchange serves as a good counter-foil to the case of The Body Shop. Although the two corporations are from two very different environments, in two very different sectors, and have very different goals and objectives, their differences crystallise the indispensable roles of virtues and character in ethical leadership and corporate social responsibility.

The Nigerian Stock Exchange (NSE) was established as the Lagos Stock Exchange (LSE) in 1960. It functioned as the LSE until 1977 when its name was changed to the NSE. The NSE is an integral part of the Nigerian Financial System, a system that has the Central Bank of Nigeria (CBN) at its apex. The CBN regulates the country's financial system through monetary policies that are formulated to create a stable economic condition. The CBN has direct control of government regulatory agencies including the Securities and Exchange Commission (SEC). The SEC focuses on non-banking institutions and regulates capital markets. The primary objective of the SEC is that of the protection of investors and capital market development. The SEC is granted a number of powers to assist it in the achievement of this objective. These include: the regulation of the capital market to prevent malpractice in security trading; the regulation of capital market trading information; regulation of the issue of new shares; the registration of individuals and institutions involved in the capital market; and the power to fine, suspend or de-list firms and individuals for securities rule violations. The NSE is a self-regulated organisation that reports to the SEC. NSE requires its market operators to subscribe to an ethical code which it describes as: 'our word is our bond'.

While integrity therefore appears to be the primary value that the NSE requires of its market operators, this value was undermined by events in February and March 2009, which show the limits of a reliance on regulation and policing as the primary framework for the supervision of financial markets. Between February and March 2009, shares in African Petroleum (AP) crashed from 293.00 Nigerian naira to 54.00 Nigerian naira, wiping 240 billion naira off the value of AP. Because the shares of AP had for many years been one of the most stable shares in Nigeria, this collapse within just eight weeks was extremely baffling. An investigation was launched, which discovered that AP had been the victim of 'share crossing', which is an illegal practice within the Nigerian securities market. As a result of the investigation, the SEC fined and suspended Nova Finance and Securities Ltd and one of its directors from trading on the Nigerian Stock Exchange. However, the records show that the then Vice President of the Nigerian Stock Exchange was the sole subscriber to Nova Finance and Securities Ltd, yet the SEC passed no comment on this (*Nigerian Muse*, 2009).

The case illustrates two very important points. First, in addition to regulation, there needs to be an ethical framework for the development of values to which institutions and individuals within the financial market will adhere. These values are needed to augment regulatory regimes in an effort to ensure that consumers are better protected and that financial crime is reduced. Secondly, principles, standards, and values have

FRAMEWORK FOR THE DEVELOPMENT OF VALUES

Values and culture of firms	Regulatory relationship
Minimum standards • Unthinking, mechanical compliance • Does as little as can get away with • Culture of dependency • Tries to abdicate decisions and responsibilities	**Policing** • Monitoring boundaries • Detecting and responding to crises • Enforcement 'lessons' • Basic training
Compliance culture • Reliant on guidance • By the book • Unaware of some risks • Bureaucratic	**Supervising / educating** • Developing ethics and competence • Looking for early warning signs • Early action to bounce firms back on track • Themed / focused visits
Beyond compliance • Risk focused, self policing • 'Buying in' at senior level • Ethos integrated into most business processes • Ethos seen as assisting business	**Educating / consulting** • Facilitating the development of competence and culture • Values scorecard • Lighter touch
Values-led business • Internalise ethos of core values • Spirit not just letter • Values focused, goes beyond rules, not just compliance • Well developed individual responsibility and a sense of involvement by all staff • Focus on prevention • Continued reassessment and improvement of approach • Awareness and discussion of ethical consideration at senior and all levels • Open relationships • Strong learning culture	**Mature relationship / benchmarking** • Reinforce good practice • Lead by example • Re-allocate resources to problem firms • Sustainable regulation

Figure 8.2   The FSA Framework

to be integrated and diffused into all aspects of the 'business as usual' activities of corporations. The case study of The Body Shop is an example of such a successful integration, while the case of the Nigerian Stock Exchange is an example of poor integration. This integration need not be complex. The United Kingdom's Financial Services Authority (FSA) Discussion Paper on Ethics proposes one such integrative model, based on three core values. These require individuals and institutions within the financial sectors to be open, honest, responsive, and accountable; to act responsibly and reliably; and to relate to colleagues and customers fairly and with respect. The FSA's integration of values and regulation is shown in Figure 8.2.

An evaluation of the NSE crisis shows that regulation alone is not enough to remove unethical behaviour, and the FSA framework shows how a regulated body might evolve into a more truly ethical organisation over time.

Conclusion

This discussion has suggested that embedded virtues form the backbone of ethical leadership behaviour. The policies, strategies, and decisions adopted by corporate leaders in the exercise of their leadership will have a ripple effect throughout corporations. The decisions of leaders influence their followers and employees, thereby impacting the organisation as a whole. Some have argued that what is really needed is better corporate governance (Amao and Amaeshi, 2008). As Sternberg observed, 'properly understood, corporate governance refers simply to ways of ensuring that a corporation's actions, agents and assets are directed at the definitive corporate ends set by the corporation's shareholders' (Sternberg, 2004:25). On this definition, corporate governance is about ensuring that directors and managers are accountable to shareholders, and that their actions are not *ultra vires*. This is particularly important in modern-day corporations where management is typically detached from ownership. As an artificial entity, corporations of necessity require directors and managers to carry out their aims and objectives. This inevitably requires the shareholders to grant certain powers and obligations to directors and managers to serve as trustees of the shareholders' interests. If we approach the discussion of corporate ethics solely from the point of view of 'corporate social responsibility', the focus tends to be on the ethical qualities of corporate leaders, because it is the decisions of these leaders, and not the decisions of the shareholders, that impact on society. If we approach the discussion of corporate ethics from the point of view of 'corporate governance', the shareholders also become involved, because of their role, through the Board, in attending to the character of the leaders acting as their agents in the execution of their roles and functions. Either way, the embedding of the virtues, from the shareholders through the Board to the leaders and employees, is indispensable if an organisation wishes to become truly ethical.

Bibliography

Agbana, G. and Adekoya, F., 'NSE Suspends Stockbroking Firm Over AP's Share Price Scam', *The Guardian*, retrieved on 27 March 2009 from www.nigerianbestforum.com/index.php?topic=26047.0;wap2OK.

Amao, O. and Amaeshi, K., Galvanising Shareholder Activism: A Prerequisite for Effective Corporate Governance and Accountability in Nigeria, *Journal of Business Ethics*, 82(1) (September2008), 119–130.

Barnard, C.I., *The Function of the Executive* (Cambridge, MA: Harvard University Press, 1938).

Baumhart, R.C., 'How Ethical Are Businessmen?', *Harvard Business Review*, 39(4) (1961) 6–19.

Begger, P.L. and Luckman, T., *The Social Construction of Reality: A Treatise in the Sociology of Knowledge* (New York: Free Press, 1967).

Bettis, R.A. and Hitt, M.A., 'The New Competitive Landscape', *Strategic Management Journal*, 16 (1995) 7–19.

Boal, K.B. and Hooijberg, R., 'Strategic Leadership Research: Moving on', *The Leadership Quarterly*, 11 (2000) 515–549.

Brenner, S.N. and Molander, E.A., 'Is Ethics of Business Changing?', *Harvard Business Review*, 55 (1977) 57–71.

Canella, Jr., A.A. and Monroe, M.J., 'Contrasting Perspectives on Strategic Leaders: Toward a More Realist View of Top Managers', *Journal of Management*, 23(3) (1997) 213–237.

Caroll, A.B., 'Corporation Social Responsibility: Evolution of a Definitional Construct', *Business and Society*, 38(3) (1999) 268–295.

Chen, J.C., Patten, D.M., and Roberts, R.W., 'Corporate Charitable Contributions: A Corporate Social Performance or Legitimacy Strategy?', *Journal of Business Ethics*, 82 (2007) 131–144.

Child, J. 'Strategic Choice in the Analysis of Action, Structure, Organisations and Environment: Retrospect and Prospect', *Organization Studies*, 18 (1997) 43–76.

Crossan, M.D., Vera, D., and Nanjad, L., 'Transcendent Leadership: Strategic Leadership in Dynamic Environments', *The Leadership Quarterly*, 19 (2008) 569–581.

D'Aveni, R., Hypercompetition: Managing the Dynamics of Strategic Maneuvering (New York: Free Press, 1994).

DiMaggio, P.J. and Powell, W.W., 'The Iron Cage Revisited: Institutional Isomorphism and Collective Rationality in Organizational Fields', *American Sociological Review*, 48(2) (1983) 147–160.

Drucker, P., *The Concept of the Corporation* (New York: John Day Publishing Company, 1946).

Garratt, B., The Fish Rots From the Head – The Crisis in our Boardrooms: Developing the Crucial Skills of the Competent Director (London: Profile Books, 2003).

Greening, D.W. and Gray, B., 'Testing A Model of Organizational Response to Social and Political Issues', *Academy of Management Journal*, 37 (1994) 467–498.

Greenleaf, R.K., Servant Leadership A Journey into the Nature of Legitimate Power and Greatness (Mahwah, NJ: Paulist Press, 2002).

Hambrick, D.C. and Mason, P., 'Upper Echelons: The Organization as a Reflection of its Top Management', *Academy of Management Review*, 9 (1984) 193–206.

Hamel, G., 'Leading the Revolution: An Interview with Gary Hamel', *Strategy and Leadership*, 29 (2001), 4–10.

Heifetz, R.A., *Leadership without Easy Answers* (Cambridge, MA: Harvard Business Press, 1994).

Hitt, M.A., 'The New Frontier: Transformation of Management for the New Millennium', *Organizational Dynamics*, 28 (2000) 7–17.

House, R.J. and Aditya, R.N., 'The Social Scientific Study of Leadership: Quo Vadis?', *Journal of Management*, 23 (1997) 409–473.

Ireland, R.D. and Hitt, M.A., 'Achieving and Maintaining Strategic Competitiveness in the 21st Century: The Role of Strategic Leadership', *Academy of Management Executives*, 19 (2005) 63–77.

Jarzabkowski, P. and Fenton, E., 'Strategizing and Organizing in Pluralistic Contexts', *Long Range Planning*, 39 (2006) 631–648.

Javidan, M. and House, R.J., 'Cultural Acumen for the Global Manager: Lessons from Project GLOBE', *Organizational Dynamics*, 29 (2001) 289–305.

Klein, K.J. and House, R.J., 'On Fire: Charismatic Leadership and Levels of Analysis', *Leadership Quarterly*, 6 (1995), 183–198.

Kotter, J.P., *A Force for Change: How Leadership Differs from Management* (New York: Free Press, 1990).

Luthans, F. and Slocum, J., 'New Leadership for a New Time', *Organizational Dynamics*, 33(3) (2004) 227.

Maak, T. and Pless, N.M., 'Responsible Leadership in a Stakeholder Society: A Relational Perspective', *Journal of Business Ethics*, 66 (2006) 99–115.

MacIntyre, A., *After Virtue: A Study in Moral Theory* (Indiana: University of Notre Dame Press, 2007).

Manz, C.C., Anand, V., Joshi, M. and Manz, K.P., 'Emerging Paradoxes in Executive Leadership: A Theoretical Interpretation of the Tensions Between Corruption and Virtuous Values', *The Leadership Quarterly*, 19 (2008) 385–392.

Mendonca, M., 'Preparing for Ethical Leadership in Organizations', *Canadian Journal of Administrative Sciences*, 18(4) (2001) 266–276.

Mendonca, M. and Kanungo, R.N., *The Ethical Dimensions of Leadership* (Thousand Oaks, CA: Sage,1996).

Meyer, J.W. and Rowan, B., 'Institutionalized Organizations: Formal Structure as Myth and Ceremony', *American Journal of Sociology*, 83 (1997) 340–363.

Nigerian Muse. (2009, 23 March). Star Information – AP's Case Against Aliko Dangote and Nova Finance and Securities. *Nigerian Muse*. Retrieved on 31 May 2009 from www.nigerianmuse.com/20090326003702zg/nigeriawatch/

officialfraud/star-information-ap-s-case-against-aliko-dangote-and-nova-finance-securities.

Osborn, R.N., Hunt, J.G., and Jaunch, R., 'Toward a Contextual Theory of Leadership', *Leadership Quarterly*, 13 (2002) 797–837.

Pearce, C.L., Manz, C.C., and Sims, Jr, H.P., 'The Role of Vertical and Shared Leadership in Enactment of Executive Corruption: Implications for Research and Practice', *The Leadership Quarterly*, 19 (2008) 353–359.

Pettigrew, A.M., 'On Studying Managerial Elites', *Strategic Management Journal*, 13 (1992) 163–182.

Prahalad, C.K. and Hamel, G., 'Strategy as a Field of Study: Why Search for a New Paradigm?', *Strategic Management Journal*, 15 (1994) 5–17.

Sirmon, D.G., Hitt, M.A., and Ireland, R.D., 'Managing Firm Resources in Dynamic Environments to Create Value: Looking Inside the Black Box', *Academy of Management Review*, 32 (2007) 273–292.

Sternberg, E., *Corporate Governance: Accountability in the Marketplace* (London: Institute of Economic Affairs, 2004).

Suchman, M.C., 'Managing Legitimacy: Strategic and Institutional Approaches', *Academy of Management Review*, 20 (1995) 571–610.

Tijjani, B., Fifield, S.G.M., and Power, D.M., 'The Appraisal of Equity Investments by Nigerian Investors, *Qualitative Research in Financial Markets*, 1 (2009) 6–26.

Waldman, D.A. and Siegel, D., 'Defining the Socially Responsible Leader', *The Leadership Quarterly*, 19 (2008) 117–131.

Waldman, D.A. and Yammarino, F.J., 'CEO Charismatic Leadership: Levels of Management and Levels-of-Analysis', *Academy of Management Review*, 24 (1999) 266–285.

Waldman, D.A., Siegel, D.S. and Javidan, M., 'Components of CEO Transformational Leadership and Corporate Social Responsibility', *Journal of Management Studies*, 43(8) (2006) 1703–1725.

Waldman, D.A., 'Best Practices in Leading at Strategic Level: A Social Responsibility Perspective, in J. Conger and R. Riggio (eds), *The Practice of Leadership: Developing the Next Generation of Leaders* (San Francisco: Jossey-Bass, 2007), pp. 224–243.

Walton, C.C., *The Moral Manger* (Cambridge, MA: Ballinger, 1988).

Whittington, R., Molloy, E., Mayer, M., and Smith, A., 'Practices of Strategising/Organising: Broadening Strategy Work and Skills', *Long Range Planning*, 36(6) (2006) 615–629.

www.berr.gov.uk/whatwedo/sectors/sustainability/what/CR/page46727.html (last accessed date 28 July 2010).

www.fsa.gov.uk/pubs/discussion/dp18.pdf (last accessed date 28 July 2010).

www.thebodyshop.com/_en/_ww/services/pdfs/Values/Ethicalpolicy hierarchyAugust06web.pdf (last accessed date 28 July 2010).

www.wbcsd.org/ (last accessed date 28 July 2010).

Yukl, G., 'An Evaluation of Conceptual Weakness in Transformational and Charismatic Leadership Theories', *Leadership Quarterly*, 10(2) (1999) 285–305.

9
Chinese Folk Wisdom: Leading with Traditional Values

Ricky Szeto

Introduction

After the establishment of modern China in 1949, the country went through several decades of political upheaval during which the Confucian education system underpinning the traditional Chinese value system was severely compromised (Bell and Waizer, 2010; Bond, 1986; Martinsons and Westwood, 1997; Davison et al., 2009). Meanwhile, economic reforms in the past three decades have brought with them the Western mindset that accompanies modern capitalism (Martinsons, 2008). However, the situation remains complex, given China's immature institutional frameworks and legal system (Davison et al., 2009). On the one hand, trends show that there is now little room for traditional Chinese values in the face of invading Western concepts. On the other hand, it appears that certain Chinese values might have an edge in a fast-changing business environment, particularly the challenge to the West of the recent financial crisis (Jian, 2009; Panzner, 2009; Sung, 2008). Indeed, previous studies have shown that the present cadre of Chinese managers still exhibit Confucian values in their business dealings, and that these values still affect the commercial behaviour of Chinese managers (Burrows et al., 2005; Chan et al., 1998; Wright et al., 2002). Traditional Confucian values still influence the Chinese in several ways, apart from through the education system (Zheng et al., 2005). One of these channels is Chinese folk wisdom, the oral tradition handed down through the 'family education'.

This study set out to discover the extent to which this Chinese folk wisdom affects the ethical decisions and behaviour of Chinese managers. In particular, this study seeks to shed light on the role of Chinese folk wisdom in guarding against unethical practices by Chinese managers.

This chapter starts with a brief literature review and discusses the forces perceived to influence the formation of business ethics alongside the economic reforms in China. The methodology employed in this research is then introduced, and the research findings are discussed. Finally, a conclusion is offered concerning the contribution of the study and directions for future research.

Literature review

Many researchers have discussed the driving forces behind the contemporary development of business ethics in China. Three major forces have been singled out: Confucianism, Maoism, and foreign business ethics (Lam, 2004; Lu, 1997; Nisbett, 2003; Whitcomb et al., 1998).

The first, Confucianism, represents the traditional Chinese culture that emphasises interpersonal relations in a society (Harvey, 1999; Lau and Kuan, 1988). Confucianism emphasises five human particular relationships: emperor and officials, father and son, brother and brother, husband and wife, and master and students. According to the Confucian teachings, keeping a harmonious relationship among different parties in a society is considered to be of the utmost importance (Whitcomb et al., 1998; Zheng et al., 2005). From this social heritage, 'trust' in relationships becomes the driving force, particularly in a turbulent business environment (Shaw, 1997, cited in Romar, 2002:124). Confucian ethics is based upon three fundamental concepts: ritual and etiquette, virtue, and the Golden Rule (Romar, 2002:127). Equally important is the Confucian emphasis on a commercial ethic that forbids cheating and the selling of poor-quality products, and a Confucian education is strong on morality, propriety, rules and regulations, laws, and the constitution (Harvey, 1999:85).

The second force is Maoism. The change of political power in China in the late 1940s, and subsequent reforms in the 1950s to 1970s, brought with them the Chinese version of Marxism, or Maoism, and revamped the Chinese education system, which had previously been dominated by Confucianism. The new China tried to replace the five major Confucian relationships with the Chinese Communist Party's ideology through changes in the education system, whereby children were separated from their parents early in their childhood (Pang et al., 1998). The Cultural Revolution further encouraged the denunciation of parents, spouses, relatives, friends, teachers and colleagues, to discourage loyalty to anyone except the Communist Party, and arguably to the people. The emphasis during this period was not on economic activity, but on class struggle and class morality (Redfern, 2005; Redfern and Crawford, 2004). The ultimate aim in this period was to remove Confucian teachings from the Chinese education system and replace them with the Party ethic.

The third force has been the gradual penetration of foreign business ethical thinking. The period of economic reform, which started in 1978, was marked by the fall of the 'Gang of Four' and the inauguration of the leadership of Deng Xiaoping, and from the 1980s started to shift the social focus from Maoism towards economic achievement. Deng's proclamation that 'to get rich is glorious' (Whitcomb et al., 1998:847) has had a profound influence on China's economic development, and profit has become an accepted goal for many contemporary Chinese people. Foreign concepts of legality and contractual duties, though not as highly respected as in the West, have begun to take root in China, while more and more business interactions are carried out with the West (Nisbett, 2003). General signs of 'convergence' with Western social values and behaviour have been fast emerging (Redfern and Crawford, 2004). Many of these Western values, however, remain in stark contrast to those of Confucianism and Maoism (Whitcomb et al., 1998; Nisbett, 2003).

In spite of this, previous research has indicated that traditional Confucian values still have influence on the business decisions made by contemporary Chinese managers (Ralston et al., 1993; Snell and Tseng, 2003; Whitcomb et al., 1998). While the Chinese educational system has long stopped offering Confucian teachings, current Chinese managers still seem to have inherited these values from their families (Jian, 2009). Despite the strenuous efforts of the Cultural Revolution to erase family ties, they have proven to be too strong to be broken. Indeed, Pang et al. (1998) have pointed out: 'the family is tied by bonds of blood and emotion, which ideally can never be untied' (p. 274). As Chinese culture is deeply rooted in Confucianism (Bond, 1986; Lau and Kuan, 1988; Zheng et al., 2005), Confucian teachings are expressed in too many ways to be entirely eliminated by the Communist Party. One of these methods is through oral tradition, handed down through families, often within the same native town or village. This method of transmitting Confucian teaching fits the agricultural mode of living of most families in mainland China. Most farmers are still virtually illiterate and can therefore only hand down their traditions by word of mouth. Many of these teachings have become folk wisdom in both rural and urban areas. Some of them, in addition to other traditional Chinese values, have been coded in colloquial sayings, such as 'Even a non-educated man has responsibility for the rise and fall of his own country' or 'Heaven's net is everywhere; though the holes are wide, no one is spared.'

This study proceeds to examine specifically whether or not Chinese folk wisdom is affecting the business ethics practised by managers in contemporary China. This is particularly important when scholars in general admit the existence of comparatively immature and competing ethical tensions in fast-developing economies like China (Martinsons, 2008; Davison et al., 2009). This study investigates whether Chinese folk wisdom has a role in guarding against unethical leadership by Chinese managers. Through a survey of practising business managers in China, an attempt is made to uncover the potential relationships between Chinese folk wisdom and ethical behaviour.

Research methodology

As it remains extremely difficult to gather information in China (Adair, 1995; Lam, 2004; Wright et al., 2002), our methodology is centered on the creation of a snowball sample similar to that used by Swecker (1998) and Xi and Wright (2001). This method is based on the work by Weiss (1994). He suggested that when information is difficult to obtain, non-probability sampling is acceptable as long as the generalisation issue has been addressed.

In this research, the participants (China mainland-born managers) in an MBA programme in the Pearl River Delta were asked to complete a questionnaire, and to persuade their peers to complete the same questionnaire. The questionnaire was self-administered and collected by hand. The sample collection was spread over several intakes of the same MBA programme, during a period of approximately two years. The research instrument used for the study was a questionnaire with 85 statements, comprising six forced-choice Likert statements followed by questions on the respondent's demographic profile. The content of the questionnaire was written first in Chinese, then translated into English for review. It was then checked by three senior Chinese colleagues, and adjustments were made. A small pilot test (n=20) then followed. In the study proper, a total of 486 sets of questionnaires were collected. The data were entered and analysed using SPSS software, showing a reliability coefficient Alpha=0.7580 indicating that the data is reliable.

This study consists of the extraction of two groups of statements from the full 85, namely those concerning Chinese folk wisdom and those concerning ethical decision-making and behaviour at work. Bivariate correlation analysis was also performed on the two groups of statements to identify their relationships because of the interval-by-interval nature of the questions.

The group of statements representing Chinese folk wisdom under study included:

QA   Even heaven will condemn him if a man does not work for his own good.

QB   Even a non-educated man has responsibility for the rise and fall of his own country.

QC   Heaven's net is everywhere; though the holes are wide, no one is spared.

QD   It is most important to have a clear conscience in whatever one does.

These four statements concerning Chinese folk wisdom were selected to test their effects on the business ethics of Chinese managers. In particular, QA and QB represent the tendency toward individualism and collectivism respectively. QC reflects the traditional Chinese thinking about 'the heaven', which implies the ultimate moral judgement. QD is related to the Confucian belief about morals coming from within, or from one's own 'heart'.

The group of statements representing business ethics decisions and behaviours consisted of the following:

Q1   International brands are built on a good foundation of trust.

Q2   I will only buy from enterprises that exhibit good ethical performance.

Q3   I will take into consideration the ethical performance of the companies in making business cooperation decisions.

Q4   Corporations must provide employees with full training to increase their trustworthiness.

Q5   Raising the standard of business ethics in a commercial environment will reduce the competitiveness of companies.

Q6   Once a contract is established, it must never be broken, even if losses might be incurred in meeting the obligation.

Q7   Even if it means incurring a loss in business, there must not be any actions of deceit.

Q8   Trust is a new strategic thinking in business.

Q9   Business ethics has nothing to do with corporate profitability.

Q10 Making ethical compromises to obtain agreement in business negotiations is unavoidable.

Results

Demographics

The resulting sample, from the total of 486 questionnaires collected, comprised 257 males and 189 females, in addition to 40 respondents who did not specify genders. The age of the sample ranged from 20 to 74. About 38.6 per cent (n=159) of the respondents aged from 20 to 30, and another 49 per cent (n=212) were 31 to 40 years old. On the respondents' education, university graduates formed the largest group, accounting for 42.8 per cent (n=208) of the sample, followed by post-secondary graduates (32.9 per cent, n=160). Only 8.4 per cent (n=41) had a Master's degree or above, and 7 per cent (n=34) were high-school graduates.

Most of the respondents worked in the industrial and services sectors, accounting for 27.4 per cent (n=133) and 21.8 per cent (n=106) of the total sample size respectively. The finance and the civil service sectors followed with much smaller groups of 7.8 per cent (n=38) and 7.0 per cent (n=34) respectively. The education sector came next (4.1 per cent, n=20), with the public services sector following at 2.9 per cent (n=14) and the scientific research sector at 2.7 per cent (n=13). The remainder were from the advertising sector (1.2 per cent, n=6), the cultural and arts sectors (1.0 per cent, n=5), and the media sector (0.2 per cent, n=1). It is worth noting that about 11.9 per cent (n=58) of the respondents had chosen 'not applicable', and 1.6 per cent (n=8) had filled in industries other than those specified in the questionnaire.

The largest group of respondents held management positions, about 28.2 per cent (n=137). By category, 14.4 per cent (n=70) identified themselves as senior executives, 6.8 per cent (n=33) as senior management and 4.9 per cent (n=24) as company owners. These results are logical given that the focus of an MBA programme is management development. A further 9.5 per cent (n=46) of the respondents indicated they were professionals, with 6.6 per cent (n=32) being frontline workers, and 5.8 per cent (n=28) being technicians. Less than 5 per cent (n=25) were in occupations other than those listed on the questionnaire.

Regarding work experience, about 14.5 per cent (n=58) had less than five years of experience, and 39.1 per cent (n=158) had 5 to 10 years of experience. Those respondents with 11 to 20 years of experience accounted for another 36.3 per cent (n=151) of the sample. Some 9.3 per cent (n=38) had had more than 20 years of experience before joining the management development programme. Among the respondents, about 46.2 per cent (n=182) had spent less than 5 years in their current jobs, and another 42.4 per cent (n=165) had already spent 5 to 10 years.

Only about 10.9 per cent (n=45) had spent more than 10 years in their current job.

On company size, about 34.3 per cent (n=138) of the respondents were from small companies with less than 100 employees, and 52.3 per cent (n=210) being from medium-sized companies with about 100 to 1,000 employees. The remaining 13.4 per cent (n=54) of the respondents worked for larger companies of over 1,000 employees. Most of the companies that respondents worked for (63.2 per cent (n=307) in the sample) were not listed companies, while 21 per cent (n=102) were. However, about 15.8 per cent (n=77) of the respondents did not reply to this question. Of all respondents, 28.8 per cent (n=140) worked in privately owned companies; 18.5 per cent (n=90) were public-sector employees; and 5.6 per cent (n=27) and 21 per cent (n=103) were employed by joint venture corporations and foreign direct investment enterprises respectively.

The results, therefore, were based on a broad consensus, but we remain mindful of Weiss's (1994) admonitions concerning possible over-generalisation.

Chinese folk wisdom statements

In Table 9.1, the results are divided into two groups. The results from statement QA (Even heaven will condemn him if a man does not work for his own good) indicate an approximately 50/50 split between the tendency to disagree (54 per cent, n=259) and the tendency to agree (46 per cent, n=221). Separately, the results of QB (Even a non-educated man has responsibility for the rise and fall of his own country) and QD (It is most important to have a clear conscience in whatever one does) show that the split between the tendency to disagree (5 per cent) and the tendency to agree (95 per cent) are on the two extremes. For QC (Heaven's net is everywhere; though the holes are wide, no one is spared), the distribution is that about 19 per cent had the tendency to disagree and 81 per cent had the tendency to agree. Though less extreme, the tendency is still skewed toward one end.

Chinese managers' ethical decisions and behaviour statements

In Table 9.2, the results are divided into three groups. The first group, including Q10 (42.7 per cent tended to disagree and 57.3 per cent tended to agree), illustrates a more or less equally distributed response between 'disagree' and 'agree'.

The second group, covering Q1 (3.8 per cent tended to disagree and 96.2 per cent tended to agree), Q2 (3.7 per cent tended to disagree and 96.3 per cent tended to agree), Q3 (7 per cent tended to disagree

Table 9.1 Answers from Chinese Managers on Chinese Folk Wisdom Statements

Question	SD	D	S/D	S/A	A	SA	Tend to disagree	Tend to agree	Mean
QA	44 (9.2%)	113 (23.5%)	102 (21.3%)	135 (28.1%)	65 (13.5%)	21 (4.4%)	54.0%	46.0%	3.26
QB	2 (0.4%)	3 (0.6%)	19 (4.0%)	82 (17.2%)	228 (48.0%)	142 (29.8%)	5.0%	95.0%	5.01
QC	3 (0.6%)	34 (7.1%)	54 (11.2%)	130 (27.0%)	170 (35.3%)	91 (18.8%)	18.9%	81.1%	4.46
QD	0 (0.0%)	6 (1.3%)	17 (3.6%)	56 (11.7%)	233 (48.7%)	166 (34.7%)	4.9%	95.1%	5.12

Table 9.2 Answers from Chinese Managers on their Ethical Decisions and Behaviour

Question	SD	D	S/D	S/A	A	SA	Tend to disagree	Tend to agree	Mean
Q1	1 (0.2%)	2 (0.4%)	15 (3.2%)	40 (8.5%)	214 (45.2%)	201 (42.5%)	3.8%	96.2%	5.26
Q2	0 (0.0%)	4 (0.8%)	14 (2.9%)	34 (7.0%)	316 (65.5%)	115 (23.8%)	3.7%	96.3%	5.08
Q3	2 (0.4%)	5 (1.0%)	27 (5.6%)	101 (21.0%)	298 (62.0%)	48 (10.0%)	7.0%	93.0%	4.73
Q4	0 (0.0%)	6 (1.2%)	11 (2.3%)	36 (7.6%)	258 (53.6%)	170 (35.3%)	3.5%	96.5%	5.20
Q5	67 (14.0%)	254 (53.0%)	79 (16.5%)	46 (9.6%)	28 (5.9%)	5 (1.0%)	83.5%	16.5%	2.43
Q6	3 (0.6%)	37 (7.6%)	71 (14.7%)	99 (20.5%)	209 (43.2%)	65 (13.4%)	22.9%	77.1%	4.38
Q7	6 (1.2%)	31 (6.4%)	70 (14.6%)	140 (29.2%)	203 (42.2%)	31 (6.4%)	22.2%	77.8%	4.24
Q8	9 (1.9%)	21 (4.4%)	37 (7.7%)	55 (11.5%)	249 (51.9%)	109 (22.6%)	14.0%	86.0%	4.75
Q9	67 (14.1%)	215 (45.4%)	96 (20.3%)	46 (9.7%)	42 (8.8%)	8 (1.7%)	79.8%	20.2%	2.59
Q10	17 (3.5%)	85 (17.6%)	104 (21.6%)	167 (34.6%)	106 (22.0%)	3 (0.7%)	42.7%	57.3%	3.56

and 93 per cent tended to agree), and Q4 (3.5 per cent tended to disagree and 96.5 per cent tended to agree) is highly skewed, where more respondents tended to 'agree'.

The third group of results, including Q5 (83.5 per cent tended to disagree and 16.5 per cent tended to agree), Q6 (22.9 per cent tended to disagree and 77.1 per cent tended to agree), Q7 (22.2 per cent tended to disagree and 77.8 per cent tended to agree), Q8 (14 per cent tended to disagree and 86 per cent tended to agree), and Q9 (79.8 per cent tended to disagree and 20.2 per cent tended to agree), was less extreme, although still skewed towards one end of the response spectrum.

Correlations on the two groups of statements

In Table 9.3, we calculate the Pearson Correlation for the statements in Tables 9.1 and 9.2. We divide the correlation results into two groups for interpretation purposes. The first group of statements covering QB and QD is found to be significantly correlated with all 10 statements (except Q10 in the case of QB) from Table 9.2.

Table 9.3 Correlation between Chinese Folk Wisdom and Ethical Leadership

		QA	QB	QC	QD
Q1	Pearson Correlation	−.117*	.273**	−.130**	.357**
	Sig. (2-tailed)	.011	.000	.005	.000
Q2	Pearson Correlation	−.062	.276**	.136**	.372**
	Sig. (2-tailed)	.173	.000	.003	.000
Q3	Pearson Correlation	−.098**	.220**	.041	.236**
	Sig. (2-tailed)	.033	.000	.370	.000
Q4	Pearson Correlation	.043	.197**	.138**	.298**
	Sig. (2-tailed)	.354	.000	.002	.000
Q5	Pearson Correlation	.192**	−.192**	.012	−.241**
	Sig. (2-tailed)	.000	.000	.800	.000
Q6	Pearson Correlation	.091*	.176**	.061	.216**
	Sig. (2-tailed)	.048	.000	.183	.000
Q7	Pearson Correlation	−.137**	.124**	.153**	.345**
	Sig. (2-tailed)	.003	.007	.001	.000
Q8	Pearson Correlation	.046	.194**	.099*	.179**
	Sig. (2-tailed)	.318	.000	.031	.000
Q9	Pearson Correlation	.138**	−.158**	−.099*	−.211**
	Sig. (2-tailed)	.003	.001	.031	.000
Q10	Pearson Correlation	.174**	−.044	−.100*	−.176**
	Sig. (2-tailed)	.000	.335	.028	.000

*Correlation is significant at the 0.05 level (1-tailed).
**Correlation is significant at the 0.01 level (2-tailed).

The second group of statements, QA and QC, are found to have significant correlations with seven statements in Table 9.2 – with the exception of Q2, Q4 and Q8 in the case of QA, and Q3, Q5 and Q6 in the case of QC. In brief, strong positive associations between the two groups of statements emerge statistically.

Discussion and implications

Chinese folk wisdom as a 'Firewall' against unethical behaviour

QA (Even heaven will condemn him if a man does not work for his own good) measures a tendency toward individualism. Since there is an approximately 50/50 split between the 'tendency' to disagree and the 'tendency' to agree, this result is ambiguous. As Romar (2002) argues, 'both Confucius and Mencius address motives of profit and self-interest'. The ambiguity in the findings may reflect a belief that these factors are neither intrinsically good or bad, but must be put into perspective, and must not blind the moral person to improper moral behaviour. Whether or not self-interest is good or bad, or agreeable or disagreeable, will depend on the respondent's perception of whether or not self-interest is handled in a moral way, and to what extent it relates to communal ends.

QB (Even a non-educated man has responsibility for the rise and fall of his own country) and QD (It is most important to have a clear conscience in whatever one does) indicate the influence of collectivism and the Confucian belief of morals coming from within or from the 'heart' respectively. Both these old Chinese sayings express Confucian values concerning the willingness to sacrifice the minority in order to ensure the survival of the majority. 'Yi' should supersede 'Li', where 'Yi' is the appropriate distribution of profits and benefits with others, and 'Li' is one's own profits and benefits (Enderle, 1997). These statements were both agreed with by approximately 95 per cent of the respondents, in agreement with many previous findings that managers in China adhere to traditional Confucian values (e.g. Lam, 2004; Ralston et al., 1993; Snell and Tseng, 2003). Thus, there is evidence to support the maintenance of these fundamental values among Chinese managers.

QC (Heaven's net is everywhere; though the holes are wide, no one is spared) reflects traditional Chinese thinking about 'the Heaven' as the ultimate resort of moral judgement. This old Chinese saying is a Taoist idea. However, since Taoism was absorbed by Confucianism (Carnogurska, 1998 cited in Snell and Tseng, 2003), Taoist philosophy is deeply integrated into the traditional Chinese values. The folk wisdom here is that righteousness does exist and people who have done wrong will ultimately receive punishment. Interestingly, approximately 19 per cent of the survey respondents disagreed with this statement. Perhaps they have seen people turning away from Confucian and Communist values to become more preoccupied with money, leading to numerous cases of dishonesty and betrayal in business (Fisher and Yuan, 1998; Harvey, 1999 cited in Snell and Tseng, 2003), yet none seems to have been punished, nor are they becoming worse off. In this connection, we see that 'Li' has its stronger stance for a certain portion (19 per cent of our sample) of Chinese managers, though a clear majority still holds the belief of ultimate moral judgement.

Overall, we conclude that Chinese folk wisdom as applied in the Chinese business context may still be a valid vehicle or means for guarding against possible unethical leadership by Chinese managers. From another perspective, we can also argue that Chinese folk wisdom may be acting as a 'firewall' to prevent a worsening of ethical leadership among Chinese managers.

An update on how Chinese managers made ethical decisions

It is noted that the responses to Q1 (International brands are built on a good foundation of trust), Q2 (I will only buy from enterprises that have good ethical performance), Q3 (I will take into consideration the ethical performance of the companies in making business cooperation decisions), and Q4 (Corporations must provide employees with full training to increase their trustworthiness) are skewed toward one end, with around 96 per cent of respondents in agreement. The underlying nature of this group of statements is that 'Yi' would bring 'Li'. In other words – it is likely that the respondents are agreeing to these statements because they have seen that ethical leadership and ethical behaviour ultimately bring profit or self-interest. Thus, ethical decisions are in line with the business goal of profit-making.

Although responses to Q5 (Raising the standard of business ethics in a commercial environment will reduce the competitiveness of the companies), Q8 (Trust is a new strategic thinking in business), and Q9 (Business ethics has nothing to do with corporate profitability) are less extreme, the tendencies still are skewed toward one end of the Likert scale (around 80 per cent generally disagreed with Q5 and Q9, while 86 per cent tended to agree to Q8). These responses clearly reflect a tendency to believe that business ethics has something to do with profitability, in line with the analysis for the group of statements described just above.

For Q6 (Once a contract is established, it must never be broken even if losses might be incurred in meeting the obligations) and Q7 (Even if it means incurring a loss in business, there must not be any actions of deceit), about 77 per cent of respondents tended to agree. This suggests that the majority still conform to Confucian values, not being completely against 'Li' and wanting to put 'Yi' into 'Li', or at least to achieve 'Li' in a moral way. The findings here support previous empirical studies that have shown that Chinese managers pay more attention to 'Yi' than to 'Li' (Lu, 1997; Nisbett, 2003).

Responses to Q10 (Making ethical compromises to obtain agreement in business negotiations is unavoidable), suggest that approximately 15 per cent are more in 'agreement' than 'disagreement'. Comparing these results with Q6, the interpretation might be that during business negotiations, it is allowable to make ethical compromises to achieve agreement, but once a contract is established, it must never be broken, even if losses may be incurred. Interestingly, there existed two sets of behaviours – the different orientation before and after making a business agreement. This phenomenon can be further explained from two perspectives. First, the responses to Q10 reflect the real situation of conducting business in the China mainland, which is perhaps more complex than is currently understood. Secondly, it is that *'guanxi'* still plays a major role in business negotiations in China. *Guanxi* remains the quickest and surest route to accomplish business goals, with acceptance and trust paramount to its establishment. A favour granted will be met by an 'unspoken promise of a favor to be returned in the future' (Pang et al., 1998). When conducting business, Chinese managers therefore tend to be practical and flexible, seeking ways to establish *guanxi* which might even lead to ethical compromise. Once a contract is signed, however, Chinese managers would ideally seek mutual compliance.

Consistencies between Chinese folk wisdom and ethical leadership

Table 9.3 suggests that the statements describing Chinese folk wisdom (QB except when against Q10, and QD in Table 9.1) are correlated significantly at the 0.01 level with all of the statements pertaining to business ethics in Table 9.2. The association between the orientation toward Chinese folk wisdom and the Chinese managers' orientation toward ethical leadership is therefore positive in general. For QD, there is a negative linear association with Q5, Q9, and Q10. All other pairs for

QD have shown positive relationships, meaning that if a Chinese manager agrees to the statement that it is most important to have a clear conscience in whatever one does, they exhibit consistency between their ethical values and ethical decisions and behaviours. Even for Q10, a Chinese manager who has a clear conscience believes that making ethical compromises to obtain agreement in business negotiations is unavoidable, although this finding may be about making ethical compromises when it is beneficial to the organisations, in order 'to ensure the survival of the majority' (Pang et al., 1998). Indeed, Lam's (2004) findings indicated that organisational benefit was a major reason for managers to commit unethical behaviours.

QB also has a negative linear association with Q5, Q9, and Q10; the others show positive relationships. Therefore, we can argue the same interpretation as for QD. Since QB is not correlated significantly at the 0.01 and 0.05 levels with Q10, the association is not so obvious, however.

Conclusions and future research

The Chinese people, even after numerous political campaigns designed to change their national collective thinking, tend to hold to traditional values embedded in 'Chinese folk wisdom'. This study suggests that these values affect their behaviour and thinking in a business context as well as in general life. Based on our data and analysis, we find that Chinese folk wisdom remains an effective carrier of Chinese traditional ethical values, despite the drastic shift in Chinese education from a Confucian mode to a Maoist mode over the previous decades. Such Chinese folk wisdom, cum Confucianism, influences the decisions and behaviour of Chinese managers, leading many scholars and researchers to regard the business ethics provided by Chinese folk wisdom as a 'firewall' to guard against unethical practice by business managers. These implications are worth noting, given the argument that China might become the economic 'locomotive' to revive the global economy after the financial crisis (Jian, 2009; Sung, 2008). Opportunities for further application of Chinese culture in China's business sector should not be rare.

Chinese traditional business practice involves a tussle between 'business' and 'ethics' in terms of 'Li' and 'Yi', where 'Yi' has traditionally received more attention than 'Li' (Enderle, 1997) in the Chinese business world. However, a new market ethic that views profit as the primary and overriding goal has emerged, following Deng Xiaoping's proclamation that 'to get rich is glorious'. As the Chinese people enjoy more economic freedom, and witness individual wealth growing at a very rapid rate among certain groups (Martinsons, 2008), these new market ethics, which contrast starkly with both Confucian and Maoist values, have become increasingly prevalent in China (Lam, 2004; Whitcomb et al., 1998). The negative associations for QD (in Table 9.1) with Q5, Q9, and Q10 (in Table 9.2) speak for 'Li' receiving more attention than 'Yi' in shaping contemporary business ethics in China. At this stage, we cannot conclude that 'Yi' or ethics is a means or an end to conducting business in China and it is possibly both. Further research along these lines would be worthwhile.

China faces an increasingly open global market. On the one hand, Westerners may think that management by trust and the adoption of international norms of business ethics in China will help improve China's competitive edge and enhance the profitability of China's companies. On the other hand, through the opening up of the market, there are equal opportunities for the West to learn how Chinese business ethics affect decision-making, and how they guard against unethical managerial practices. We have argued that there are three main forces influencing business ethics in China: Confucianism, Maoism, and foreign business ethics. This study has provided empirical evidence about the influence of Confucianism, handed down through Chinese folk wisdom, in the Chinese business world. In the face of signs of a re-reliance or resurrection of Confucianism in Chinese government policy, as a means to consolidate support for implementing nationwide policies like financial reforms, the impact that Chinese folk wisdom is already having on China's business sector should be worth further investigation. Our study hopes to act as a catalyst in this endeavour.

Note

Acknowledgment, with thanks: this chapter is an edited version of my original paper in *Journal of Public Affairs*, 2010, and is published by permission of John Wiley & Sons Ltd (Chinese folk wisdom: Implications for guarding against unethical practices by Chinese managers; by R. W. F. Szeto, *Journal of Public Affairs*, 10(3), Copyright © 2010, John Wiley & Sons Ltd).

Bibliography

Adair, J.G., 'The Research Environment in Developing Countries', *International Journal of Psychology*, 30(1) (1995) 643–62.

Bell, D.A. and Waizer, M., 'Reconciling Socialism and Confucianism?: Reviving Tradition in China', *Dissent*, 57(1) (2010) 91–101.

Bond, M.H., *The Psychology of the Chinese People* (Hong Kong: Oxford University Press, 1986).

Burrows, G.R., Drummond, D.L., and Martinsons, M.G., 'Knowledge Management in China', *Communications of the ACM*, 48(4) (2005) 73–6.

Carnogurska, M., 'Original Ontological Roots of Ancient Chinese Philosophy', *Asian Philosophy*, 8(3) (1998) 203–213.

Chan, A., Wong, S., and Leung, P., 'Ethical Beliefs of Chinese Consumers in Hong Kong', *Journal of Business Ethics*, 17(11) (1998) 1163–1170.

Davison, R.M., Martinsons, M.G., Ou, C.X.J., Murata, K., Drummond, D., Li, Y., and Lo, H.W.H., 'The Ethics of IT Professionals in Japan and China', *Journal of the Association for Information Systems*, 10(11) (2009) 834–859.

Enderle, G., 'A Worldwide Survey of Business Ethics in the 1990s', *Journal of Business Ethics*, 16(14) (1997) 1475–1483.

Fisher, C.D. and Yuan, A.X.Y., 'What Motivates Employees? A Comparison of US and Chinese Employees', *International Journal of Human Resource Management*, 9(3) (1998) 516–528.

Harvey, B., ' "Graceful Merchants": A Contemporary View of Chinese Business Ethics', *Journal of Business Ethics*, 20(1) (1999) 85–93.

Jian, J., 'Confucianism a Vital String in China's Bow. Greater China', 29 October (2009). Retrieved from *Online Asia Times*: www.atimes.com/atimes/China/KJ09Ad01.html on 23 December 2009.

Lam, C.F., 'Understanding the Ethical Decisions and Behaviors of Hong Kong Business Managers: An implication for Business Ethics Education', *Management Research News*, 27(10) (2004) 69–77.

Lau, S.K. and Kuan, H.C., *The Ethos of the Hong Kong Chinese* (Hong Kong: Chinese University Press, 1988).

Lu, X., 'Business Ethics in China', *Journal of Business Ethics*, 16(14) (1997) 1509–1518.

Martinsons, M.G., 'Relationship-based E-Commerce: Theory and Evidence from China', *Information Systems Journal*, 18(4) (2008) 331–356.

Martinsons, M.G. and Westwood, R.I., 'Management Information Systems in the Chinese Business Culture: An Explanatory Theory', *Information and Management*, 32(5) (1997) 215–228.

Nisbett, R., *The Geography of Thought: How Asians and Westerners Think Differently...and Why* (New York: Free Press, 2003).

Pang, C.K., Roberts, D.and Sutton, J., 'Doing Business in China – the Art of War?' *International Journal of Contemporary Hospitality*, 10(7) (1998) 272.

Panzner, M., 'China Calls For US Change After Financial Tsunami' (2009). Retrieved from Panzner's website: http://panzner.typepad.com/ on 22 December 2009.

Ralston, D.A., Gustafson, D.J., Cheung, F.M., and Terpstra, R.H., 'Differences in Managerial Values: A Study of U.S., Hong Kong and PRC Managers', *Journal of International Business Studies*, 24(2) (1993) 249–275.

Redfern, K., 'The Influence of Industrialisation on Ethical Ideology of Managers in the People's Republic of China', *Cross Cultural Management*, 12(2) (2005) 38–50.

Redfern, K. and Crawford, J., 'An Empirical Investigation of the Influence of Modernisation on the Moral Judgements of Managers in the People's Republic of China', *Cross Cultural Management*, 11(1) (2004) 48–61.

Romar, E.J., 'Virtue is Good Business: Confucianism as a Practical Business Ethics', *Journal of Business Ethics*, 38(1/2) (2002) 119–131.

Shaw, R.B., *Trust in the Balance: Building Successful Organizations in Results, Integrity and Concern* (San Franciso: Jossey-Bass, 1997).

Snell, R.B. and Tseng, C.S., 'Images of the Virtuous Employee in China's Transitional Economy', *Asia Pacific Journal of Management*, 20(3) (2003) 307–313.

Sung, Y.W., 'China Bucking the Financial Tsunami'. Manila: 11th International Convention of East Asian Economic Association 2008, 15–16 November (2008).

Swecker, P.R., Validation of Organizational Practice Statements in the Indonesian Work Environment, Unpublished DBA thesis (Perth, Western Australia: Murdoch University Press, 1998).

Whitcomb, L.L., Erdener, C.B., and Li, C., 'Business Ethical Values in China and the U.S', *Journal of Business Ethics*, 17(8) (1998) 839–852.

Weiss, R., *Learning From Strangers: The Art and Method of Quantitative Interviewing* (New York: Free Press, 1994).

Wright, P., Szeto, W. and Cheng, T.W., 'Guanxi and Professional Conduct in China: a Management Development Perspective', *International Journal of Human Resource Management*, 13(1) (2002) 156–182.

Wright, P., Szeto, W. and Cheng, E., 'Business Networking in the Chinese Context: Its Role in the Formation of Guanxi, Social Capital and Ethical Foundations', *Management Research News*, 29(7) (2006) 425–438.

Xi, S. and Wright, P., 'Developing and Validating an International Business Negotiator's Profile: The China Context', *Managerial Psychology*, 16(5) (2001) 364–389.

Zheng, Y.B., Lin, M.C., Nonaka, A.and Boem, K., 'Harmony, Hierarchy and Conservation: A Cross-Cultural Comparison of Confucian Values in China, Korea, Japan and Taiwan', *Communications Research Report*, 22(1) (2005) 109–117.

10
Leading Ethically: What Helps and What Hinders

Kurt April, Kai Peters, Kirsten Locke, and Caroline Mlambo

Introduction

Ethics is concerned with moral obligation, responsibility, social justice, and the common good. It is about defining the practices and rules – written and unwritten – which inform responsible conduct and behaviour between individuals and groups in order to maintain, or enhance, the common good. Everything we do has a consequence, such that ethics is fundamental to the very essence of who we are, and what we value, both as individuals and as people. This chapter presents the findings of a study that aimed to identify those enablers that seem to help individuals to live and act ethically, and those stumbling blocks that prevent them from translating a theoretical knowledge of ethics and morals into action. The sample involved 646 middle managers enrolled on the MBA programmes of the University of Cape Town (South Africa) and Erasmus University (Netherlands). The chapter explains the approach taken and presents the findings, as a contribution to the debate on the practical steps that might increase ethical behaviour in individuals.

Enablers

Our theoretical starting point for the enablers of ethical behaviour utilises a virtue ethics approach. Virtue ethics, or character ethics, directs our attention not just to questions about what is the ethical thing to do, or how we are to act ethically, but to questions about what it means to be an ethical sort of person (Mahoney, 1998). The four cardinal (*cardes*, 'hinges') virtues of Aristotle and Greek philosophy – *justice*, *wisdom* (prudence), *courage* (fortitude), and *moderation* (self-control, temperance) form the basis of Western ethics. The intellectual virtue of wisdom is education-based, while the moral virtues of justice, courage, and moderation are practice-based. All other virtues are derived from these four. Mahoney (1998:191) argues that the particular contribution of virtue theory to business ethics is to emphasise that there is really no substitute for integrity: the trustworthiness, loyalty, and moral courage of the individual person working within the company for its best interests. It was Plato who noted that the way to virtue was through knowledge of the Good. According to him, if we knew without a doubt that virtue was always for our good, and that justice is always more profitable than injustice (the central teaching of *The Republic*), then we would have no motive for preferring vice. Lantos (1999:222) explains that 'the ethical person chooses the moral course of action regardless of personal sacrifice'. April et al. (2000) believe that authenticity and ethics are linked, arguing that 'in order to become an authentic leader, it is important to know where one stands on important moral and professional issues and then act accordingly'. Persons of character do not allow situations to be the determining force behind their actions (Scarnati, 1997:25), since 'what we have worked hard to achieve during our lifetime can be quickly lost if the basic principle is seriously violated'.

Stumbling blocks

However, situational social psychologists argue that the notion of ethics is not global (Alzola, 2006), but that it evolves according to time and culture (Svensson and Wood, 2003), and varies by individual, place, and time. It is therefore situation-specific (Annas, 2006). The main proponents of the situationist thesis (Doris, 1998 and 2002; Harman 1999, 2002 and 2003; Zimbardo, 1971, 2004 and 2007) largely base their views on findings from experimental psychology. Arjoon (2008) summarises five types of situational contexts, which studies show can lead to ethical sub-optimisation. First, *obedience to authority*, originating from Milgram's (1974) Yale University electric shock experiments and Zimbardo's (1971) Stanford Prison experiments. Secondly, *mood effects*, which can be characterised as organisational culture, deriving from Isen and Levin (1972). Thirdly, *bystander* studies (Asch, 1951; Latane and Darley, 1968 and 1970; Latane and Rodin, 1969) point to conformity when a given behaviour is called for. Fourthly, the *Good Samaritan* or hurry factor (Darley and Baston, 1973) shows that people tend not to stop when that would be the right thing to do. Lastly – *consistency*. Studies carried out among schoolchildren have shown that children who are consistently honest at school are not necessarily honest at home, or vice versa (Hartshorne and May, 1928). Within the business ethics literature, situationist authors (Gandossy and Sonnenfeld, 2005) have shown how many of the recent corporate crises like Enron, Shell, Tyco, and WorldCom can be traced back to a range of these factors, with organisational obedience to authority looming largest. Positioning situational social psychology as a necessary cause of immoral behaviour is of course incorrect. What the situationists simply identify is that certain situations more often than not lead to bad behaviour. The debate between proponents of virtue ethics and the situationists has long been seen as a dichotomy but need not be constructed as such (Webber, 2006). That said, the situational factors identified as encouraging negative behaviours have been used to provide a framework of classification for the stumbling blocks in this study.

Methodology

Our research base comprised 646 middle managers enrolled on the MBA programmes of the University of Cape Town and Erasmus University. Participants were given the following definition of 'ethics':

> *Ethics is concerned with moral obligation, responsibility, social justice and the common good, and can both be taught and also exist instinctively in an individual. Ethics are a set of moral principles or rules of conduct (virtues) by which human beings live in relation to other human beings, nature, God and/or themselves, and against which human actions and proposals may be judged good or bad, or right or wrong, in a particular context. These rules of conduct, recognised in respect of a particular class of human actions, when acted upon through choice among equally plausible alternatives by an individual, shape his/her character (lived virtues/values/ principles). In other words, ethics are not simply a series of norms or values to be imposed as a template upon people, but rather imply a rational, discursive practice on the part of the individual – and are most evident at a time of ethical dilemma. The main factors which most likely cause people to compromise ethical standards are: pressure to meet unrealistic business objectives/deadlines, desire to further one's career, and the desire to protect one's livelihood.*

We encouraged the research respondents to write their own personal stories, and to self-report their experiences relating to stumbling blocks and enablers. We also asked them to report on the practical actions that they employed to live and work ethically. When we received the written situated-experiences of the research respondents, we analysed the data using a five-step blueprint (Srnka and Koeszegi, 2007:35):

Our analysis of the 646 self-reported documents identified 255 different mentions (in 10 separate themes) of enablers, and 98 different mentions (in six separate themes) of stumbling blocks. Additionally, respondents mentioned 176 different practical actions/recommendations (in 10 separate themes) which they took in their own lives in order to be more ethical. The findings are listed in Table 10.1 (enablers), Table 10.2 (stumbling blocks), and Table 10.3 (actions), respectively. The enablers and the stumbling blocks were both grouped by theme, then grouped with the cardinal virtues and the rules/regulations situational corrector. Lastly, the behaviours and actions listed by respondents that might encourage and further develop ethics were coded and are presented by theme.

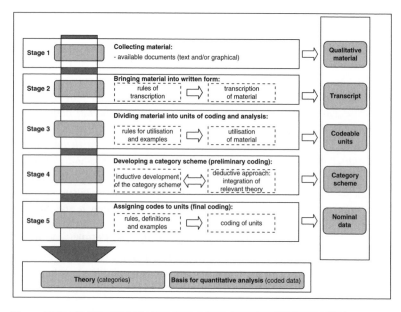

Figure 10.1   Blueprint for the Qualitative Analysis Process
Source: adapted from Srnka and Koeszegi, 2007

Table 10.1   Frequency – Enablers

Themes of enablers mentioned	Listings
Upbringing	57
Spirituality	54
Mentors and role models	45
Honesty, courage and integrity	37
Self-control	21
Conscience	17
Standing up for own beliefs	8
Codes of conduct	8
Self-knowledge	7
Defining moments	1

Findings – enablers

Table 10.1 shows the frequency of enablers mentioned, in descending order. The enablers are then discussed under the headings of the virtues of justice, wisdom, courage, and moderation.

The virtue of justice

Standing up for your beliefs

P38 wrote: '*Whenever I am placed in a difficult or grey situation with two or more choices where morality/ethics is questionable, I refer to this instant in my life and ask myself which of the two options is the more difficult. Experience has shown me that the more difficult choice is the ethical option, and because of past experiences having resulted in awful circumstances, I now always choose the high road, that is, I practice greater self-control and avoid unethical temptations.*'

Conscience

Scarnati (1997:26) argues that 'dedication to the virtue of honesty establishes an internal warning system called "conscience" that will assist in keeping us upright and out of unethical situations'. People who listen to their conscience experience deep fulfilment even in the midst of difficulties and challenges (Covey and Merrill, 1994:185). P89 agreed and wrote: '*My conscience is one factor that enables me to keep grounded into the issues of ethics. This is not to suggest that it prohibits me from engaging in unethical acts, but often than not it prevents me from becoming too far involved and makes me to realize that my actions were being contrary to the* norms of a decent person. *My conscience causes me to realise that although there are no legal obligations involved, there are major issues about keeping one's word, about being honest about being fair, that are values that need to be considered and applied if we are to live in a society that is both satisfying and at least relatively stable.'* Badaracco (2006:34) argues that 'a moral compass is useful for questions of right and wrong but in most organisations, however, the hardest choices arise when right conflicts with right'. P139, however, believed: *'It is the conviction that you know that you will be able to sleep at night, that what you are doing will make the world a better, safer place that enables us to be ethical.'* P481 argued that: *'There have been times in the past where I have done something I have been ashamed of. Afterward I feel very uncomfortable, and anxious. Often this is only relieved if I admit to someone what I have done.'* Holian (2006:1134), however, warns that sometimes increased awareness of ethical issues can lead to an increased perception of uncertainty, risk and overload, which paralyses decision-making.

Self-knowledge

Much in the same way as Augustine's documented early education in the fourth century, which through contemplation and self-reflection led to an awakening to his personal beliefs, a re-reading of his personal value narratives, and the formation of his ethics (upward ascent of the soul), P210 argued: *'Knowing my values and beliefs and being true and honest with myself, and being able to distinguish the right from the wrong, are enablers for me to always strive to be a better person and do the right things'*, while P449 claimed: *'I feel that by being aware of the influence of ethics on my judgements, I am able to adjust my values and behaviour whenever needed.'* P442 concurred: *'There are times when I have applied my ethics in business at the cost of short-term financial gain, but I have slept well at night and I do not regret for one second having done that. I feel that in the long-term I have made the right decision.'*

The Virtue of wisdom

Upbringing

Odom and Green (2003:67) argue that 'early education experiences and family influences are going to have the most critical impacts on the integrity of future business leaders and their willingness and ability to be value driven'. P400 concurred and stated: *'Every building that lasts is built on solid foundations. Similarly when we build our "self" – our character or personality – we need a solid platform to build on. It is therefore vital that we have an ethical foundation that we use to judge our actions or view-points.'* P122 also argued: *'I have the good fortune to have been guided by my mother, who even though she had not progressed beyond grade 8 at school, taught me to live a life based on consideration for others, to know the difference between right and wrong and to act in accordance with that knowledge, and if in doubt, to consult somebody who knows.'* P391 also related to folklore and stated: *'My adult life therefore draws back and is shaped mostly by my fundamental beliefs, which were infused in me by my grandmother. In her pursuit to instil moral instincts in me, she would sometimes tell me mystical stories that would make me differentiate between good and bad, and mostly discourage me from what our society perceived as bad.'* P232 questioned the usefulness of a protected upbringing and stated: *'I am proud of where I come from and, by and large, I think that the morality that was instilled in me has helped to shape the person I am. However, as I have grown into an adult I have trouble at times assimilating these values with the realities of my adult life, which appear more complex.'*

Spirituality

P41 claimed: *'It is my belief that there is a higher force that we are all responsible and accountable to. I am talking about my belief in the Bible and what it teaches about the existence of God, that God is love and that God created the universe. I use the Bible to understand love, which is the call message that God tries to send to every mankind. In believing in the ethics and authentic values through following the Bible, I create a special bond with God.'* P119 concurred and stated: *'My sense of right and wrong has been greatly influenced by my religion. I am aware of God watching me and am aware of the profound influence the rigid code of conduct that my religion requires of me and its effect on my everyday life.'* P254 contrasted the Christian and Muslim beliefs and argued: *'I am a practicing Muslim and my religion is a huge cornerstone of what I define as good or bad behaviour. The Quran does not have a set of commandments similar to that in the Bible. Instead, the Quran defines specific guidelines on what is acceptable and what is not. These guidelines form the principles on which I base my ethics and values.'* Shipka (1997) advises that it is through spirit that we infuse deeper meaning and purpose to our lives. Through our spirituality we also unleash untapped unlimited creative potential; we comprehend our connection to reach others and all life.

Mentors and role models

Odom and Green (2003:67) argue that 'when leaders are truly trans-formational and serve as role models of ethical behaviour, a positive culture will permeate the whole organisation'. P38 agreed and stated: '*I believe that mentors serve as a beacon of light and morality especially when faced with difficult decisions. I am fortunate enough to have had a number of mentors to date.*'

The virtue of courage

Honesty/courage and integrity

P332 viewed honesty as '*a non-negotiable policy but when faced with sensitive issues, I have had to temporarily compromise on my policy and hold back on my honesty*'. However, Lewis (1952) wrote: 'We might think that provided you did the right thing, it did not matter how or why you did it – whether you did it willingly or unwillingly, sulkily or cheerfully, through fear of public opinion or for its own sake. But the truth is that the right actions done for the wrong reason do not help to build the internal quality or character called a virtue and it is this quality or character that really matters.' P120 by contrast believed ethics required: '... *the courage to make an unpopular decision without concern for personal consequences*'. P266 believed: '*Honesty and integrity allow the clear projection of one's own intentions and thoughts.*'

The virtue of moderation

Self-control

P456 argued that: '*Self control, in this respect, is a matter of choice and personal attitude. Control of noticing feeling at a particular moment, awareness of recognising what is wrong or right and having the courage to act against it or not.*' P455 agreed and stated: '*I am strongly convinced that you always have a choice whether you adapt to your standards or adapt to the environment. By having that choice it also means you are in control.*' P282 believed that '*self control helps to avoid unethical temptations*'. P12 stated: '*I noticed that if someone firmly believes and defends his/her opinion properly, people respect that person more than a person who is always happy to go along with the rest of the group and has never expressed an opinion for himself/herself.*'

Codes of conduct

P282 stated: '*I am an accountant by profession, and the professional body that sets the accounting standards stipulates that accountants must practice by the highest levels of morals, ethics and integrity. I even signed an oath with regards to this.*' April and Wilson (2007) argue that rules not backed up by punishment will normally not be adhered to. In South Africa, the corporate governance guidelines provided by King (King, 1991) are used by most companies to set ethical standards.

Findings – stumbling blocks

Table 10.2 shows the frequency of stumbling blocks mentioned, in descending order. The stumbling blocks are then grouped by the five factors derived from the social psychology literature: obedience to authority, mood effects, the bystander/Good Samaritan factors, and the factor of consistency.

Obedience to authority

P446 stated: '*I know I like to be part of a group. I sometimes even adapt myself to become part of certain groups. This sometimes can result in feeling the peer pressure, wanting to change my natural personality. I know though that this peer pressure does not go that far that I will change myself and act against my own values and beliefs.*' P119 concurred and stated: '*My stumbling blocks have been doing what others are doing in a certain situation, not willing to be personally accountable for the decisions.*' P229 also wrote: '*I should have left the company the first time I came to the realisation that I did not approve of the way we did business. I was afraid that I might not find another well-paying job, or I may have to move and start a new life again.*' P93 viewed '*ethical behaviour in the workplace as something that is being driven very strongly by procedures and standards. Unfortunately the compliance to these is not always very good. An example is discrimination during recruitment, as well as disciplinary procedures. In the end, the ethics of any business depends on the ethics of the people working in that business and therefore you need to start with the people.*'

Table 10.2   Frequency – Stumbling Blocks

Themes of stumbling blocks mentioned	Listings
Bottom-line mentality	34
Organisational influences	31
Fear	21
Peer pressure	8
Compliance	2
Humour	2

Mood effects

Mood effects, or an organisational culture that promotes unethical behaviour, are clearly drivers. P514 wrote: *'I cannot fail to mention that I come from Peru, where unethical behaviour like bribing, are "tools" and common practice to move ahead, when primarily dealing with governmental bureaucracy. To me, it is hard to imagine a business entity, which along their lifetime did not bribe and not only in Peru, but I can attest that in all of Latin America. This might seem tough and dark, but it is reality; furthermore, I believe that given the collective unconsciousness in my mother-home society this is a common practice and some may argue, needed. Western ethical behaviour amidst this scenario will be tough to fulfil.'* P37 justified unethical conduct by stating: *'If a person has no financial option whether or not they stay in the job it may well serve their interest to accept the unethical manner of doing business, even if it is in contrast to their own moral code.'* P129 also argued that: *'At other times, Lucifer whispers equally sweetly into my ear and tells me that money is good and by working hard, I am actually servicing humanity in my own sweet way!'* P10 argued that: *'Although at a personal level I might consider myself moral or ethical in my conduct, business life poses its own challenges on a daily basis.'* P9 claimed: *'In an organisation, if one is not in a position of power, it is sometimes very difficult to act ethically even if one wants to. One is forced to conform to the organisation's expectations.'* P501 also argued that: *'Another big stumbling block regarding ethics is the feeling that my contribution towards a better world is so small, that my effort does not matter.'* P35 concurred with P9 and P501, and stated: *'Although I did employ an ethical and moral approach in my own day to day professional activities, I was not placed in a senior enough position where I could challenge those that do things for their own personal gain and recognition within the company. I suppose that this is one of the main reasons why I decided to leave the company at the end of the day.'*

The bystander/good samaritan factors

These factors can lead to an emphasis on profits at the expense of service. P14 argued that: *'In organisations, I have been involved in dilemmas ... It was very definitely a case of profit first and morality, ethics, social responsibility, etc. a distant second.'* P273 stated that: *'Sometimes I become too focused on the bottom-line on a specific project, and then ethical dilemmas that may previously have caused me to rethink my relationship with the client are given less prominence. There are lots of grey areas between what is right and wrong; the lines become even more blurred when focused on the bottom-line.'* P120 believed that making shareholders happy drove him to: *'... manipulate financial results if I can get away with it to make the shareholder happy, or profits at the expense of environmental degradation, and the attainment of huge bonuses as the expense of others.'* P275 agreed with the view of a life of comfort and claimed: '*One of the driving forces behind my ambition to succeed is to be able to provide for my mom, siblings and children what I never had. In the quest of this, I sometimes lose sight of the bigger picture and adopt a bottom-line mentality.'* P275 stated that: '*One of my challenges is exposing the snake in the suit. I know what she is doing is wrong and causing much unhappiness in a few people's lives. I know the right thing to do is to expose her to her superiors at work so that she can be dealt with, and the situation rectified. For years I have been ignoring this, not to upset the apple cart.'*

Consistency

P228 argued: '*I found this quite challenging; working in an environment where corruption is an integral part of daily life in both the public and the private sectors. I resisted offers on some occasions but on others the offers were too tempting to resist. As I think back, I realise that on those occasions where I did not act ethically, I convinced myself that my efforts alone were likely to be isolated and will do little to fight corruption. I also found solace in the thinking that it was not so bad "earning" a commission when you acted as a middleman in a corrupt deal. It was the desire to earn another "buck" that led me into seeking justification for things that were certainly morally incorrect.'* P477 stated: '*When I want immediate or physical gratification, it is amazing to see how I can rationalise my own behaviours and treat those events as if they live in a vacuum, and hence have no impact on my wholeness.'*

Table 10.3   Practical Actions Frequency

Themes of practical action/recommendations	Appearances
Act in accordance with my values and beliefs	29
Increase self-awareness	17
Develop, make use of and value my support network	14
Religion/Spirituality	12
Act with courage	11
Practice reflection, meditation and mindfulness	11
Be open, honest and transparent	10
Embrace diversity	9
Heighten awareness and exposure	9
Other	54

Findings – practical actions

The respondents made the following recommendations as to what can be done as far as ethics and morals are concerned. These are listed in descending order of frequency of mention in Table 10.3.

Act in accordance with my values and beliefs

In my definition for ethics, I am not only going to focus on being able to tell what is right and wrong, but also being able to act on what I believe to be right.

This guideline ranked first in terms of nominations. Respondents felt that it was extremely important to act in accordance with their values and beliefs if they were to improve their ethical performance in any way.

I will, through practice, act in accordance with what I believe more often and be brave [enough] to disagree with anyone who compromises my beliefs.
And that is where I think the crux [with] ethics lies. It is not whether you know the difference between 'right' and 'good', it is about whether you know the difference, but choose to ignore it for your own gain. I therefore think that the secret to becoming a better, more ethical person is just to do what you know is right in your heart. If everybody lived [according] to this simple rule, we would have a lot better, happier, more loving world out there.

One respondent highlighted the fact that she needs to take action, even if she believes that the small role she plays cannot make a difference.

The final step is acting on your moral decision. I must have the confidence in my abilities to do what is correct. I have often felt that one person cannot make a difference and therefore I don't even try. However I must recognise that one person can make a difference, even if it is a small difference and therefore I must be willing to act.

Another questioned himself as to whether his ethical behaviour was driven by principles or was based on a fear of consequences. He felt that his true challenge lies in being ethical and acting in accordance with his values and beliefs, even if it went against mainstream thinking.

What became evident under this guideline is that respondents felt they needed clarity on their 'moral code' and 'value proposition' before enacting what they believed to be right.

> *My goal is to cultivate my moral code according to the purest form of known truth. This means that I must have my perception of 'what is the truth' under a microscope. Tied firmly to this mission is to ensure that my every action matches my moral code. That my decisions are in perfect tandem with my theoretical beliefs of right and wrong.*

Increase self-awareness

This guideline received the second most mentions. Most respondents discussed the importance of checking their values and refining them if necessary.

> *Ethics have always been important to me and I was brought up with a strong set of values. I think that this helped me to get through some difficult periods in my life. As I move on through my life, and from continent to continent, I will regularly have to make a reality check on my set of values and readjust when necessary.*
>
> *I recognise that to attain effective self-leadership I must be able to determine what I stand for and have a system of reviewing these as, and when, time and space allow.*

Others felt that by being fully self-aware, they would be in a better position to stand their ground.

> *If I know what is right and what is wrong I will be able to stand my ground in any situation and defend this.*

Self-awareness links to self-discipline, and five respondents also felt that by instilling greater self-discipline within themselves they would be better able to stick to their beliefs and perform in an ethical fashion.

Develop and make use of a support network

This guideline received the third most nominations. Several respondents mentioned that they would consider using a mentor to guide their ethical behaviour.

> *Kerns (2003) also recommends wisdom and knowledge as important enablers to distinguish between right and wrong. In this regard, I believe*

that mentors (Odom and Green, 2003) will serve as a beacon of light and morality, especially when faced with a difficult decision.

In my future career in business, I will have to deal with many ethical issues. My personal action plan that will help me develop the competencies I will need to handle these issues effectively is, firstly to have a mentor or a positive role model. I will use my mentor as a sounding board whenever I am unsure of the next steps to take – in business, or in life in general.

Others suggested surrounding themselves with those they believed to have high moral and ethical standards.

I will certainly attempt to surround myself with ethical people as this can certainly aid good ethical behaviour, as suggested by Reilly and Myroslaw (1990).

I must become acquainted with, and seek guidance from, those whom I believe live their lives with humility and integrity.

Religion/spirituality

Religion/spirituality received the fourth most mentions.

The adage goes that without God everything is justifiable, so people can never be held accountable for their actions. God demands fairness and that we do what is right and good (Is. 56:1) because, in the end, we will all be judged (Rev. 20:12). It is the standard I have set for my life because I'll be held to account.

Instead of determining my ethics by what is socially acceptable, I need to ask myself what is acceptable to God. Failing to do so, ethics becomes nothing more than etiquette, a reflection of time- and spatial-specific norms. Without genuine integrity and 'fundamental character strength', life's challenges will eventually expose my true motives (Covey, 2004:22).

Act with courage

Respondents highlighted this guideline 11 times. Several felt that they needed to act with courage, especially when going against the flow.

When I feel that I have authority in a matter and where I have influence over others, it is much easier for me to make ethical decisions. However, when I am not in control I find it easier to go with the flow instead of standing up for what I believe in. I need to become braver and learn that I do not necessarily have to hurt anyone by not going along with his or her decisions.

I will endeavour to stand my ground on ethical issues despite that this has a potential to sideline me and hinder my career progression.

Others mentioned being courageous in terms of setting goals and boundaries for themselves.

My quest is to be more courageous in setting goals and boundaries for myself.

Practise reflection, meditation and mindfulness

This guideline was cited 11 times.

I will be mindful of everything happening around me and continue being resolute in my beliefs of right and wrong.

Acting in an ethical way requires more than simply knowing what is right. Knowing what is right but failing to act upon this knowledge still constitutes unethical behaviour. It is important, therefore, that I am honest with myself and that I reflect upon my actions.

Being in the present, and noticing my body sensations, helps me to sense what is right and what is wrong. Usually my body does not lie – I just have to be open to such intuition.

Be open, honest and transparent

The respondents highlighted the importance of being open, honest and transparent as a way to enhance enablers and overcome stumbling blocks within this seed.

In this situation I find [one of] my stumbling blocks is that [I live] in Africa, where bribery is rife, thus leading and encouraging unethical behaviour. I need to speak out and be more transparent with my surroundings and [thereby] allowing me to be true to myself.

Two respondents mentioned the importance of not judging others based on their personal ethical standards.

I must try not to judge others by my everyday ethical standards.

Embrace diversity

Respondents highlighted this guideline nine times. They recognised the fact that different communities have different ethical standards, and that these need to be understood and embraced.

> *I will endeavour to explore more ways of identifying perceptions of ethical standards, and also try to accept the standards that I do not agree with.*
>
> *When I think 'ethics', I need to constantly challenge myself to think outside my own mindset in order that I can accommodate different perspectives and cultures.*

Heighten awareness and exposure

> *Practise constant integrated awareness.*

'Heighten awareness and exposure' was cited nine times. One respondent felt that she needed to increase her awareness of the fact that her decisions have an effect on others.

> *The first important step in ethical decision-making is to recognise that your decision has an effect on others. When making a decision we must ask who will be affected by my actions. If a person does not recognise a moral issue they will not employ moral decision-making schemata and instead make the decision according to other schemata, such as economical rationality. I generally am able to recognise that people will be affected by the decisions I make.*

Others felt that it was important to 'keep up with the times'.

> *Be aware of the influence of the times in which I 'currently' live.*

Other

Respondents offered several other suggestions as to practical actions.

Seven respondents felt it important to accept *accountability* as part of improving their ethics.

> *In my experience one's ethical stance is inextricably linked to authenticity, accountability and being in control. Kerns (2003) claims that ethics can be compromised when one is not taking accountability for their actions or they lack self-control. The capacity to take the ethical path requires a*

commitment to the value of acting with temperance. Through improving my accountability and internal orientation I will ensure that my ethical standpoint will never be questioned.

Six respondents listed as a guideline *'Treat others as you would like to be treated.'*

In order to become more ethical, I need to make a deliberate choice to apply the Golden Rule in my daily life, namely 'Do for others just what you want them to do for you' (Luke 6:31).

Six respondents also felt that they could take an active role in their ethics progression by focusing on *building education and learning into their lives* as much as possible.

I plan to take the 'Before the Whistle Blowers' elective course [as part of my] MBA in order to understand the legislative and corporate governance frameworks [controlling] unethical behaviour. This will give me the skills to proactively influence my company's commitment to ethics, and help me make informed decisions on how to encourage ethical behaviour in the workplace. I can be the agent of change in any company I work for.

I have to be open to diverse ethics and keep myself informed and educated at all times, especially when getting in contact with people from different cultural backgrounds.

Linked to this, two respondents recommended *sharing this knowledge and learning with others.*

My family up-bringing and education to date has made working at this company easy. This is endorsed by Fransworth and Kleiner (2003:130–140) when they stated that 'education serves to reinforce existing values and encourage their application. Early education experiences and family influences are going to have the most crucial impacts on the integrity of future business leaders and their willingness and ability to be value driven'. My personal challenge is to ensure that I pass on to my children the true value of abiding by their ethics.

As a transformational leader I must serve as a role model of ethical behaviour, 'if I achieve that a positive culture will permeate the whole organization' (Odom and Green, 2003).

Focusing specifically on learning about ethics, four respondents had found it helpful to *engage with the philosophical concept of ethics* specifically.

> *I finally discovered that I have to engage in the philosophical concept of ethics to understand it better.*
>
> *In understanding the philosophical concept I believe I will be able to implement it sustainably in my life and day-to-day actions.*
>
> *I believe that it would be more useful to study both the opposing and agreeing value set and, in this way, try to get a better idea of the arguments. It should be easier to construct a stronger argument by analysing both sides. I try to be strongly moral and ethical, but because of my innate curiosity and sceptical bent, I get confused by the blurring lines and grey areas I discover. I've often thought that it would be much easier to live by a simple moral code, such as that which George W. Bush, ex-President of the USA, advocates: a world where everything is black or white, good or evil (his famous 'axis of evil' speech), with or against 'us'. Things are set in stone, there are rules. But rules that are unquestioned are equal to dogma, something I just cannot agree to. I need to question, to search, to wonder – and when I find, I must remember the poet Kahlil Gibran's words, 'say not, "I have found the truth", but rather, "I have found a truth"'.*

Six respondents mentioned that it was important to *never compromise.*

> *Svensson and Wood (2003) contend that the activity of examining one's moral standards or the moral standards of a society, and asking how these standards apply to our lives and whether these standards are reasonable or unreasonable. I believe I still have a long way to go when it comes to ethics especially in view of the alignment and political pressures at work, I will endeavour to stand my ground on ethical issues despite that this has a potential to sideline me and hinder my career progression.*
>
> *I will never indulge in any activity that could dent my dignity.*
>
> *Listen to my gut feeling. If it does not feel right it probably is not. No compromises.*

Four respondents advised others to choose to operate in *environments which support ethical behaviour.*

> *Another useful tool that, in the future, would empower me to continue practising these values is finding a work environment that allows and supports ethical behaviour.*

Learning from your mistakes was a guideline listed three times and, connected with this, two respondents felt it important to improve their *self-esteem*: *'In case I fall down, I must learn to stand up, lift my head up and walk tall, never looking back.'*

Other guidelines that were mentioned included the importance defining a sense of purpose, decreasing self-preoccupation, and practising forgiveness. One respondent recommended the Buddhist philosophy of 'First, do no harm', and another commended a maxim of 'continuous improvement, not destination perfection'.

Conclusion

Locus of control is defined as a personality construct reflecting a belief or perception about who controls a person's behaviour and life events (Connolly, 1980). It was the generalised belief of the majority of our research repondents that behavioural outcomes are under one's personal control (internal locus), rather than being dependent on outside forces, luck, or powerful others (external locus) (Rotter, 1966). Power does not rest solely on belief about locus of control, but action emanating from such belief is often required. Our research highlighted the fact that such action was often inward-focused, that is, drawing strength from one's upbringing, one's defining moments, one's spirituality, one's conscience; exercising self-control, using honesty, courage, and integrity; standing up for one's beliefs and using mentors to lean on (enabling individuals) to encourage the upholding of codes of conduct. Our respondents emphasised the fact that such action often counted as some of their most difficult life experiences which, when reflected upon and learnt from, became the crucibles that forged their characters, developed their internal powers, and gave them a sense of freedom to handle difficult circumstances in the future, and to inspire others to do so as well (enabling environments).

However, individual behaviour, we found, is bound by contextual constraints. Therefore, ethics is essentially a methodological attempt to make sense of our individual and social moral experience, such that rules for governing (constraining) human conduct, rules identifying the societal values worth pursuing (constraint), and the character traits deserving development (constraint) are highlighted and made to be the norm. Bandura (1986) identified self-efficacy as, perhaps, the single most important factor in promoting changes in behaviour. Despite literature suggesting that individuals can rise above their circumstances through their own independent will, fear is a very dominant stumbling block with respect to ethics. And individuals who challenge the status quo or the order of things, or seek to shift ethical constraints, may suffer personally. Indeed, our research respondents identified, in the main, organisations and society as the key stumbling blocks. These were the stumbling blocks which the respondents most often had to tolerate to be able to meet their financial commitments, often at the expense of fulfilment, self-worth, authenticity and ethical living.

Note

Acknowledgment, with thanks: this chapter is an edited version of our original paper in *Journal of Public Affairs*, 2010, and is published by permission of John Wiley & Sons Ltd (Ethics and leadership: Enablers and stumbling blocks; by K. April, K. Peters, K. Locke and C. Mlambo, *Journal of Public Affairs*, 10(3), Copyright © 2010, John Wiley & Sons Ltd).

Bibliography

Alzola, M., 'On the existence of character traits and the plausibility of Aristotelian virtue ethics', Proceedings of the 14th International Symposium on Ethics, Business and Society, IESE Business School, Barcelona, Spain, 18–19 May 2006.

Annas, J., 'Virtue Ethics and Social Psychology', *A Priori*, 2 (2003) 20–34.

April, K., Macdonald, R., and Vriesendorp, S., *Rethinking Leadership* (Kenwyn: University of Cape Town Press, 2000).

April, K. and Wilson, A., 'In Search of Ethics', *Journal for Convergence*, 8(1) (2007) 16–18.

Arjoon, S., 'Reconciling Situational Social Psychology with Virtue Ethics', *International Journal of Management Reviews*, 10(3) (2008) 221–243.

Aristotle, *Nicomachean Ethics*, trans. D.P. Chase (London: J.M. Dent and Sons, 1911).

Asch, S., 'Effects of group pressures upon the modification and distortion of judgment' in Guetzkow, H. (ed.), *Groups, Leadership, and Men* (Pittsburgh: Carnegie Press, 1951).

Badaracco, J.L., *Questions of Character: Illuminating the Heart of Leadership through Literature* (Boston: Harvard Business School Press, 2006).

Bandura, A., *Social Foundations of Thought and Action: A Social Cognitive Theory* (Upper Saddle River, NJ: Prentice Hall, 1986).

Connolly, S.G., 'Changing Expectancies: a Counselling Model based on Locus of Control', *The Personnel and Guidance Journal*, 59(3) (1980) 176–180.

Covey, S.R., *The 8th Habit: From Effectiveness to Greatness* (London: Simon and Schuster, 2004).

Covey, S.R. and Merrill, A.R., *First Things First: To Live, To Love, To Learn, To Leave a Legacy* (London: Simon and Schuster, 1994).

Darley, J. and Baston, D., 'From Jerusalem to Jerico: a Study of Situational and Disposition Variables in Helping Behaviour', *Journal of Personality and Social Psychology*, 27 (1973) 100–108.

Doris, J., 'Persons, Situations and Virtue Ethics', *Nous*, 32 (1998) 504–530.

Doris, J., *Lack of Character: Personality and Moral Behaviour* (Cambridge and New York: Cambridge University Press, 2002).

Fransworth, R. and Kleiner, B., 'Trends in Ethics Education at U.S. Colleges and Universities', *Management Research News*, 26(2/3/4) (2003) 130–140.

Gandossy, R. and Sonnenfeld, J., 'I See Nothing, I Hear Nothing: Culture, Corruption and Apathy', *International Journal of Disclosure and Governance*, 2(3) (2005) 228–243.

Gibran, K., *The Prophet* (Harmondsworth: Penguin Books, 2003).

Harman, G., 'Moral Philosophy Meets Social Psychology: Virtue Ethics and the Fundamental Attribution Error', *Proceedings of the Aristotelian Society*, 99 (1999) 315–331.

Harman, G., 'The Nonexistence of Character Traits', *Proceedings of the Aristotelian Society*, 100 (2002) 223–226.

Harman, G., 'No Character or Personality', *Business Ethics Quarterly*, 13(1) (2003) 87–94.

Hartshorne, H. and May, M., *Studies in the Nature of Character Volume 1: Studies in Deceit* (New York: MacMillan, 1928).

Holian, R., 'Management Decision-making, Ethical Issues and Emotional Intelligence', *Management Decision*, 44(8) (2006) 1134.

Isen, A. and Levin, P., 'Effect of Feeling Good in Helping: Cookies and Kindness', *Journal of Personality and Social Psychology*, 21 (1972) 384–388.

Kerns, C.D., 'Creating and Sustaining an Ethical Workplace Culture' (2003) http://gbr.pepperdine.edu/033/ethics.html (accessed 15 April 2010).

King, G.R., 'Back to Accountability', *Management Decision*, 29(8) (1991) 1–6.

Lantos, J.D., 'The Inclusion Benefit in Clinical Trials', *Journal of Paediatrics*, 134(2) (1999) 130–131.

Latane, B. and Darley, J., 'Bystander Interventions in Emergencies: Diffusion of Responsibility', *Journal of Personality and Social Psychology*, 8 (1968) 377–383.

Latane, B. and Darley, J., *The Unresponsive Bystander: Why Doesn't He Help?* (New York: Appleton and Century Crofts, 1970).

Latane, B. and Rodin, J., 'A Lady in Distress: Inhibiting Effects of Friends and Strangers or Bystander Intervention', *Journal of Experimental Psychology*, 5 (1969) 189–202.

Lewis, C.S., *Mere Christianity* (London: Harper Collins, 1952).

Mahoney, J., 'Cultivating Moral Courage in Business', *A European Review*, 7(4) (1998) 187–188.

Milgram, S., *Obedience to Authority: An Experimental View* (New York: Harper and Row, 1974).

Odom, L. and Green, M.T., 'Law and the Ethics of Transformational Leadership', *Leadership and Organisation Development Journal*, 24(2) (2003) 62–69.

Reilly, B.J., and Myroslaw, J.K., 'Ethical Business and the Ethical Person', *Business Horizons*, 33(6) (1990) 23–28.

Rotter, J., 'Generalized Expectancies for Internal versus External Control of Reinforcement', *Psychological Monograph*, 80 (1966) 609.

Scarnati, J.T., 'Beyond Technical Competencies: Honesty and Integrity', *Career Development International*, 2(1) (1997) 22.

Shipka, B., *Leadership in a Challenging World: A Sacred Journey* (Boston: Butterworth-Heinemann, 1997).

Srnka, K.J. and Koeszegi, S.T., 'From Words to Numbers: How to Transform Qualitative Data into Meaningful Quantitative Results', *Schmalenbach's Business Review*, 59 (2007) 29–57.

Svensson, G. and Wood, G., 'The Dynamics of Business Ethics: a Function of Time and Culture – Cases and Models', *Management Decision*, 41(4) (2003) 350–361.

Webber, J., 'Virtue character and situation', *Journal of Moral Philosophy*, 3 (2006) 192–213.

Zimbardo, P., 'The Power and Pathology of Imprisonment', *Congressional Record*, 15 (1971) 10–25.

Zimbardo, P., 'A Situationist Perspective on the Psychology of Evil: Understanding How Good People are Turned into Perpretators', in Miller, A. (ed.), *The Social Psychology of Good and Evil: Understanding our Capacity for Kindness and Cruelty* (New York: Guildford, 2004).

Zimbardo, P., *The Lucifer Effect: Understanding How Good People Turn Evil* (New York: Random House, 2007).

Part III
Perspectives for the Future

11
Beyond Compliance
James M. Lager

What's past is prologue

Once again, governments worldwide are seeking to impose new rules and restrictions on financial institutions and their leaders. It's an age-old and predictable pattern – a scandal leads to cries of outrage, followed by legislation, regulation, and increased enforcement. It's also a Newtonian approach to human behaviour, the belief that for every action there is or should be a reaction, and that an effective way to curb the normally encouraged drive to acquire is to make certain methods of acquisition unlawful. The problem is that human behaviour is much harder to describe and to predict than the effect of a force on a body in motion, so the blunt instrument of law and enforcement frequently strikes the wrong target, leading to unexpected consequences.

Inapt governmental response

Of course, government officials are compelled to respond to public outcry, and despite the maxim that ethics cannot be legislated, it remains relatively expedient and politically attractive to respond to business scandal by increasing the sanctions for abusive or deceptive business conduct. Unfortunately, the evidence that the threat of incarceration at any level deters white-collar crime is at best equivocal (Gustafson, 2007; Simpson, 2002; Weisburd et al., 1995). Indeed, for deterrence to be effective, an individual must know the legal rule, be willing and able to apply that knowledge to a decision, and to be able to determine that the threat of punishment exceeds the benefit of the offending conduct. Since these three prerequisites for effective deterrence rarely exist, reliance on deterrence to change behaviour, in the words of one critic, appears 'wildly misguided' (Robinson and Darley, 2004). Even when the three prerequisites are present, deterrence will be ineffective in those cultures where an individual might be 'caught up in...social pressures of the group' (Robinson and Darley, 2004:205), which is likely to occur frequently in organisations since group-based loyalty can supersede loyalty to society (Anand et al., 2005:13).

Though incarcerating an individual will incapacitate them for a while and *may* occasionally deter others, the threat of punishment, no matter how severe, has been an ineffective method for *promoting* ethical behaviour (Moohr, 2007). Most criminologists have concluded, instead, that an individual's perception of the probability of getting caught is a greater deterrent than the severity of the sanction (Buell, 2008). Accordingly, vigorous monitoring and internal controls that dramatically increase the perception by potential offenders that they will be caught are more likely to reduce ethical misconduct than are draconian penalties. But if constant monitoring is effective in deterring specific conduct, there are huge costs for the increased internal controls and surveillance, ultimately paid either by consumers in higher prices for goods and services, or by taxpayers for government surveillance. Further, excessive monitoring of employees can also reduce trust, and displace intrinsic with extrinsic motivation (Hess, 2007).

The incentive to declare success remains

Of course, regardless of any mandated internal controls or other mechanisms imposed, business leaders continue to strive to meet or exceed performance expectations, and to deliver benefits to stakeholders – the more the better. This obvious incentive to show positive business performance increases the likelihood that 'misleading disclosures' will be made to the investing public, which increases in line with the extent to which an executive's compensation and marketability is tied to performance (Donoher and Reed, 2007). Because legal regulation will not sate investor appetite for profits nor remove the profit incentive, the regulation of business behaviour may have the potential to change organisations' methods of production or acquisition, but is unlikely to have an impact on business or leader ethics. Moreover, new proscriptive laws and regulations can frequently fail even in preventing the specific harm intended. For example, despite the US enactment of the Foreign Corrupt Practices Act, US companies continue to pay bribes at about the same rate as companies from other developed countries (Hess and Ford, 2008:313). Furthermore, even new laws and regulations that appear to be effective can actually cause more unethical conduct, as the new rules generate new evasions and drive offenders underground (Vaughan, 1983). Perhaps most seriously, by converting ethical problems into legal ones, compliance has ascended as the principal measure of propriety, with sometimes alarming results (Vaughn, 1990:432). Indeed, though perhaps justifiable from a utilitarian perspective, the elevation of law above ethics goes some way towards explaining the appalling treatment of prisoners by US forces at Abu Ghraib and elsewhere, enabling many US military and political leaders to argue that waterboarding a detainee 119 times was lawful and compliant, without regard to higher standards of compassion and human decency.

The nostrums of codes of conduct and related training

Many organisations use a similar, quasi-legislative approach to ethics, by establishing codes of conduct that specify the behaviours expected and prohibited, usually coupled with a threat of discipline for the non-compliant. Such codes are often required by government (for example, see Federal Acquisition Regulation § 52.203–13(c)(1), 2008). Knowing what is required, however, does not always translate into doing what is required (Michaelson, 2006:245), and there is little empirical evidence that employee codes affect employee behaviour (Krawiec, 2003; Newberg, 2005; Pelletier and Bligh, 2006; Weaver, 1995). Anecdotally, Enron's 65-page Code of Conduct of Business Affairs – which all employees were required to read and sign for – was waived by Enron's Board at least three times (Jennings, 2003), and is now legendary for its failure to prevent unethical conduct. Section 406(b) of the Sarbanes-Oxley Act was enacted in response to Enron's waivers, and now requires US publicly traded companies to disclose whether they have waived their Ethics Code (Title 15, United States Code, section 7264). Similar notorious examples of a corporate code's failure to govern corporate behaviour can be found worldwide (Webley and Werner, 2008), which, at a minimum, should belie the notion that leaders can assure good organisational ethics by adopting a code.

Whether encouraged or required by law, or because it is now so common it is considered best practice, organisations typically require their employees to attend training about codes of conduct and governing ethics laws and rules. Indeed, US Sentencing Guidelines suggest that organisations with formal compliance training will receive favourable treatment in criminal sentencing (US Sentencing Guidelines Manual, § 8B2.1(b)(4)(A), 2008). Unfortunately, ethics training 'is often focused exclusively on conformity to Sarbanes-Oxley and other regulatory and rules-based legislation – and not on clarifying values and fostering integrity to those values and to enduring principles' (Covey, 2006:61). Further, the more legalistic the training, the more likely it will draw the participants' attention to some small factual variation that would convert the conduct from illegal to lawful. This will often inadvertently teach employees how to skirt the intention of the rule yet remain compliant. Unethical but compliant leaders can behave similarly. Instead of attending training, they engage attorneys, accountants, and other experts to find ways around troublesome ethics, tax, and other inconvenient laws.

Neither does a lack of training or not knowing the rules do much to explain ethical failure. According to a 2005 ethics survey, improper training or ignorance that a particular action was unethical is only the fifth most likely cause of ethical lapse, behind pressure to meet unrealistic goals, the desire for career enhancement, the need to assure continued employment, and working in an environment with poor morale (American Management Association, 2006:59), all factors beyond the reach of legislation. Even if poor training were a significant factor in ethical failure, requiring employees to attend training does nothing to ensure that content is learned or that attitudes are changed. Training is also very expensive, not just to pay for the trainers, facilitators, and materials, but for the opportunity cost to leaders and others attending. These costs, of course, are also ultimately passed on to consumers or taxpayers.

The ethical failure of compliance leadership

Leaders are nevertheless required to assure that their organisation complies with governing laws and regulations, if only to protect themselves and their organisations from economic sanction. But a leader who strives for compliance is unlikely to lead an ethical organisation (Lager, 2009), and may miss key opportunities to increase workplace efficiency. For example, compliance with the equal employment laws may vitiate legal liability for discrimination, but will hardly assure that the workplace provides an equal opportunity for all, or that the unique talents of employees, partners, and other stakeholders are well applied. Mere compliance with wage and hour laws will do little to attract and retain employees, and compliance with occupational safety rules will not guarantee a safe workplace, or reduce insurance costs, or prevent legal actions from injured employees. And though Sarbanes-Oxley may produce a compliance-friendly audit trail and impose penalties for violating governance standards, it can guarantee neither good governance nor the creation of an ethical culture that fosters responsible behaviour (Mintz, 2005:595).

Culturally attuned ethical leadership

In contrast with the compliance leadership contemplated by legislation and many corporate codes, ethical leadership can have several positive organisational effects. Employees in organisations with strong ethical leadership are more committed to their organisations, more ethically aware, and more willing to report problems (Treviño et al., 2003). Research shows that less unethical behaviour is observed in organisations that support ethical conduct through cultural systems that emphasise employee and public welfare (Treviño and Weaver, 2003:263). And the promotion of a moral organisation by senior managers, supported by an adherence to ethical standards, leads not only to reduced misconduct, but to higher job satisfaction (Heminway, 2008; Andreoli and Lefkowitz, 2009).

Acknowledging that law and regulation provides an inferior gauge for assessing ethics is a key first step for an ethical leader. Instead of being satisfied with measuring compliance against legal requirements, ethical leaders should establish a baseline for some of the indicia of an ethical culture in their organisation, such as how much misconduct is observed, whether employees feel comfortable reporting misconduct, whether employees believe they are being treated fairly, or whether employees are pressured to overlook certain matters (Kaptein and Avelino, 2005). Occupational frauds are much more likely to be discovered by tips than by external audits or internal controls (Association of Certified Fraud Examiners, 2008). From the results of an ethics audit of this kind, it may be possible to identify the actions or systems that would best correlate with positive ethics-related outcomes, unique to each organisation's mission and environment (Kaptein (A), 2009).

Regardless of the results of an ethics audit or assessment, the literature is replete with studies showing that leadership is crucial to assuring ethical organisational behaviour (Carlson and Perrewe, 1995:831 and 836). Leaders who integrate and measure ethics in their organisations' operations, and who are mindful of the messages they send, can have a great impact on organisational culture, which in turn has the greatest influence in determining ethical outcomes (Treviño and Weaver, 2003:235). Leaders are perhaps best positioned to influence an organisation's culture, and to act as role models for subordinates about appropriate organisational behaviours (Grojean et al., 2004; Dickson et al., 2001), which in turn impacts on other corporate agents (Schwartz et al., 2005). To set a good example, leaders must be ethical role models who make visible the ethical challenges they face and the standards they apply to their resolution. Having top managers set a good example and keep promises has a statistically significant impact on several ethics-related outcomes (Ethics Resource Center, 2006). Leader modelling of 'doing the right thing', the celebration of employees who have made hard ethical decisions, and the rewarding of ethical action by recognition and financial awards (Treviño and Weaver, 2003:261), are all ways to demonstrate that ethics is an organisational way of life, not just a method to mollify oversight authorities (Heminway, 2008).

To flourish, an organisation's commitment to ethics must extend beyond the top leader to other executives and supervisors. A lack of alignment among top management can result in mixed signals and ambiguous messages to employees, negatively affecting climate and employee trust (Lankau et al., 2007). Naturally, ethical action must accompany the rhetoric, and unethical activity must not be justified as necessary or 'acceptable', as is so often the case (Ivancevich et al., 2008). Lofty statements proclaiming an organisation's high ethical standards will only engender cynicism if the values they espouse are inconsistent with the values in action (Schein, 2004:29f.). Those leaders who permit unethical conduct to recur – whether because of inattention, conflict avoidance, or through rationalised compromise – cannot reasonably expect ethical conduct from their employees (Gebler, 2006; Vance and Trani, 2008).

Though there is at least one study finding that a positive ethical climate can be obtained without the usual elements of a formal compliance programme (Andreoli and Lefkowitz, 2009:326), many commentators have stressed that most successful value-based systems will have some elements of a compliance programme (Hess, 2007; Treviño and Weaver, 2003). Regardless of whether cost-effective or efficacious, typical ethics structures such as codes of conduct, employee hotlines, and training will need to be present if they are required by legislation or other external pressures. But formal ethics systems will have little influence on behaviour unless they are supported by cultural systems (Treviño and Brown, 2004). Indeed, it is the general lack of supportive cultural systems in organisations that may explain the results of a longitudinal study showing that, despite the general increase in the scope of ethics programmes in the United States between 2004 and 2008, no significant change in the seven dimensions of ethical culture examined could be found (Kaptein (B), 2009).

More effective than the usual compliance-based ethical system are values-oriented or integrity-based programmes. These focus not on compliance, but on maintaining a culture where ethical issues can be discussed, where ethical behaviour is rewarded, and where the organisation's values are incorporated by its leaders into strategic decisions (Hess, 2007; Weaver and Treviño, 1999). Less unethical behaviour is observed in organisations that support ethical conduct by cultural systems emphasising employee and public welfare (Treviño and Weaver, 2003), and a values orientation is 10 times more effective in obtaining ethics-related outcomes than the most effective training technique (Ethics Resource Center, 2008: Table 2). Other research has found that a values orientation is a more important influence than a compliance-based effort on several indicia of a good ethical climate, including better ethical awareness, employee commitment and integrity, readiness to disclose 'bad news' to superiors, and the belief that organisational decisions are better because of the ethics programme (Treviño and Weaver, 2003). A values-oriented approach also contributes to increased organisational commitment by employees (Regan, 2007), which has a salutary effect on morale, motivation, and performance.

Where typical compliance structures are already present, ethical leaders should modify them so they support an ethical, not just a compliant, culture. For example, instead of an organisational code of conduct that just restates legal requirements and makes lofty statements; a leader could engage staff in identifying the core values that drive organisational behaviour. Once identified, these core values, such as integrity, fairness, and care for others, should be integrated into the code of conduct to provide a compass for employees at every level to consider when making important decisions. Shared involvement in identifying what is important not only creates norms and shared expectations, but also sends an important signal that ethics and those making ethical decisions will be supported (Treviño, 2005).

Training too can have an important role if, instead of achieving begrudging attendance, it accomplishes thoughtful consideration of available choices and helps employees to make good, not just compliant, decisions. The most effective ethics training is interactive, and includes case analysis and a consideration of ethical dilemmas (Ethics Resource Center, 2008:n3). And though seemingly self-evident, studies show that employees are more likely to make an ethical choice in situations when they can identify which of the available choices are ethically sound

(Coughlan and Connolly, 2008). This is harder than it might appear, particularly when employees are asked to consider competing values, instead of simply applying a specific rule to a situation regardless of the ethical nature of the outcome.

Individuals in organisations tend to seek out the information and contacts they need for their work, and typically ignore information perceived as extraneous. Insulated by this relative lack of external information, daily work behaviour is typified by compliance with organisational routines that pose no ethical issues. In this environment, an employee's decision to acknowledge the presence of an ethical issue can be uncomfortable, particularly when they are asked to choose among competing options, to question others with whom they may have important relationships, or even to defend their own conduct (Reagan, 2007:948f.). Choosing to acknowledge and act on ethical issues thus requires self-awareness and the courage to overcome conflict aversion or other intrapersonal tendencies, and is often reflexively avoided. But the presence of this discomfort can in itself trigger the realisation that there is an ethical dilemma to be resolved (Gaudine and Thorne, 2001). Training that helps overcome this tendency to ignore ethical issues – or hide from them by donning rule-based blinders – can be essential to promote their recognition and resolution.

Conclusion

Efforts to criminalise and regulate the conduct of business leaders have never proved successful in creating ethical conduct. Instead, these efforts result in organisational cultures where compliant behaviour is often mistaken for ethical behaviour, and paradoxically can actually guide criminals and those willing to disregard ethical considerations to shield their activity with apparent or actual compliance. It is not surprising, therefore, that legally mandated corporate ethics programmes, largely focused as they are on compliance with myriad applicable restrictions, would have little success in promoting ethical behaviour.

To be an ethical leader, leaders must do more than engage compliance professionals and ensure robust compliance. Ethical leadership requires recognition that the legal standards for compliance are merely that: standards, not goals for, or measures of, ethical conduct. Leaders who properly relegate compliance to a subordinate role are better able to integrate ethical values into the fabric of their organisation through responsible ethical leadership. Assuming that the leaders are by and large virtuous, the resulting genuine concern for employees and other stakeholders will naturally encourage behaviour that comports with most legislative and regulatory commands, reducing legal exposure and costs for insurance and compliance, while simultaneously enhancing productivity and organisational brand. Therefore, while governments may require facial compliance, authentic ethical leaders will require more.

Note

The opinions and views expressed in this chapter are the author's alone and are not intended to reflect the US Government Accountability Office's institutional views. Acknowledgment, with thanks: this chapter is an edited version of my original paper in *Journal of Public Affairs*, 2010, and is published by permission of John Wiley & Sons Ltd (Governments demand compliance, ethics demands leadership; by J. M. Lager, *Journal of Public Affairs*, 10(3), Copyright © 2010, John Wiley & Sons Ltd).

Bibliography

American Management Association, *The Ethical Enterprise: Doing the Right Things in the Right Ways, Today and Tomorrow: A Global Study of Business Ethics 2005–2015* (2006).

Anand, V., Ashforth, B.E., and Joshi, M., 'Business as Usual: the Acceptance and Perpetuation of Corruption in Organizations', *Academy of Management Executive*, 19(4) (2005) 9–23.

Andreoli, N. and Lefkowitz, J., 'Individual and Organizational Antecedents of Misconduct in Organizations', *Journal of Business Ethics*, 85(3) (2009) 309–332.

Association of Certified Fraud Examiners, 'Report to the Nation on Occupational Fraud and Abuse' (2008). Retrieved from the ACFE Web page on 16 April 2010 from www.acfe.com/documents/2008-rttn.pdf.

Buell, S.W., 'The Upside of Overbreadth', *New York University Law Review*, 83 (2008) 1491–1564.

Carlson, D.S. and Perrewe, P.L., 'Institutionalization of Organizational Ethics through Transformational Leadership', *Journal of Business Ethics*, 14(10) (1995) 829–838.

Coughlan, R. and Connolly,T., 'Investigating Unethical Decisions at Work: Justification and Emotion in Dilemma Resolution', *Journal of Managerial Issues*, 20(3) (2008) 348–365.

Covey, S., *The Speed of Trust: The One Thing That Changes Everything* (New York: Free Press, 2006).

Dickson, M.W., Smith, D.B., Grojean, M.W. and Ehrhart, M., 'An Organizational Climate Regarding Ethics: the Outcome of Leader Values and the Practices that Reflect Them', *Leadership Quarterly*, 12(2) (2001) 197–217.

Donoher, W.J. and Reed, R., 'Employment Capital, Board Control, and the Problem of Misleading Disclosures', *Journal of Managerial Issues*, 19(3) (2007) 362–378.

Ethics Resource Center, 'Critical Elements of an Organizational Ethical Culture' (2006). Retrieved from the ERC's Web page on 16 April 2010 from www.ethics.org/resource/critical-elements-organizational-ethical-culture.

Ethics Resource Center, 'Improving ethical outcomes: the role of ethics training' (2008). Retrieved from the ERC's Web page on 14 March 2010 from www.ethics.org/fellows/fellow-publications.asp.

Fiske, S.T., Harris, L.T., and Cuddy, A.J.C., 'Why Ordinary People Torture Enemy Prisoners', *Science*, 306(5701) (2004) 1482–1483.

Gaudine, A. and Thorne, L., 'Emotion and Ethical Decision-making in Organizations', *Journal of Business Ethics*, 31(2) (2001) 175–187.

Gebler, D., 'Creating an Ethical Culture: Values-based Ethics Programs Can Help Employees Judge Right from Wrong', *Strategic Finance*, 87(11) (2006) 28–34.

Grojean, M., Resick, C., Dickson, M., and Smith, D., 'Leaders, Values, and Organizational Climate: Examining Leadership Strategies for Establishing an Organizational Climate regarding Ethics', *Journal of Business Ethics*, 55(3) (2004) 223–241.

Gustafson, J., 'Cracking down on White-collar Crime: an Analysis of the Recent Trend of Severe Sentences for Corporate Officers', *Suffolk University Law Review*, 40 (2007) 685–701.

Heminway, J.M., 'Does *Sarbanes-Oxley* Foster the Existence of Ethical Executive Role Models in the Corporation?', *Journal of Business and Technology Law*, 3 (2008) 221–242.

Hess, D. and Ford, C.L., 'Corporate Corruption and Reform Undertakings: a New Approach to an Old Problem', *Cornell International Law Journal*, 41(2) (2008) 307–346.

Hess, D., 'A Business Ethics Perspective on Sarbanes-Oxley and the Organizational Sentencing Guidelines', *Michigan Law Review*, 105 (2007) 1781–1816.

Ivancevich, J.M., Konopaske, R., and Gilbert, J.A., 'Formally Shaming White-collar Criminals', *Business Horizons*, 51(5) (2008) 401–410.

Jennings, M.M., 'A Primer on Enron: Lessons from a Perfect Storm of Financial Reporting, Corporate Governance, and Ethical Culture Failures', *California Western Law Review*, 39 (2003) 163–262.

Johnson, C.E., *Ethics in the Workplace: Tools and Tactics for Organizational Transformation* (Thousand Oaks, CA: Sage Publications, 2007).

Kaptein M. and Avelino, S., 'Measuring Corporate Integrity: a Survey-based Approach', *Corporate Governance*, 5(1) (2005) 45–54.

Kaptein, M., 'Ethics Programmes and Ethical Culture: a Next Step in Unraveling Their Multi-faceted Relationship', *Journal of Business Ethics*, 89(2) (2009A) 261–81.

Kaptein, M., 'The Ethics of Organizations: a Longitudinal Study of the U.S. Working Population', *Journal of Business Ethics*, 92(4) (2009B) 601–618.

Krawiec, K., 'Cosmetic Compliance and the Failure of Negotiated Governance', *Washington University Law Quarterly*, 81 (2003) 487–544.

Lager, J.M., 'Overcoming Cultures of Compliance to Reduce Corruption and Achieve Ethics in Government', *McGeorge Law Review*, 41(1) (2009) 63–83.

Lankau, M.J., Ward, A., Amason, A., Ng, T., Sonnenfeld, J.A. and Agle, B.A., 'Examining the Impact of Organizational Value Dissimilarity in Top Management Teams', *Journal of Managerial Issues*, 19(1) (2007) 11–34.

Michaelson, C., 'Compliance and the Illusion of Ethical Progress', *Journal of Business Ethics*, 66 (2006) 241–251.

Mintz, S.M. 'Corporate Governance in an International Context: Legal Systems, Financing Patterns and Cultural Variables', *Corporate Governance*, 15(5) (2005) 582–597.

Moohr, G.S., 'On the Prospects of Deterring Corporate Crime', *Journal of Business and Technology Law*, 2 (2007) 25–41.

Newberg, J.A., 'Corporate Codes of Ethics, Mandatory Disclosure, and the Market for Ethical Conduct', *Vermont Law Review*, 29 (2005) 253–295.

Pelletier, K.L. and Bligh, M.C., 'Rebounding from Corruption: Perceptions of Ethics Programme Effectiveness in a Public Sector Organization', *Journal of Business Ethics*, 67(4) (2006) 359–374.

Regan, Jr, M.C., 'Moral Intuitions and Organizational Culture', *Saint Louis University Law Journal*, 51 (2007) 941–986.

Robinson, P.H. and Darley, J.M., 'Does Criminal Law Deter? A Behavioural Science Investigation', *Oxford Journal of Legal Studies*, 24 (2004) 173–204.

Schein, E.H., *Organizational Culture and Leadership* (San Francisco: Jossey-Bass, 2004).

Schwartz, M.S., Dunfee, T.W. and Kline, M.J., 'Tone at the Top: an Ethics Code for Directors', *Journal of Business Ethics*, 58(1) (2005) 79–100.

Simpson, S., *Corporate Crime, Law, and Social Control* (Cambridge: Cambridge University Press, 2002).

Treviño, L.K. and Brown, M.E., 'Managing to be Ethical: Debunking Five Business Ethics Myths', *Academy of Management Executive*, 18(2) (2004) 69–81.

Treviño, L.K. and Weaver, G.R., *Managing Ethics in Business Organizations: Social Scientific Perspectives* (Stanford: Stanford University Press, 2003).

Treviño, L.K., 'Out of Touch: The CEO's Role in Corporate Misbehavior', *Brookyn Law Review* , 70 (2005) 1195–1211.

Treviño, L.K., Brown, M.and Pincus, L.H., 'A Qualitative Investigation of Perceived Executive Ethical Leadership: Perceptions from Inside and Outside the Executive Suite', *Human Relations*, 56(1) (2003) 5–37.

Vance N. and Trani, B., 'Situational Prevention and the Reduction of White Collar Crime', *Journal of Leadership, Accountability and Ethics*, 6(4) (2008) 9–18.

Vaughan, D., *Controlling Unlawful Organizational Behaviour: Social Structure and Corporate Misconduct* (Chicago: The University of Chicago Press, 1983).

Vaughn, R.G., 'Ethics in Government and the Vision of Public Service', *George Washington Law Review*, 58 (1990) 417–450.

Weaver G.R. and Treviño, L.K., 'Compliance and Values Oriented Ethics Programs: Influences on Employees' Attitudes and Behaviour', *Business Ethics Quarterly*, 9(2) (1999) 315–335.

Weaver, G.R., 'Does ethics code design matter? Effects of ethics code rationales and sanctions on recipient's justice perceptions and content recall', *Journal of Business Ethics*, 14(5) (1995): 367–385.

Webley S. and Werner, A., 'Corporate Codes of Ethics: Necessary but not Sufficient', *Business Ethics: A European Review*, 17(4) (2008) 405–415.

Weisburd, D., Waring, E., and Chayet, E., 'Specific Deterrence in a Sample of Offenders Convicted of White-collar Crimes', *Criminology*, 33(4) (1995) 587–607.

12
A Moral Compass for the Global Leadership Labyrinth

Lindsay J. Thompson

Introduction

Globalisation, with its undisputed opportunities and benefits, constitutes a moral challenge (Bok, 2002; Combs, 2002; Singer, 2004; Starke-Meyerring, 2005). Postmodern worldviews now contest the dominance of secular, enlightenment values as the foundation of moral decision-making. They also challenge the elegant secular theories of human behaviour – rational choice, neoclassical economics, and humanist philosophy – that emerged in the modern era as a dominant discursive framework for understanding, negotiating, and explaining human values.[1] Although the modern embrace of reasoned secularism may have emerged as a pragmatically peaceful path to circumvent the perils of religious and tribal warfare in negotiating value conflicts, it requires a suspension of spiritual identity that is deeply offensive to some and outright unacceptable to other participants in an expanded world stage. The 2008 global economic meltdown lends credence to warnings from proponents of traditional morality about the corrosive effects of competitive free market capitalism as a rational foundation for world order (Ellul, 1984). Initiatives such as the Global Compact exemplify a growing insistence that human values should anchor wealth creation. Diverse stakeholders from nations, multinational corporations, and small businesses expect leaders to incorporate rather than exclude claims of religion, culture, and ethnic values, in response to their environment. This environment contains both macro threats, like climate change, resource shortages, pandemic pathogens, financial volatility, economic insecurity, and political instability, and micro threats, like competition, new product roll-out, job relocation, restructuring, and the elimination of product lines or business units. To be effective, leaders need tools for engaging and managing the affective, visceral dimensions of human values, and the moral will to move forward to accomplish goals. Those accustomed to rational argument, bolstered by quantitative analysis and the moral anchor of their personal values, can find themselves woefully ill-equipped for the challenges of leadership in a global arena of competing and conflicting value claims.

Drawing on premises derived from the natural and social sciences, this chapter develops the moral compass as a constructive model of discernment, dialogue, consensus-building, and decision-making. It is designed to create common moral ground across social boundaries and values, and across the competing claims of religion, ethnicity, and culture.[2] The moral compass model maps an alternative to agenda-driven culture wars and superficial conformity, welcoming the majority of people in the world who cannot – or will not – imagine morality without religion, while honouring the integrity of secularists, atheists, and agnostics who reject with equal vehemence the constraints of religion. The moral compass blends moral theory with emerging research theories in neuroscience, anthropology, cultural studies, and leadership, to conceptualise the tensions of moral contradiction as the dimensions of a complex but coherent framework of human morality. This enhanced understanding of human moral complexity provides the conceptual tools for framing and integrating moral experience in a way that opens the possibility of building moral solidarity with others across the room or across the world.

The leadership labyrinth

Personal morality operates within the wisdom tradition of a particular culture. The 'labyrinth' of leadership is the location of leaders within the web of their own cultural experience yet, in a multicultural, pluralist world, charged with responsibilities and duties that involve a relational web of diverse individuals located within their own cultural experiences. A leader cannot – and usually should not be expected to – reject or deny their cultural roots. As Clifford Geertz has observed, human beings are 'incomplete or unfinished animals who complete or finish ourselves through culture – and not through culture in general but through highly particular forms of it. We are extremely dependent on a certain sort of learning: the attainment of concepts and application of specific systems of symbolic meaning' (Geertz, 1973). Yet leaders in the era of globalisation must be able to expand their moral horizons well beyond their own limited experience and the wisdom of their own cultures.

Theseus, the Ancient Greek hero of the Labyrinth, represents timeless leadership qualities of character, intelligence, courage, and imagination, as a hero who ventures into an alien realm to rescue a group of his own people taken as hostages. The image of the Labyrinth, an ancient symbol of complexity and choice, is an intricate pattern of winding, interconnected and dead-end paths found all over the world in public squares and gardens, and in sacred spaces such as the cathedral at Chartres, Asian temple grounds, and Native American pyramid complexes. It is also a reminder that the modern leadership dilemma of high-risk competing choices and demands is not new. The Labyrinth is as old as humanity's quest for wisdom and certainty in an environment of confusion, complexity, and uncertainty. In a globally conscious environment, leaders cannot escape the inexorably moral character of leadership.

Rather than avoid the moral demands of leadership or impose the values of their own moral traditions, leaders need to understand the broadly universal character of their moral role as leaders, as well as the highly particular circumstances and events that shape their own moral character and the characters of the people and organisations they lead. A thoughtful and critical understanding of personal morality within a wider context of culturally constructed moral meaning is not unlike the chef who acquires an 'objective' knowledge and understanding of food chemistry, nutrition, appetite, and taste to deepen her personal appreciation of food to become a better chef. In that process, she learns that even though individual food tastes vary and are influenced by cultural cuisines, there are elements of food and eating traditions that are common to all people and cultures. In this process, whether in the realm of morality or food, understanding the vital role of strong emotional attachments to traditions of family, culture, and ethnicity as the social glue of communities and cultures provides a mechanism for building wider moral communities and new wisdom traditions. The ability to construct new wisdom traditions linked to those already established can become the social glue of moral meaning that enables people to maintain a sense of continuity, order, and purpose while adapting to fast-paced disruptive change.

These general observations lead to the following basic premises about the moral effectiveness of contemporary leaders:

1. Morality is a culturally situated human structure.
2. Moral direction is the work of leaders.
3. Contemporary leaders face the moral demands of new, untested challenges that preclude a reliance on any single wisdom tradition for moral guidance.

The conditions defined by these premises constitute the Leadership Labyrinth of complexity, competing claims, and conflicting demands, in which moral direction is expected from leaders but cannot be credible without substantive collaboration between leaders and stakeholders. To do this effectively requires a working knowledge of human moral functioning.

The human structure of morality

Human beings are the foundation of morality. Although there is considerable variation in how human values are interpreted, the moral claim of human life and welfare is generally regarded as universal (Bok, 2002; Nussbaum, 2003; Sen, 1999; Singer, 2004), and is affirmed as such by the majority of nations in the UN Declaration of Human Rights. The nomenclature of ethics ('good' and 'bad') and morality ('right' and 'wrong') is derived from this fundamental claim. Wisdom traditions of family, tribe, religion, culture, philosophy, and science are systems of moral guidance grounded in the shared responsibility to preserve, protect, and promote human flourishing. Wisdom traditions share a common structure rooted in uniquely human neurochemistry and in the self-conscious experience of embodiment under conditions of interdependence. The physical, emotional, spiritual, and intellectual connection among humans informs the creation and mediation of moral meaning. Recent brain research has reinforced established cultural theories about the emotional, physical, and spiritual dimensions of language and values (Berger and Luckmann, 1967; Changeux et al., 2005; Cohen, 2000; Damasio, 1999; Douglas, 2002; Durkheim and Fields, 1995; Geertz, 1973a). The growing body of theoretical and empirical research on the physiology, psychology, and sociology of human values suggests that morality is an inherent human capability and need.

Morality is organic, dynamic, and multidimensional. There is much in natural sciences research to suggest that morality is 'hard-wired' into the human organism (Bionolo and DeAnna, 2006; Casebeer and Churchland, 2003; Damasio, 1999, 2001; Szasz, 1996; Thompson, 1999; Wilson, 1975).[3] Despite the modern bias towards reason as a privileged mode of moral meaning, there is ample evidence that human moral sensibilities are far more complex and multidimensional. From the moment of birth (and before), the meaning of the human encounter with the world is mediated through the physical body. This encounter is further mediated and interpreted by thought and feeling. Each individual learns to organise these experiences through the concepts and language of their family and community. The structure of morality, therefore, emanates from and reinforces natural human capabilities for meaning and connection, mediated through experience. Values are expressed in stories and images, rules, symbolic practices, and reasoned behaviour. The person is a creation of the culture and the culture is the creation of its human members. Reflexive theories of culture and individuality as mirrors of each other span the ages, from Ancient Greece to the discussions of contemporary anthropology (Bourdieu and Nice, 2004; Bourdieu and Wacquant, 1992; Plato and Waterfield, 1993). Both individual and collective structures of moral meaning reflect the complex natural structure of the human organism. This structure can be represented schematically.

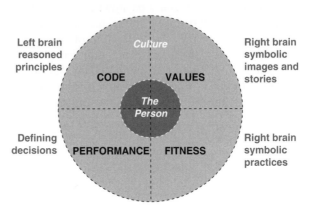

Figure 12.1   The Structure of Moral Meaning

Social scientists have long theorised morality as a natural human capability that develops over time (Dewey, 1924; Gilligan, 1988; Kohlberg, 1984; Piaget, 1972). Based on observational studies of human brain activity in situations involving moral dilemmas, Green observed that moral judgement engages emotions and emotional processing, a view that challenges the traditional modern view of morality as a primarily rational 'higher cognition' thought process (Greene, 2001; Greene et al., 2004). These studies corroborate the pioneering work launched by Nobel economists Amos Tversky and Daniel Kahneman, demonstrating the role of emotional biases in the formation of judgements (Gilovich et al., 2002; Kahneman et al., 1982). The heuristics and biases studies following Tversky and Kahneman emphasise conditions of risk, danger, and uncertainty as especially subject to emotional bias in the formation of judgement, theorising a dual-processing system of judgement that differentiates between two complementary systems of reasoning, the intuitive and the rational (Gilovich et al., 2002; Sloman, 2002). Taken together, these findings suggest an organic structure of morality associated with the way human beings form moral judgements and act upon them.

Wisdom traditions are systems of moral guidance. Given the lengthy human journey to adulthood, an adult's morality is largely a function of their membership of a community of shared moral meaning. The system of values, rules, symbolic practices, and reasoned behaviour constitutes the generic structure of moral meaning. Each human group, from the microculture of the family to the macroculture of the community of nations, develops a tradition of shared wisdom reflecting its unique convergence of people, relationships, events, and circumstances. This tradition idealises heroes and shares legends that symbolise values and virtues worthy of emulation as well as dangers to be avoided. A concomitant code of rules and a repertoire of symbolic practices emerges to instil habits of virtue, to reinforce values, and to commemorate symbolic heroes and events. These structures are the embedded moral compass through which a community defines good, bad, right, wrong, honourable, and dishonourable. While traditions can appear to be radically divergent, the generic structure is remarkably similar, as illustrated by comparing two local wisdom traditions, College and America.

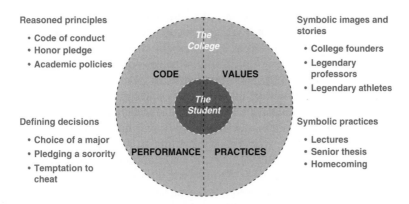

Figure 12.2 The Wisdom Tradition of the College

Wisdom traditions are embedded in wisdom communities. Wisdom traditions capture the moral imagination and will, but they are also fluid, porous, and malleable. They create and reinforce a sense of shared identity, purpose, and destiny among group members. They do this through structured experiences that fulfil a human need for consonance between personal embodiment, the surrounding social order,

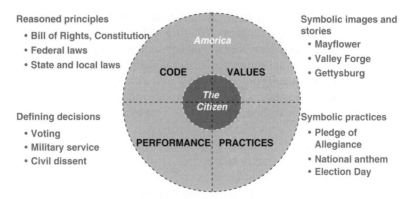

Reasoned principles
- Bill of Rights, Constitution
- Federal laws
- State and local laws

Symbolic images and stories
- Mayflower
- Valley Forge
- Gettysburg

America

CODE   VALUES

The Citizen

Defining decisions
- Voting
- Military service
- Civil dissent

PERFORMANCE   PRACTICES

Symbolic practices
- Pledge of Allegiance
- National anthem
- Election Day

Figure 12.3   The Wisdom Tradition of America

and a given cosmology or worldview (Douglas, 1982). Anthropologists have observed and theorised extensively the power of structured symbolic stories (myth) and practices (ritual) as the social glue of communities in the formation of self-consciousness (Cohen, 1994; Douglas, 1986; Epstein, 1978; Leach, 1976; Turner, 1986). The cultural legitimisation of identity (who one is and can become) and agency (what one does and can do) imposes moral imperatives and constraints, explicitly codified in law and normative social rules, that reflect values embedded in the symbolic structure of myth and social practice in a seamless web of inescapable moral meaning. The symbolic structure of received values is the 'moral default' position to which people often revert under the stress of danger, risk, and uncertainty. However powerful, the cultural context of individual moral identity and agency is neither total nor absolute. Individuals are, in fact, capable of critical agency and can assert their unique values and moral will in an ongoing series of negotiations that influence and shape the culture, usually subtly and slowly, but sometimes dramatically. The dramatic tension of these negotiations is especially evident at the margins of cross-cultural encounter, when people perceive the need or expectation for the identification and maintenance of strong ties with more than one culture. This negotiation is as commonplace as the first few weeks of any child's adjustment to preschool, and as monumental as the creation of a Palestinian state.

The moral work of leaders

The work of leaders is almost always understood to have a moral dimension, and the character of leaders is a prominent theme in wisdom traditions. Confucius observed that the strongest form of leadership was to set a good example (Confucius et al., 1998). Greek and Roman philosophers and historians emphasised character and virtue as essential qualities which all citizens – and especially leaders – should cultivate (Aristotle and Greenwood, 1909; Cicero; Plato and Bloom, 1991; Plato and Waterfield, 1993; Plutarch, 1969; Suetonius; Virgil and Ruden, 2008). The reflections of the Roman Emperor Marcus Aurelius on the duties and character of leadership were recently republished as a popular paperback (Aurelius et al., 2006), and ancient epics continue to engage modern readers and audiences, even as new mythic heroes emerge from current events, illustrating the human penchant for leadership stories of character and moral struggle. The literature on the character and ethics of leaders is extensive, but a few general themes highlight the moral dimensions of leadership.

Leadership is a moral trust. Leaders are moral agents with responsibilities towards others. This is true in the obvious sense that leaders who act on behalf of others' interests need to be trustworthy in carrying out the duties entrusted to them. Leaders are also entrusted with stewardship of the legacy of a community or organisation. It is therefore not just the current members of a group whose interests are at stake in the decisions and actions of a leaders; the entire community of stakeholders, present and future, bear the consequences of those decisions and actions. The ability to fulfil the moral trust of leadership is the pivotal stage on which new leaders emerge to replace established leaders who have failed to fulfil their promise.

Conditions of threat are the moral test of leadership. Epic heroes of mythic history feature leaders at momentous crossroads where lives, countries, and futures hang in the balance. Conditions of danger, risk, and uncertainty that threaten human life and flourishing activate the complex process of moral judgement (Kahneman et al., 1982). Risk, danger, and uncertainty are often the right-versus-right 'defining moments' that challenge the moral imagination and resourcefulness of leaders (Badaracco, 1997; Kidder, 1996). Conditions of threat highlight the role of the leader in rallying stakeholders to establish a direction and take effective action. Forces of threat can be either external forces endangering the community or internal challenges to established rules and order. In either case, the authentic leaders are those who are first to recognise and respond to the threat. Forces of threat can be those external forces endangering the community, or internal challenges to established rules and order. The authentic leaders are those who are first to recognise and respond to these threats. Although the notion of threat usually conjures up negative events such as natural or human-induced catastrophes, positive conditions and opportunities can be threats when they involve uncertain consequences of benefit and burden for human beings. The leader who abuses power by garnering unfair benefits for friends, or neglects considerations of justice and care in managing prosperity, or fails to anticipate the needs of those who depend on them falls just as short in the moral test of leadership as the one who fails to recognise or respond to a disaster. Failing the moral test of leadership is a classic trope of regime transformation, in which a formerly powerless or obscure person emerges with a heroic resolve to protect, rescue, and restore integrity to the community.

Leaders interpret and adapt wisdom traditions to meet new challenges. In traditional cultures, people are united with each other and their leaders by a shared wisdom tradition on which they mutually rely for guidance in the face of adversity. Members of traditional communities share this 'moral default' position of symbolic values. Confident that the entire community understands the tradition, leaders are adept at enlivening its symbols, images, stories, and rituals with the concrete detail of new situations. Throughout American history, for example, leaders have adapted its cherished ethos of freedom and equality far beyond the limited scope envisioned by the founders, by extending full rights and privileges of citizenship to women, African Americans, Chinese, Native Americans, and people without property. When the anchor of tradition is reinterpreted in light of new circumstances, it demonstrates utility and continuity by stretching to meet new demands for moral direction. For over a century, cultural historians and museum curators have been collecting and cataloguing the artifacts of traditions that have failed to adapt. The ongoing dance of leadership between a community and its leaders negotiates the rhythm and pace of change so that people feel securely anchored in the wisdom of their tradition, and continue both to believe in and to be faithful to it. When either of these conditions fails, the tradition eventually fails, either because the tradition no longer works, or because its members no longer see themselves as its faithful adherents. As scholars from diverse disciplines have demonstrated, the creative interpretation and adaptation of a tradition keeps it alive (Geertz, 1983; O'Donnell, 1998; Schneider and Somers, 2006; Sittungkir, 2004).

Globalisation and the moral performance of leaders

In recent years leadership ethics has emerged as a growing field of scholarship, involving a wide range of disciplines and perspectives

(Aguilar, 1995; Dalla Costa, 1998; Doh and Stumpf, 2005; Hitt, 1990; Høivik, 2002; Kanungo and Mendonca, 1996; Keohane, 2006; Klein, 2002; Krass, 1998; Maak and Pless, 2006; Piper et al., 1993; Sergiovanni, 1992; Shapiro and Stefkovich, 2005; Spears, 1995; Starratt, 2004). The consensus of modern scholarship on leadership ethics is that integrity, character, and ethics are not just important, but that they constitute the core of leadership responsibility (Ciulla, 2004).

This shift towards ethics as the heart of leadership has emerged in the wake of new theories that have revolutionised the fundamental understanding of leadership, moving away from authoritarian, mechanistic models towards collaborative, organic models based on authentic relationships and shared interests. The concept of transformational leadership, first popularised by James McGregor Burns, begins with the moral mandate of leadership. Transformational leadership models have altered the practice of leadership in organisations throughout the world to focus on the relational nexus of leaders and followers, revising and reinventing organisations through people (Bass, 1998; Burns, 1978; Kouzes and Posner, 2002). More recently, the challenge of managing the exponential growth of knowledge has highlighted the distinction between the kind of leadership needed to solve technical problems, and the more complex leadership needed to envision and strategise the deep change necessitated for survival in complex, competitive environments. Ronald Heifetz defines this situation as the adaptive leadership challenge (Heifetz, 1994).

Adaptive leaders create new knowledge to meet new challenges. The concept of adaptive leadership focuses on the role of leaders both in constructing knowledge to understand the pressure of adaptive dynamics and in using that knowledge to lead change more effectively (Heifetz, 1994). Heifetz defines leadership itself as the mobilising of people to do the work of developing solutions to problems for which there are no answers. This 'adaptive work' builds the answers by clarifying and resolving value conflicts, and developing strategies that bridge the gap between aspirational values and the status quo. By its very nature, adaptive work is collaborative. No one person can possibly develop the knowledge required for deep organisational change, but many people working together throughout the organisation can. The leader is the person who engages these people with the problem and each other in creating a solution. Many of the problems of contemporary organisations and societies are new situations for which there are no answers and for which adaptive work is the only feasible response.

Adaptive leaders are not necessarily authorities. People expect authorities to lead, but the work of adaptive leadership is not always done by those in authority. Sometimes the work of being in authority – directing, protecting, defining roles and responsibilities, managing conflict, and enforcing norms – conflicts with the purpose of adaptive work. Or authorities can be so absorbed in the demands of their work, especially when competitive pressures create high levels of organisational stress, that they have blind spots in their aspirational vision. In these situations, anyone who recognises the adaptive challenge can learn to be an adaptive leader by beginning to work on the challenge, especially if that work is begun in collaboration with others in the organisation. Collaboration is also important to build ownership and commitment to adaptive work throughout the organisation, in preparation for the inevitable resistance from those unwilling or unable to change. Adaptive leaders who are also in positions of authority, however, can minimise these hazards, because they have far more resources at their disposal to manage the environment, expectations, and pace of change (Heifetz, 1994).

The moral challenges of globalisation invite the creation of new wisdom. The work of adaptive leadership can be difficult, dangerous, and engaged in the crux of moral challenges. Much of the new knowledge created in response to adaptive challenges involves values, insight and will, as much as cognition and the analysis of empirical evidence. Leaders of global organisations with multiple stakeholders with allegiance to diverse wisdom traditions must adapt to the moral demands of those new, untested challenges that preclude reliance on either secular reason or any single wisdom tradition for moral guidance. It can no longer be assumed that members of a global organisation share the wisdom traditions of their leaders or with each other. Yet, they must rely on the wisdom of shared values and moral will to build organisations adapted to conditions of pluralism, complexity, and the interconnectedness inherent to the context of globalisation. The challenge of creating, capturing, and delivering sustainable value in a relentlessly competitive environment is further complicated by increasingly vocal stakeholders claiming their rights and championing their values. Yet, it is no longer defensible to discount those voices in the interests of increased profitability, especially when human talent is the currency of value in a knowledge economy. The adaptive challenge for leaders is to tap into these sources of potential dissent and discontent as a source of enhanced strategic value. This involves engaging not only their cognitive intelligence, but also their moral and social intelligence, and their imagination and commitment.

The moral compass

One aspect of the emerging adaptive leadership role in global organisations is to identify and respond effectively to those adaptive challenges involving conditions of risk, danger, and uncertainty that call for new wisdom as well as new knowledge. The adaptive work of building new collaborative wisdom, with its multidimensional engagement of human emotional and intuitive neuro-processing, is far more complex than the skill of building new knowledge. Leaders who do this effectively need models and skills that facilitate intrapersonal and interpersonal insight, and openness to communication and connection across boundaries that have sometimes been traditionally understood as impermeable. The moral compass is one such model, an intentionally neutral, generic concept of human morality that privileges no single wisdom tradition yet can apply to all. In using this model as a starting point for conversation about values, leaders can begin the process of creating new wisdom traditions that link the personal conscience of diverse stakeholders in a shared moral vision, adapted to the new challenges and circumstances of globalisation.

The moral compass model builds on a generic understanding of human morality in a schematic representation of moral meaning and experience: vision, code, fitness, and performance. A moral compass can be described as the framework of internalised values and behaviour people use to realise the good and to avoid or manage the bad in themselves, in others, and in their social and material environment. While each community, organisation, and institution is endowed with a moral compass, most modern individuals belong to several communities, and are constantly negotiating the embedded wisdom traditions of these communities.

For example (see Figure 12.4), Jason might be a practising Buddhist, a physician in a Catholic hospital, a board member of his community association, the spouse of a Jew, the son of atheists, and a member of the Green Party. Each of these affiliations constitutes membership of a community of sorts, with a wisdom tradition to which Jason may consider himself somewhat aligned. Consciously or not, Jason is seeking consonance between his internal morality and the moral frameworks of his meaningful affiliations, so he is constantly renegotiating and refining his personal moral compass. As a result, his personal moral compass is a composite of multiple compasses in his relational network of morality, embedded and expressed in his character, habits, decisions, relationships, actions, and preferences. The more conscious and intentional he is about

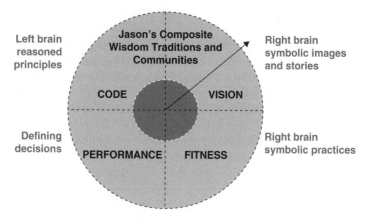

Figure 12.4   Jason's Moral Compass

the content of his moral compass, the more authentically he can align his personal values with the moral compass of each of these communities.

The moral compass intentionally decouples religion from morality and allows for diverse religious and non-religious interpretations of morality. The model is represented by a circle in two intersecting hemispheres. These hemispheres are the physical/metaphysical and the rational/intuitive aspects of morality. These in turn produce four quadrants: *Vision* – symbolic moral vision as the intuitive 'moral default' position of core values; *Code* – cognitive moral rules; *Fitness* – concrete symbolic practices of moral fitness; and *Performance* – moral performance in concrete behaviour and decisions. As previously noted, people constantly seek consonance among these aspects of their internal moral compass, as well as between their personal moral compass and that of their communities (Douglas, 1982). The model is applicable to individuals, groups, organisations, and communities as a tool for establishing a generic moral framework that links diverse social identities and locations to structures of shared meaning, without distorting or encroaching upon either. The moral compass can be used to clarify personal morality and to build moral solidarity in work teams, organisations, or communities of diverse membership.

Moral vision

Moral vision is the 'true north' of the moral compass. It is the spiritual, affective aspect of moral identity expressed in the power of myth, narrative, and those images that represent core values. It is the story we tell to explain who we are. Core values may be expressed in words like *truth, justice, freedom, friendship, world peace*. But moral meaning expressed in compelling imagery and models of subjectivity shapes both conscious and unconscious perception, as well as our interpretation of events, experiences, and nature, in the formation of a subjective identity and worldview. The twentieth-century movie myth, *Star Wars*, is a powerfully persuasive vehicle for representing the values of courage, loyalty, and tenacity. Sophisticated secularists may reject religious mythology and ritual, but everyone has an internalised mythic morality of idealised characters, stories, experiences, and images to anchor moral identity. Adults may consider mythology to be a primitive form of spirituality, or a remnant of childhood, but an active, mature moral imagination can continue to inspire moral fitness throughout life, and contribute to the capacity for building moral solidarity with others. Researchers have examined the skill of visionary leaders like Martin Luther King, Jr and former US President Ronald Reagan in their use of symbolic imagery to create moral solidarity, demonstrating that people build shared identity through myth and ritual systems (Kertzer, 1988).

Moral code

An intentional, normative moral code is the rational aspect of moral identity that complements the symbolic, intuitive moral vision. Many people rely on religious codes such as the Ten Commandments, the Five Pillars, or the Eightfold Path as their primary source of moral principles, but most people refine and elaborate their basic code as they study and learn through experience. A system of reasoned beliefs and normative principles reflects a coherent understanding of the self as a moral agent in a complex relational and material environment. A moral code is often expressed in moral theories according to formal methods of moral reasoning. Professions, organisations, and communities frequently adopt moral codes, just as law and public policy express the moral code of a civic community. A reasoned moral code frames the moral parameters of life, and defines acceptable choices within a wide range of domains like work, parenting, personal care, sexual relationships, and recreation. Modern life is codified in discursive knowledge (sometimes with competing rules) about the right way to approach every human endeavour from birthing to dying. In building a moral code it is important to examine the consonance between the values represented in one's moral vision and the moral principles underlying the code. The neuroscience and heuristic bias studies referenced earlier suggest that when there is dissonance between a rational moral code and intuitive moral vision, people are more likely to follow their vision (Damasio, 1999, 2001; Gilovich et al., 2002; Kahneman et al., 1982).

Moral fitness

Moral fitness is the symbolic aspect of moral agency. It is ritualised action that expresses and reflects the vision and values of moral identity. The disciplined cultivation of character is a traditional element of religious practice. This includes the conditioned ability to assume moral responsibility for both recognising and responding effectively to those moral challenges that require decision or action. Ritualisation, however, is a human capacity that should not be conflated with religion. The postmodern reinvention of the self includes practices of cultivated dispositions aimed at freeing oneself to become what one values. Moral practice includes a regimen of moral fitness to cultivate virtues, overcome vices, create dispositions of moral awareness, and build moral community. These moral fitness practices are highly elastic, enabling individuals to internalise, interpret, and enact moral identity in unique and innovative ways, using forms that may themselves be inelastic. People with religious affiliations may align their moral fitness practice with religious rituals and spiritual disciplines. Secularists and atheists may use moral fitness practices to create, refine, and reinvent themselves. Moral fitness practices also reflect the innate human capacity for marking the moral significance of events or passages. People use meals, filling in journals, walking, bicycling, quiet time, social gatherings, anniversaries, and a host of other activities as concrete ways of cultivating desired dispositions, or of orienting the self according to an internalised moral identity. For most people, there is a strong social dimension to moral fitness, whether or not this is formally acknowledged.

Moral performance

Performance is the 'proof of the pudding' – the intentional aspect of moral agency demonstrated in concrete decisions and behaviour. Morality is actualised in the concrete experience of real problems, dilemmas, and conflicts that need to be resolved. These are the moments when moral vision, code, and fitness are put to the test in shaping and defining the character of individuals, communities, and organisations. From the most personal struggles of integrity to the global distribution of wealth, effective moral performance involves preparing for defining moments by developing an intentional strategy for recognising and managing them when they occur. This rational, deliberative aspect of moral performance is complemented by all of the other three aspects of moral identity and agency brought to bear on the situation. While it is the immediate urgency of moral problems and dilemmas that is most likely to draw people from diverse locations into engagement in search of a solution, their ability to perform effectively can be enhanced by strong development in all aspects of the moral compass. What is most evident from the body of research lying behind the model of the moral compass is the weight of the moral iceberg that lies below the surface of visible choices and behaviour. Understanding this, adaptive leaders create opportunities that invite moral engagement and solidarity before there is a crisis.

Conclusion

A moral compass is more than a metaphor. It is a conceptual tool that enables adaptive leaders to create new wisdom traditions by linking the diverse stakeholder collection of personal conscience with a larger community of shared values and moral will. In a complex world filled with competing demands and conflicting claims, leaders can apply the model to their own organisation with its diverse stakeholder groups to structure both personal and collective moral discernment, dialogue, and decision-making. By being more aware of their own moral compass and how it works, they will be more able to recognise moral challenges, articulate their values, and make decisions that align with these values. They will also be better equipped to engage others in conversations about values to enhance moral solidarity in shared decisions. Without presuming a conclusive or irrefutable body of knowledge, the moral compass model described here builds on a reasonably constructed body of theory and evidence. It therefore emerges as a credible model for facilitating the adaptive work of moral leadership.

Notes

1. For a relevant discussion of postmodernity as an aspect of globalisation, see 'Postmodernism and Business Ethics' (Calton, 2008) and 'Postmodernism' (Roy, 2008) in the *Encyclopedia of Business Ethics and Society* (Kolb, 2008).
2. For a discussion of constructivist theories as applied to cognition and learning see Piaget and Vygotsky (Smith et al., 1997). For constructivism as applied to adult learning see Caffarella, Baumgartner, and Mezirow (Merriam et al., 2007; Mezirow, 2000). For constructive approaches to leadership see Heifetz on adaptive leadership (Heifetz, 1994).
3. For more on the origins of sociobiology and morality see Harvard biologist Edward O. Wilson whose book *Sociobiology: The New Synthesis* launched the field of sociobiology, making the controversial assertion (among others) that ethics should be separated from philosophy, at least temporarily, to be studied as a part of natural sciences (Wilson, 1975, 1998, 1999).

Bibliography

Aguilar, F.J., *Managing Corporate Ethics: Learning from America's Ethical Companies How to Supercharge Business Performance* (New York: Oxford University Press, 1995).

Aristotle and Greenwood, L.H.G., *Aristotle Nicomachean Ethics: Book Six* (Cambridge: University Press, 1909).

Aurelius, M., Hammond, M., and Clay, D., *Meditations* (London; New York: Penguin Books. 2006).

Badaracco, J., *Defining Moments : When Managers Must Choose between Right and Right* (Boston, MA: Harvard Business School Press, 1997).

Bass, B.M., *Transformational Leadership: Industrial, Military, and Educational Impact* (Mahwah, NJ: Lawrence Erlbaum Associates, 1998).

Berger P.L. and Luckmann, T., *The Social Construction of Reality: A Treatise in the Sociology of Knowledge* (New York: Doubleday Anchor Books, 1967).

Bionolo, G. and DeAnna, G. (eds), *Evolutionary Ethics and Contemporary Biology* (Cambridge: Cambridge University Press, 2006).

Bok, S., *Common Values* (Columbia, MO: University of Missouri Press, 2002).

Bourdieu P. and Nice, R., *Science of Science and Reflexivity* (Chicago: University of Chicago Press, 2004).

Bourdieu P. and Wacquant, L.J.D., *An Invitation to Reflexive Sociology* (Chicago: University of Chicago Press, 1992).

Burns, J.M., *Leadership*, 1st edn (New York: Harper and Row, 1978).

Calton, J., 'Postmodernism and Business Ethics', in Kolb, R.W. (ed.), *Encyclopedia of Business Ethics and Society Vol. 4* (Thousand Oaks: Sage Publications, 2008).

Casebeer, W.D. and Churchland, P.D., 'The Neural Mechanisms of Moral Cognition: A Multiple-Aspect Approach to Moral Judgment and Decision-Making', *Biology and Philosophy*, XVIII(1) (2003) 169–194.

Changeux, J.P., Christen, Y., Damasio, A.R., and Singer, W., SpringerLink Online Service (2005). 'Neurobiology of Human Values' from http://dx.doi.org/10.1007/3–540–29803–7.

Cicero, *De Officiis*, Public Domain.

Ciulla, J.B., *Ethics, the Heart of Leadership*, 2nd edn (Westport, CN: Praeger, 2004).

Cohen, A.P., *Self Consciousness: An Alternative Anthropology of Identity* (London; New York: Routledge, 1994).

Cohen, A.P., *Signifying Identities: Anthropological Perspectives on Boundaries and Contested Values* (London; New York: Routledge, 2000).

Combs, G.M., 'Meeting the Leadership Challenge of a Diverse and Pluralistic Workplace: Implications of Self-Efficacy for Diversity Training', *Journal of Leadership and Organizational Studies*, VII(4) (2002) 1–16.

Confucius, Ames, R.T. and Rosemont, H., *The Analects of Confucius: A Philosophical Translation*, 1st edn (New York: Ballantine Pub. Group, 1998).

Dalla Costa, J., *The Ethical Imperative: Why Moral Leadership Is Good Business* (Reading, MA: Addison-Wesley, 1998).

Damasio, A.R., *The Feeling of What Happens: Body and Emotion in the Making of Consciousness*, 1st edn (New York: Harcourt Brace, 1999).

Damasio, A.R., *Unity of Knowledge: The Convergence of Natural and Human Science.* (New York: New York Academy of Sciences, 2001).

Dewey, J., *Democracy and Education: An Introduction to the Philosophy of Education* (New York: The Macmillan Company, 1924).

Doh J.P. and Stumpf, S.A., *Handbook on Responsible Leadership and Governance in Global Business* (Cheltenham, UK; Northampton, MA: Edward Elgar, 2005).

Douglas, M., *Natural Symbols: Explorations in Cosmology* (New York: Pantheon Books, 1982).

Douglas, M., *How Institutions Think*, 1st edn (Syracuse, NY: Syracuse University Press, 1986).

Douglas, M., *Purity and Danger: An Analysis of Concept of Pollution and Taboo* (London; New York: Routledge, 2002).

Durkheim, E. and Fields, K.E., *The Elementary Forms of Religious Life* (New York: Free Press, 1995).

Ellul, J., *Éthique de la Liberté* (Génève: Labor et Fides, 1984).

Epstein, A.L., *Ethos and Identity: Three Studies in Ethnicity* (London; Chicago: Tavistock Publications, Aldine Pub. Co., 1978).

Geertz, C., *The Interpretation of Cultures: Selected Essays* (New York: Basic Books, 1973).

Geertz, C., *Local Knowledge: Further Essays in Interpretive Anthropology* (New York: Basic Books, 1983).

Gilligan, C., *Mapping the Moral Domain: A Contribution of Women's Thinking to Psychological Theory and Education* (Cambridge, MA: Center for the Study of Gender, Education, and Human Development Distributed by Harvard University Press, 1988).

Gilovich, T., Griffin, D.W., and Kahneman, D., *Heuristics and Biases: The Psychology of Intuitive Judgement* (Cambridge; New York: Cambridge University Press, 2002).

Greene, J.D., 'An fMRI Investigation of Emotional Engagement in Moral Judgement', *Science*, 293(5537) (2001) 2105.

Greene, J.D., Nystrom, L.E., Engell, A.D., Darley, J.M., and Cohen, J.D., 'The Neural Bases of Cognitive Conflict and Control in Moral Judgment', *Neuron*, XX(2) (2004), 389–400.

Heifetz, R.A., *Leadership without Easy Answers* (Cambridge, MA: Belknap Press of Harvard University Press, 1994).

Hitt, W.D., *Ethics and Leadership: Putting Theory into Practice* (Columbus: Battelle Press, 1990).

Høivik, H.W., *Moral Leadership in Action: Building and Sustaining Moral Competence in European Organizations* (Cheltenham; Northampton, MA: Edward Elgar, 2002).

Kahneman, D., Slovic, P. and Tversky, A., *Judgment under Uncertainty: Heuristics and Biases* (Cambridge; New York: Cambridge University Press, 1982).

Kanungo R.N., and Mendonca, M., *Ethical Dimensions of Leadership* (Thousand Oaks, CA: Sage Publications, 1996).

Keohane, N.O., *Higher Ground: Ethics and Leadership in the Modern University* (Durham: Duke University Press, 2006).

Kertzer, D.I., *Ritual, Politics, and Power* (New Haven: Yale University Press, 1988).

Kidder, R., *How Good People Make Tough Choices: Resolving the Dilemmas of Ethical Living*, 1st Fireside edn (New York: Simon and Schuster, 1996).

Klein, S., *Ethical Business Leadership: Balancing Theory and Practice* (New York: Peter Lang, 2002).

Kohlberg, L., *The Psychology of Moral Development: The Nature and Validity of Moral Stages*, 1st edn (San Francisco: Harper and Row, 1984).

Kolb, R.W., *Encyclopedia of Business Ethics and Society* (Thousand Oaks, CA: Sage Publications, 2008).

Kouzes, J.M. and Posner, B.Z., *The Leadership Challenge*, 3rd edn (San Francisco: Jossey-Bass, 2002).

Krass, P., *The Book of Leadership Wisdom: Classic Writings by Legendary Business Leaders* (New York: Wiley, 1998).

Leach, E.R., *Culture and Communication: The Logic by Which Symbols Are Connected : An Introduction to the Use of Structuralist Analysis in Social Anthropology* (Cambridge, UK; New York: Cambridge University Press, 1976).

Maak, T. and Pless, N., *Responsible Leadership* (London; New York: Routledge, 2006).

Merriam, S.B., Caffarella, R.S., and Baumgartner, L., *Learning in Adulthood: A Comprehensive Guide*, 3rd edn (San Francisco: Jossey-Bass, 2007).

Mezirow, J., *Learning as Transformation: Critical Perspectives on a Theory in Progress*, 1st edn (San Francisco: Jossey-Bass, 2000).

Nussbaum, M.C., 'Capabilities as Fundamental Entitlements: Sen and Social Justice', *Feminist Economics*, IX(2) (2003) 33–59.

O'Donnell, J.J., *Avatars of the Word: From Papyrus to Cyberspace* (Cambridge, MA: Harvard University Press, 1998).

Piaget, J., *Judgment and Reasoning in the Child* (Totowa, NJ: Littlefield, Adams, 1972).

Piper, T.R., Gentile, M.C., and Parks, S.D., *Can Ethics Be Taught?: Perspectives, Challenges, and Approaches at Harvard Business School* (Boston, MA: Harvard Business School, 1993).

Plato and Bloom, A.D., *The Republic of Plato*, 2nd edn (New York, NY: Basic Books, 1991).

Plato and Waterfield, R., *The Republic* (Oxford and New York: Oxford University Press, 1993).

Plutarch, *Vitae Parallelai*, Ziegler, K. (ed.) (Leipzig: Teubner, 1969).

Roy, A., 'Postmodernism', in Kolb, R.W. (ed.), *Encyclopedia of Business Ethics and Society*, Vol. 4, (Thousand Oaks, CA: Sage Publications, 2008) 1641–1643.

Schneider, M. and Somers, M., 'Organizations as Complex Adaptive Systems: Implications of Complexity Theory for Leadership Research', *The Leadership Quarterly*, XVII(4) (2006), 351–365.

Sen, A.K., *Development as Freedom* (New York: Anchor Books, 1999).

Sergiovanni, T.J., *Moral Leadership: Getting to the Heart of School Improvement*, 1st edn (San Francisco: Jossey-Bass Publishers, 1992).

Shapiro, J.P. and Stefkovich, J.A., *Ethical Leadership and Decision Making in Education: Applying Theoretical Perspectives to Complex Dilemmas*, 2nd edn (Mahwah, NJ: Lawrence Erlbaum, 2005).

Singer, P., *One World: The Ethics of Globalization* (New Haven: Yale University Press, 2004).

Sittungkir, H., 'On Selfish Memes: Culture as Complex Adaptive System', *Journal of Social Complexity*, II(1) (2004) 20–32.

Sloman, S. 'Two Systems of Reasoning' in Gilovich T. and Kahneman, D., editors, *Heuristics and Biases: The Psychology of Intuitive Judgement* (Cambridge; New York: Cambridge University Press, 2002) 379–396.

Smith, L., Dockrell, J., and Tomlinson, P., *Piaget, Vygotsky, and Beyond: Future Issues for Developmental Psychology and Education* (London; New York: Routledge, 1997).

Spears, L.C., *Reflections on Leadership: How Robert K. Greenleaf's Theory of Servant-Leadership Influenced Today's Top Management Thinkers* (New York: J. Wiley, 1995).

Starke-Meyerring, D., 'Meeting the Challenges of Globalization: A Framework for Global Literacies in Professional Communication Programs', *Journal of Business and Technical Communication*, XIX(4) (2005) 468–499.

Starratt, R.J., *Ethical Leadership*, 1st edn (San Francisco: Jossey-Bass, 2004).

Suetonius, *Vitae Caesarii*, public domain.

Szasz, T.S., *The Meaning of Mind: Language, Morality, and Neuroscience* (Westport, CN: Praeger, 1996).

Thompson, P., 'Evolutionary Ethics: Its Origin and Contemporary Face', *Zygon*, XXX(3) (1999), 473–484.

Turner, V.W., *The Anthropology of Performance*, 1st edn (New York, NY: PAJ Publications, 1986).

Virgil, and Ruden, S., *The Aeneid*. (New Haven: Yale University Press, 2008).

Wilson, E.O., *Sociobiology: The New Synthesis* (Cambridge, MA: Belknap Press of Harvard University Press, 1975).

Wilson, E.O., *Consilience: The Unity of Knowledge*, 1st edn (New York: Knopf : Distributed by Random House, 1998).

Wilson, E.O., *The Diversity of Life* (New York: W.W. Norton, 1999).

13
Spiritually Anchored Leadership
Fahri Karakas

Introduction

This chapter introduces a new framework for analysing and capturing the range of different leadership value systems. Building on the concept of 'career anchors' (Schein, 1990), this chapter introduces the concept of 'spiritual anchors', those patterns of deeply held spiritual motives, values, and attitudes that provide direction, meaning, wholeness, and connectedness to a person's life or work. Based on a concept of spirituality derived from the Sufi tradition, supplemented by qualitative interviews conducted with 32 managers in Turkey, this article develops a typology of spiritual anchors, each of which can be thought of as the spiritual DNA of a person, or a fractal of that person's holistic value system. The spiritual anchors stem from nine Sufi paths. Each of the spiritual anchors refers to a unique way of perceiving and practising spirituality. People from each of the anchors have a different perspective, and make a unique contribution to organisational life.

This chapter argues that these nine spiritual anchors are the underlying basis of leadership values and team roles in organisations. This study is intended to help to fill the gap of holistic theories in the current values literature by expanding the extent of our knowledge about: a) different value compasses of leaders; b) individual style differences; and c) different team roles in organisations, based on the idea of spiritual anchors. The chapter has three parts. First, the case is made for the need for an integrative model of spiritual anchors. Secondly, the methodology of the research is described and the results of the qualitative data analysis are presented. The nine spiritual anchors are illustrated using interview data, with respondents being classified based on the spiritual anchors they have. Finally, the study concludes with a note about the implications that arise both for researchers and for practitioners.

Part 1 – The case for an integrative model

The paper introduces and describes nine spiritual anchors, representing different value compasses of leaders in organisations. The call to rediscover the spiritual roots, characteristics, and dynamics of leaders in organisations is timely for a number of reasons, not least because of the crisis of confidence in leadership which accompanied the recent 2008 global financial crisis (Hutton, 2008; Steenland and Dreier, 2008; Greenhalgh, 2008). This crisis led to the collapse of a number of high-profile financial institutions and administrations around the world, and led to declines in world stock indexes, culminating in increased unemployment and job losses worldwide. Recent critics have highlighted the ethical roots of the crisis, which has made many question those in leadership positions at the time (Greenhalgh, 2008; Steenland and Dreier, 2008; Heuvel and Schlosser, 2008).

Meanwhile, over the past decade, scholars report a dramatic and steady increase in interest in workplace spirituality among management researchers and practitioners, particularly in North America (Cavanagh, 1999; Tischler, 1999; Giacalone and Jurkiewicz, 2003). Howard argues that this explosion of interest in spirituality is a new dimension of management, and that it is 'probably the most significant trend in management since the 1950s' (Howard, 2002:230). This movement has been described as a major transformation, where 'organisations which have long been viewed as rational systems are considering making room for the spiritual dimension, a dimension that has less to do with rules and order and more to do with meaning, purpose, and a sense of community' (Ashmos and Duchon, 2000:134). This new spiritual dimension embodies employees' search for simplicity, meaning at work, self-expression, creativity, and their interconnectedness to something higher (Marques et al., 2007; Lips-Wiersma and Mills, 2002).

The growing interest in spirituality at work is evident not only in journals and bookstores, but also in corporations, corporate meeting rooms, and the business world in general. A growing number of organisations, including corporations such as Intel, Southwest Airlines, and Sears, are reported to have incorporated spirituality in their corporate strategies and cultures (Konz and Ryan, 1999; Wagner-Marsh and Conley, 1999). Although the increasing popularity and interest in spirituality at work has been well documented (Duchon and Plowman, 2005; Markow and Klenke, 2005; Fry, 2003; Mitroff and Denton, 1999; Ashmos and Duchon, 2000), controversy remains over the multiple meanings and definitions of 'spirituality at work' (Giacalone and Jurkiewicz, 2003; Hicks, 2002; Kinjerski and Skrypnek, 2004; Dent et al., 2005). In the past decade, more than 70 definitions of spirituality have been introduced, yet a widely accepted definition is yet to emerge (Markow and Klenke, 2005). However, in most of these definitions, spirituality has been described as a subjective phenomenon, focusing on the inner life and on the experiences and feelings of the individual. The multiplicity of these definitions naturally reflects the variety of ways in which individuals experience spirituality in their life. A key challenge for research, therefore, is to delve into these inner worlds to understand the complexity and diversity of their spiritual experiences. This study uses the construct of 'spiritual anchors' to inquire into this inner world, using qualitative interviews, and will therefore resist the temptation to add an artificially neat definition of spirituality to the literature.

Spiritual anchors

The concept of a 'spiritual anchor' originates from the spiritual principles of Sufism, the spiritual and philosophical tradition well developed in Anatolia. Sufism can be defined as a lifelong Islamic discipline which builds character and the inner life by purifying the heart spiritually and investing it with virtues. It is also known as the mystical philosophy of Islam, focusing on diminishing the ego in multiple ways including the regulation of physical needs. Its aim is to attain the pure love of God as the ultimate satisfaction. In the Islamic world, Sufi paths of transformation have been used as tools for enhancing self-awareness and self-growth for centuries (Uzunoglu, 1999). Nine paths of transformation represent the different ways through which spiritual development occurs and, due to their spiritual power, have been used by mystics for centuries. They have recently been introduced to the Western world by the Russian mystic, Gurdjieff, and the system has been popularised as the 'Enneagram' (Riso and Hudson, 2000).

Because until recently the Sufi tradition was an oral one, there are few written references to spiritual paths or anchors in Islamic sources before the twentieth century, where there are references to different spiritual paths in the works of the leading Islamic scholar Said Nursi (1925). The spiritual paths served as a means for self-observation and study, guiding people to spiritual unfolding and God-consciousness. Based on the assumption that the spiritual paths originate from the unique configuration of spiritual anchors in individuals, and that spiritual anchors form the basis of spiritual diversity among organisational leaders, this study argues that leadership styles can be both mapped and explored using this concept. The spiritual anchors are based on universal human values such as truth, wisdom, justice, inspiration, creativity, courage, honesty, and compassion. Although these values are beginning to be recognised in the spirituality literature, it seems that they are often listed without any systematic effort to be comprehensive. This study provides the missing unifying framework that illustrates the holistic and multidimensional nature of these values, using concepts from Sufism integrated with patterns in qualitative data.

Defining the anchors

This study builds on Schein's seminal work on career anchors and applies the concept to the emerging field of workplace spirituality. Schein (1990) conducted a panel study of 44 Sloan School of Management alumni to study the interaction of personal values and career events in the lives of managers in organisations. As a result, he introduced the concept of career anchors, encompassing the motives, values, and attitudes which give stability and direction to a person's career. In this usage, a career anchor is a motivational or attitudinal syndrome which guides the person's career and acts as the core motivator of that person.

As a development of this, the concept of a spiritual anchor refers to the pattern of deeply held individual assumptions, values, and priorities that provide direction, wholeness, meaning, and connectedness to that person's life or work. We can describe a spiritual anchor as the underlying structure of unique spiritual needs, attitudes, and motives of that individual. A spiritual anchor is a composite dynamic potential in every individual, affecting their spiritual needs, motives, and attitudes.

While each individual has different spiritual values, needs, attitudes, dreams, hopes, aspirations, and passions about their own life and future, each individual also has different spiritual gifts, talents, and strengths. Spiritual anchors can be used to define the variety of these spiritual differences. Because a spiritual anchor is a fractal of an individual's spiritual life, their spiritual anchor acts as a lens through which to see the patterns and dynamics of their whole life. Like a hologram, spiritual anchors show the same features at different levels of examination – from the closest look at the smallest element to the most distant view of the whole universe. A spiritual anchor is that concern or value which the person will not give up, if a choice has to be made. This is because their spiritual anchors reflect a person's essence, and lie at the heart of their identity.

Part 2 – The research

Methodology

Qualitative data for this chapter comes from a sample of 32 cases of a study of managers and professionals in Turkey. The sample consisted of 32 professionals and managers (engineers, fundraisers, sales managers, and IT professionals) in a variety of different sectors (financial services, manufacturing, software, and telecommunications) and civil initiatives in Istanbul, Turkey. The aim was to include individuals from a wide range of organisations, work contexts, job roles, and positions. Table 13.1 provides demographic information for the whole sample.

The target respondents were interviewed about their search for meaning, their spirituality at work, their perceptions of their own spiritual values, their individual views of the ideal, and their values about organisations. The interviews varied between 80 minutes and 2.5 hours in length. The aim was to reveal individual stories of spirituality, with a special focus on individual values, needs, and attitudes. The interviews were conducted in Turkish. Open questions were used, and interviewees were allowed to speculate freely on their thoughts and feelings concerning their own spiritual universe. Sample questions included: How would you describe your spiritual life? Reflecting on your inner life, what are your priorities, guiding principles, and spiritual core values? What derives meaning, hope, and faith in your life? How would you define yourself spiritually? Can you describe an experience at work that made you reflect on your spiritual values?

Table 13.1   Demographic Information of the Sample

Gender	**62.5% men**	**37.5% women**
Education (degree)	28% postgraduate	68% undergraduate
Organisation	82% businesses	18% NGOs
Nationality	92% Turkish	8% other
Position	31% managerial	69% professional
	Mean	**Range**
Age	27.7	22–35
Years of experience	4	0.5–12

*n = 32

When do you really feel vital, authentic, and alive? Which spiritual values and principles are indispensable in your work? Why do you think so?

Methodologically, a grounded theory approach was used in the analysis (Glaser and Strauss, 1967), with a focus on material specifically related to spirituality, values, and individual differences. The interview transcripts were read to extract data on how these individuals thought about their personal definitions, descriptions, or conceptions of their spirituality and values. An analytic memo was then composed for each case, enumerating the relevant material found (Patton, 2002). These memos were then reviewed for patterns, with particular attention being paid to the diversity and multiplicity of recurring themes regarding spirituality and values. Iterating this data with theory on the spiritual paths (Nursi, 1925; Uzunoglu, 1999), emerging themes were compared, using the Sufi paths, to code and cluster the findings, using the method of constant comparison advocated by Glaser and Strauss (1967).

This process produced a number of building blocks for a tentative theoretical framework (Patton, 2002). First – a set of profiles capturing similarities and differences in descriptions of spiritual values, needs, attitudes, preferences, and experiences. Secondly – a catalogue of different kinds of value compasses and team roles. Thirdly – a set of memos capturing the richness, texture and interaction of spiritual experiences at work, individual values, and behavioural manifestations of values at work. These building blocks were used to generate a typology of anchors, resulting in nine distinct spiritual anchors accompanied by specific sets of values.

Results

The interviews revealed a number of common themes about what these leaders were looking for spiritually in their work. The data suggested that there were implicit theories in the minds of the participants regarding their values and spirituality, their spiritual needs, motives, attitudes, and behaviours. For some leaders, spirituality is intrinsically related to building high-quality connections with other people. For others, spirituality is inherently individual, and reflects a search for meaning and a deeper understanding of self. And for others, spirituality is linked with creativity, self-expression, and inspiration at work. The data set suggests that spiritual anchors can explain and reflect the implicit theories in the minds of the participants regarding their own value compasses and spiritual motives.

The resulting taxonomy provides a framework of nine different spiritual anchors, nine different sets of value compasses, and nine different team roles likely to arise from these orientations (See Appendix 13A.1 and 13A.2 at the end of this chapter). The nine anchors are: perfection, compassion, passion, inspiration, investigation, dedication, appreciation, determination, and cooperation. The anchor framework provides an integrative model with which to examine the diversity of spiritual values within organisations. Each anchor will be considered in turn, before the implications of these findings are explored.

Spiritual anchor 1: perfection

A number of managers make it very clear that their fundamental spiritual motivation is to reach perfection in their lives. '*I continuously find myself struggling towards perfection,*' one said. These managers are idealists in their pursuit of excellence. This perfectionism is defined through attention to details, rules, and principles. '*Generally I am the one on the team who stresses high quality standards and details regarding the project.*' Another put: '*Even a minute detail is very important because excellence comes with the details. So, I make sure that all the procedures are systematically followed throughout the process.*' This requires relentless effort and discipline to reach the ideal standards. Rules, processes, principles, plans, details, and protocols are important. Inevitably, the more idealised one imagines the world and struggles for it, the higher stress s/he puts on the self. This is because they imagine a 'utopian picture'. One respondent clearly stated: '*This requires constant questioning, self discipline and self control. I am the strictest judge of myself.*' This spiritual state also has implications for how the manager positions him or herself in relation to other team members: '*Even if my team members say that I have done a perfect job, I am still not comfortable because I feel that it could be better.*'

Therefore, the spiritual anchor of 'perfection' is about the universal spiritual need to be right, to act ethically and to reach perfection. This spiritual anchor represents the 'transcendence' dimension in human life. The internal voice tells the individual to reach the ideal, seek perfection, be responsible, live life the right way, improve the world, and achieve excellence. The value compass of managers having this anchor is set on values such as objectivity, order, rationality, quality, perfection, honesty, integrity, truthfulness, self-discipline, consistency, and self-control. Behavioural manifestations of this anchor include: enforcing moral values in decision-making, pointing out and correcting mistakes and wrong deeds, telling the truth, seeking out the highest ethical standards, acting as a guardian/auditor by overseeing the application of ethical principles, enforcing self-discipline, walking the talk, and preventing any forms of corruption.

Spiritual Anchor 2: Compassion

A number of respondents make it very clear that what motivates them spiritually is compassion. What distinguishes this group is that the internal voice tells these managers to help people, serve people, care about people, be compassionate and kind to people, develop empathy and rapport, and reach hearts. Spiritual values on this anchor are charity, compassion, altruism, kindness, appreciation, sincerity, helpfulness, nurturing, modesty, and affection.

Spiritual Anchor 2 is about the universal spiritual need to love and be loved. *'We are the avant-garde of love; we don't have time for hostility,'* one manager said. Another stated: *'Love all the creation because of the Creator.'* This spiritual anchor is centred on the innate drive to form social relationships and to develop mutual caring commitments with other humans. This spiritual anchor represents the 'interconnectedness' dimension in human life. People, relationships, and feelings are at the core of this spiritual anchor.

Behavioural manifestations of the 'compassion' anchor include: making people feel valued and important, organising charity activities, transcending own immediate self-interests for the sake of others, donating for a common cause; helping weak, disabled, or troubled people by meeting their needs, building rapport and compassion in the workplace, communicating with and by hearts, paying individualised attention to every person, greeting colleagues sincerely, smiling compassionately, serving other people, and offering them moral and emotional support.

Sub-theme 1: Sensitivity to people
'For me, people and love come before profits or loss. Business is essentially about people. If everyone on the team is satisfied, we will produce better outcomes for our stakeholders. I always try to stress the values that tie us together: Love, compassion, generosity, helping, caring, empathy, belonging and cooperation. If we can flourish these values in our company, we can convey them to our customers as well.'

'I find my identity by helping, pleasing and warming the hearts of people important in my life.'

Sub-theme 2: Attention to relationships, feelings, needs
'I make an extra effort to meet the needs of my friends. I pay attention to feelings of people. I imagine that there is a sign on every

person's forehead that reads, "Make me feel valued and important". I track down all the birthday dates of my colleagues and I organize birthday parties for them. Sometimes I feel burnout and I neglect my own needs because I focus so much on other people's needs.'

Spiritual Anchor 3: Passion

A number of respondents have talked about how work gives meaning to their lives and contributes to their spiritual well-being. These managers stressed how they believed in the necessity of hard work as an end in itself and as a form of prayer. They mentioned how they loved their job and viewed their work as a path to spiritual maturation and growth.

Spiritual Anchor 3 is about the universal spiritual need to progress, to be productive and to be ethically successful in life. This spiritual anchor represents the 'work ethics' dimension in human life. Work in daily life in organisations can essentially be a sacred and spiritual task, and accepted as an additional form of worshipping and prayer. Ethical success and productivity are at the core of this spiritual anchor. The internal voice tells the individual to work hard, be focused, motivate people, achieve goals, focus on results, perform well, and make an impact. Spiritual values on this anchor are conscientiousness, persistence, ambition, self-development, productivity, ethical success, effort, zeal, and diligence. Behavioural manifestations in organisations include: striving for the well-being of the organisation, acting as a model of conscientiousness by working hard, motivating other colleagues to work better, setting and achieving challenging objectives individually and at the group level, persisting in the face of hardships, loving own work, and conveying passion at work.

Sub-theme 1: Persistence and hard work
'When you analyze influential leaders, you see that these people are very persistent and they try harder than most others do. I believe in one thing: There is nothing as failure, but there are people who lose their faith and hope.'

'My job means more than just work for me. It is my passion; it is my way of life. The workplace is the place where I thrive, where I learn and where I grow. My workplace is my natural habitat and I shine there.'

Sub-theme 2: Focus on motivation, goals, and achievements
'My mind often operates as follows: What does it take to succeed here? How can I reach the objective? What are the probable obstacles? What are my strategies to overcome them?'

Spiritual Anchor 4: Inspiration

A number of leaders have expressed a strong spiritual need to search for a deeper meaning and inspiration as part of their work. Some respondents mentioned that they wanted to create something new and creative that can be identified with them. What distinguishes this group is that the internal voice tells these leaders to search for meaning, seek authenticity, bring beauty, express feelings, avoid being ordinary, explore identity, create deep union, foster creativity, design aesthetically, and develop a personal vision. Spiritual values on this anchor are self-awareness, creativity, sensitivity, emotional honesty, depth, authenticity, equanimity, self-expression, and reflection. Deep feelings, self-expression, and creativity are important.

Spiritual Anchor 4 is about the universal spiritual need to discover and express oneself. This spiritual anchor represents the 'self-awareness and reflection' dimension in human life. This anchor embodies the universal path of art, beauty and aesthetics. Inspiration, authenticity, and intuition are at the core of this spiritual anchor. Behavioural manifestations in organisations include: bringing in authentic and unique perspectives; searching for organisational identity and soul; searching for a deep sense of meaning and purpose at work; expressing own feelings; appreciation of the sorrowful aspect of life; decorating organisational settings aesthetically; and using powerful stories and metaphors to express spirituality.

Sub-theme 1: Creativity and intuition
'I feel I should come up with something affecting and authentic; with depth, insight and style. I should feel passionate about my work. The process should be a peak experience. The product should be a unique contribution. I select projects which are compelling, yet distinct.'

'I view our work as creating a piece of art. The process of creating a masterpiece is not orderly. It is a chaotic and nonlinear process. It involves inspiration and passion. It involves turmoil and emergence. It involves tragedy and fascination.'

Sub-theme 2: Concern for aesthetics, meanings, and depth
'I try to share my sincere feelings with my coworkers. I love inspiring people. I try to build special relationships with my coworkers. There is a true gift hidden in everyone. Every person is special and deep. Everyone has a potential to discover own unique richness and gift. Everyone should discover the best of self, the hidden beauty inside.'

Spiritual Anchor 5: Investigation

A number of respondents make it clear that what motivates them spiritually is to learn and know more. These leaders generally work on creating new knowledge with their team members. What distinguishes this group is that the internal voice tells these leaders to search for knowledge, seek information, do research, use intellect, read and understand, develop insight, explore, think analytically, and develop knowledge. *'The greatest book to be read is the human being. The Universe is within the human, the human is within the Universe,'* one leader said. Spiritual values of leaders having this anchor are wisdom, insight, understanding, intellectual mastery, enlightenment, curiosity, learning, and foresight. Intellectual focus, specialisation, and observation are important for these leaders.

Spiritual Anchor 5 is about the universal spiritual need to understand and know about the world and the universe. This spiritual anchor represents the 'learning and searching for meaning' dimension in human life. This anchor embodies the universal path of science and knowledge. Behavioural manifestations include: being involved in research, trying to discover and make sense of the world, creating and sharing knowledge, trying to know deeply about phenomena, searching for wisdom at work, and designing knowledge-based strategies for the organisation.

Sub-theme 1: Science and wisdom
'I've always wanted to be in a role of doing research, discovering things, creating knowledge and understanding deeply. I love thinking and discovering in the name of God. Science is a sacred and spiritual activity in Islam and it is definitely the most valuable and dear activity for me.'

Sub-theme 2: Emphasis on intellectual focus, knowledge, and learning
'I can read, study or work on my computer for hours without interruption. I tend to forget the outside world when I am dealing with information. Full concentration is necessary to create and generate knowledge.'

Spiritual Anchor 6: Dedication

A number of respondents state that what motivates them spiritually is to be dedicated for a larger cause and to be part of a community. *'We are a great community here and I want to be a part of this,'* one leader said. What distinguishes this group is that the internal voice tells these leaders to be part of the community, be cautious, foster loyalty, protect group norms, act responsibly, and contribute to the common good. Spiritual values on this anchor are loyalty, trust, commitment, faithfulness, reliability, dedication, responsibility, dependability, and trustworthiness. *'I care about brotherhood and sincerity, not only in this world but also in the other world,'* a leader said. *'I would like to die in the middle of a process of an active duty and community work. I would decline any leadership, any ranks, any status, reputation, or honor in this world,'* another put.

Spiritual Anchor 6 is about the universal spiritual need to feel part of something bigger and to belong to a community. This spiritual anchor represents the 'trust and loyalty' dimension in human life. Group identification, sense of loyalty and belongingness, willingness to take on responsibility, and commitment to larger efforts are at the core of this spiritual anchor. Behavioural manifestations in organisations include: carrying out duties and obligations as a loyal member; ensuring a close atmosphere of trust; taking precautions and action in difficult times; and guarding and protecting the fundamental values of the organisation.

Spiritual Anchor 7: Appreciation

A number of managers make it very clear that their core spiritual motivation is to appreciate and be thankful for the good things in life. These leaders are generally champions of new ideas and innovative projects in organisational life. They seem to be visionaries who are oriented towards the future. The internal voice tells these leaders to be hopeful about the future, create a vision, be positive and cheerful, explore alternatives, search for originality, foster innovation, discover, seek adventure, and come up with bright ideas and inventions. Spiritual values on this anchor are enthusiasm, hope, gratefulness, positive thinking, openness, innovativeness, imagination, novelty, and flexibility. Positive energy, fun, and joy are essential.

Spiritual Anchor 7 – 'appreciation' – is about the universal spiritual need to appreciate the good aspects of life and be hopeful about the future. This spiritual anchor represents the 'gratefulness and enthusiasm' dimension in human life. It embodies the spiritual path of hope. Hope and optimism are at the core of this spiritual anchor. Participants anchored here state that they perform most energetically, creatively, and enthusiastically when they appreciate people and the world around them. Some participants said no matter how bad things got; they had the hope and faith that all would work out well somehow.

The belief that there is a guiding plan that governs all lives gives them a sense of resilience and hope. In this sense, spirituality is inextricably connected with hope, positive thinking, and optimism. Behavioural manifestations in organisations include: appreciating the good aspects of life; feeling grateful; using and encouraging intellectual stimulation for innovation; inspiring people to create novel ideas; starting new projects and brainstorming; articulating a vision for the betterment of the world around them; instilling hope; and encouraging positive thinking.

Sub-theme 1: Vision and exploration

'I am fascinated with big plans and grand visions. I have an enthusiasm for visionary projects and I share this enthusiasm with my friends. I can energize people with my passion and ideas. I have a feel for the future, for the big picture and for what it takes to be there.'

Sub-theme 2: Hopes and dreams

'We are the children of our hopes and dreams. Hopes and dreams of a better life, better organization, better society and a better world. Our hopes are our driving forces. We live with our hopes. Every born child in the world is the biggest reason for us not to lose our hopes; because this is an indication that God still loves us and has hopes, mercy as well as plans for us. In our organization, we do not want to be realists. We are idealists. Reality is boring. Facts cannot inspire us. Ideas can.'

Spiritual Anchor 8: Determination

These respondents emphasise that their core spiritual motivation is to be determined and courageous and to have a lasting impact. '*I am here to protect the rights of my team members and to open up their ways,*'one said. These leaders care about ensuring and maintaining social justice around them. They are always there to protect the rights of the weak. '*I am responsible for nurturing and protecting all my team members – physically, emotionally, spiritually, and mentally,*' one said. The internal voice tells these leaders to take initiative, be assertive, act as a courageous leader, implement change, realise dreams, maintain justice, make a contribution, and have a lasting impact. These leaders care about their social responsibility to make a lasting impact and to make a sustainable contribution to the lives of people around them. These leaders are assertive about being a leader and being in charge: '*While acting as a manager in this organization, I am aware of the heavy responsibilities of being a just and an able leader. I am responsible for taking initiative and action to take this organization ahead.'* These leaders, therefore, seem to share the values of justice, magnanimity, self-reliance, decisiveness, courage, willpower, independence, assertiveness, and confidence.

Spiritual Anchor 8 is about the universal spiritual need to be determined to protect and maintain social justice. This spiritual anchor represents the 'sense of community, social justice and responsibility' dimension in human life. This anchor embodies the spiritual path of will and courage. Behavioural manifestations of this value compass include: managing people with justice and fairness, leading people to good and noble causes, ensuring equitable allocation of resources, protecting the rights of the minorities and the weak, preventing any form of injustice, taking risks for the common good, ensuring the well-being of people, and preventing chaos.

Spiritual Anchor 9: Cooperation

A number of leaders make it very clear that what motivates them spiritually is cooperation and harmony. These leaders talk about the importance of tranquillity, wisdom, silence and reflection in their lives. *'Just being patient and listening to everyone's opinions respectfully makes a huge difference in terms of the spiritual health of our team,'* one leader said. What distinguishes this group is that the internal voice tells these leaders to be connected with everyone, stay calm, respect everyone, be patient, get along with people, listen to them with empathy, search for middle solutions, develop consensus, and build dialogue. Spiritual values on this anchor are patience, tranquillity, dialogue, receptivity, tolerance, universality, peace, balance, harmony, contemplation, naturalness, interdependence, and wholeness.

Spiritual Anchor 9 is about the universal spiritual need to achieve inner peace and to be in harmony with the universe. This spiritual anchor represents the 'wholeness and balance' dimension in human spirituality. It embodies the universal path of dialogue and tolerance. Moderation and balance are at the core of this spiritual anchor. Participants anchored here feel that spirituality is itself related to the deep feeling of the interconnectedness of everything and it is important for them to search harmony and wholeness in the universe. As respect for diversity and consensus are essential, followers of this path can excel in turning diversity into richness in social and organisational life. Behavioural manifestations of this value compass include: Accepting and tolerating diversity, showing tolerance for and being sensitive to individual differences, trying to turn differences into complementary synergy, focusing on the larger picture, mediating and resolving conflicts peacefully, fostering patience and tranquillity at work, seeking out consensus in collective decision-making processes, achieving inner peace and tranquillity, giving everyone a voice in meetings, and enhancing dialogue with all stakeholders.

Sub-theme 1: Harmony, peace, and cooperation
'I try to be connected to all my team members and do my best to build peaceful relationships with them. I do not remember any case where I lost my temper and had conflict with any of them. One of the most important requirements for effective team work is the spirit of collaboration and harmony among us. If we foster a cooperative group climate, every member will contribute to the group by his or her unique gifts and views.'

Sub-theme 2: Balance and moderation
'I tend to see some truth in multiple perspectives, which are seemingly opposite. This attitude brings in synthesis and balance. Seemingly conflicting views may actually be reconcilable if we try to see the big picture.'

Sub-theme 3: Patience and listening
'I try to listen to everyone with empathy and without any judgments. My colleagues generally come to me when they have something to share or when they have a problem. I think I give people a sense of being heard and understood. Everything will turn out well in the end. No need to get nervous and stressful. We should do whatever we can do and then just trust the divine intervention.'

Part 3 – Implications

Based on qualitative interviews, this chapter has developed a typology of spiritual anchors. Using this typology, leaders can be classified on the basis of the reasons they give for their core values, what they are seeking in life, and how they see themselves in teams. Any given leader may be anchored in more than one area, but, for the respondents in this study, it proved possible to identify one major spiritual anchor which seemed to be their guiding force. While the respondents in this study identified the Sufi tradition as part of their spiritual worldview, Sufism shares many common spiritual principles with Christianity, Judaism, and other world religions. Thus, the spiritual anchors that emerge may be more generally useful in exploring the value anchors in other cultural and spiritual contexts. For example, Arslan's (2001) empirical work comparing the work ethic values of Protestant British, Catholic Irish and Muslim Turkish managers found more similarities than differences in terms of spiritual values among these managers. Further research therefore could test the portability of these spiritual anchors into different contexts.

This exploratory study suggests several implications for future research. As has already been mentioned, the results may not be generalisable to different cultural contexts and different samples. Participants in this small qualitative study were relatively young, highly educated, and working as managers and professionals in Turkey. Spiritual anchors may operate differently for different people in diverse cultures or organisational settings, and more research on this would elucidate the extent to which the construct of a spiritual anchor is universal or particular. As well as their generalisability, the spiritual anchor construct itself could be refined through additional empirical research. The qualitative data in this study mostly relied on the self-perceptions and attitudes of the respondents. More empirical research is needed to measure and observe the actual behaviours of managers with a given spiritual anchor. Mixed designs combining in-depth qualitative methods and large-scale survey data could be used to inquire into the nature and scope of spiritual anchors and their behavioural manifestations. As this exploratory research attempts to open up a new space, there conceptual ambiguities remain in the definitions and boundaries of spiritual anchors. The terms used are not precise and, while this is partly a deliberate choice to reflect the richness, depth, and density of the concepts, with further research some of these ambiguities could be resolved. This would provide a more rigorous taxonomy.

Nevertheless, this research suggests a number of general implications for leaders and organisations. First, this study contributes to the spirituality at work literature in identifying a range of different meanings and expressions of spirituality at work. The definitions and conceptions of spirituality offered by respondents in this sample support suggestions made by some researchers (Mitroff and Denton, 1999; Duchon and Plowman, 2005) that the construct of spirituality is more complex and multidimensional than it is often assumed. These findings highlight the value of multiple interpretations and definitions when it comes to workplace spirituality, indicating that there are many different paths to achieve the positive incorporation of spirituality at work. The idea of spiritual anchors can also be used as a powerful metaphor in organisational life to articulate spiritual differences in the workplace.

Secondly, the key theoretical contribution of this study is the introduction of the new construct of spiritual anchors as the nine different paradigms or faces of human spirituality. They form the underlying basis of different leadership values and team roles in organisations, enabling us to live in depth, and to live with meaning, purpose, and joy. Spiritual anchors form the basis of our deeply held values, guiding our life and work practices and characterising our personal search for meaning and purpose in life.

Thirdly, this study contributes to the values literature, illustrating how different value sets link with the diverse spirituality of leaders. The findings are in line with what Butts has called 'time-honored, life-affirming, and unifying values' (Butts, 1999:329), which include truth and wisdom (illuminating the mind and heart), trust and justice (leading to organisational and societal well-being), inspiration and creativity (leading to innovation), collective harmony and wholeness (leading to synergy), compassion and charity (enhancing love among people), and deeper meaning (leading to higher purpose). Although some of these values have been recognised in the literature on values and spirituality, this study has made a systematic effort to contribute to this literature by offering a comprehensive framework.

Fourthly, this study contributes to critical leadership studies in identifying an alternative epistemological position in contrast to the dominant positivist paradigm. Research findings in this study reveal multiple interpretations and meanings attached to a leader's value-set. Further qualitative research in leadership could benefit from those holistic and interdisciplinary perspectives that capture the diverse spiritual anchors of different leaders. Further research that combines rational and 'trans-rational' logic and provides new ways to model the non-linear, complex patterns of spirituality could provide new and innovative perspectives on leadership.

Fifthly, the results of this research can be used by leaders to develop deeper self-awareness through individual reflection. The road to becoming a conscious, authentic, and spiritual leader involves personal spiritual reflection, growth, and transformation. Reflecting on and exploring spiritual anchors enables a leader to discover the underlying structure of their own spiritual strengths, needs, attitudes, and motives. Leaders who can assess and evaluate their unique spiritual gifts and skills can utilise these talents and strengths in their leadership practice. Leaders who reflect on their spiritual anchors can discover the essence of their inner wholeness to channel their search for meaning and purpose at work.

Sixthly, leaders can use the idea of spiritual anchors to create supportive team and work environments for employees, centred on spiritual awareness, wisdom, and openness to diversity. The art, craft, and science of spirit-catching, mind-growing, soul-quaking leadership require the possession of deep awareness of the spiritual needs, values, priorities, and strengths of team members. Modern leadership is about discovering and embracing colleagues as whole persons, acknowledging not only their cognitive faculties but also their social, emotional, and spiritual faculties, to engage their hearts, minds, and spirits. Leaders who are aware of spiritual anchors can therefore act as catalysts for individual growth.

Seventhly, the results of this research could be used in career and role counselling to match individuals to tasks in team settings, because each of these spiritual anchors can be associated with specific team roles, as illustrated in Appendix 13A.2. As colleagues explore their spiritual anchors, they can discuss their respective spiritual values, needs, strengths, and attitudes. While it is always dangerous to confuse the positive and the normative, knowing about the natural inclinations of team members can only help to create more harmonious workplaces.

Eighthly, the model of spiritual anchors has implications for spiritual diversity in the workplace. Organisations should encourage their leaders to express their own spirituality at work. In the post-September 11 era, debates over religious conflict and tolerance have become global (Hicks, 2003). Moreover, workplaces of today are more diverse and multicultural than ever before. Since spirituality is a highly individual experience, it is necessary to respect and value individual inner landscapes, values, and perspectives (Krishnakumar and Neck, 2002). Promoting 'one right path' or favouring a specific spiritual or religious framework will not work in these diverse work environments (Hicks, 2003). A culture of respect for diverse spiritualities should be cultivated in the workplace through codes of conduct as well as through the values of tolerance and compassion (Milliman et al., 2003; Milliman et al., 1999; Kouzes and Posner, 1995).

Finally, the results of this research can be used by organisations to design more enabling work environments for leaders and employees who have diverse spiritual needs at work. It is important for organisations to acknowledge these spiritual needs, values, priorities, and preferences. HR and OD professionals stress the importance of engaging

Appendix 13A.1 Spiritual Anchors

Spiritual anchor	Sufi paths	Spiritual dimension in human life	Universal spiritual need	Sub-themes	Value compasses: Defining set of values
SA1 Perfection	Path of truth	Transcendence	To be right, act ethically, reach perfection	Perfectionism, discipline Attention to details, rules, principles	Objectivity, truthfulness, order, rationality, quality, self-discipline, idealism, judgement, consistency, efficiency, discipline, control
SA2 Compassion	Path of love	Interconnectedness	To love and be loved	Sensitivity to people Attention to feelings, relationships	Affection, service, charity, empathy, gentleness, mercy, altruism, forgiveness, kindness, sincerity, helpfulness, nurturing
SA3 Passion	Path of work	Work ethics	To progress, be productive, be successful	Persistence and hard work Focus on motivation, and goals	Conscientiousness, striving, persistence, perseverance, ambition, self-development, ethical success, effort, diligence, hard work
SA4 Inspiration	Path of authenticity	Self-awareness and reflection	To discover and express oneself	Creativity and intuition Concern for aesthetics, meaning, and depth	Self-awareness, creativity, sensitivity, aesthetics, authenticity, equanimity, beauty, self-expression, reflection
SA5 Investigation	Path of wisdom	Learning and search for meaning	To understand/ know about the world/ universe	Science and wisdom Emphasis on knowledge, learning	Science, comprehension, insight, knowledge, understanding, enlightenment, learning, foresight, curiosity

SA6 Dedication	Path of trust	Trust and loyalty	To feel part of something bigger	Focus on loyalty and responsibility	Loyalty, commitment, reliability, obedience, caution, dependability, trustworthiness, honesty, integrity, belonging
SA7 Appreciation	Path of hope	Gratefulness and enthusiasm	To be resilient and hopeful about the future	Vision and exploration Optimism Hopes and dreams	Exploration, openness, thanksgiving, hope, enthusiasm, gratefulness, innovativeness, imagination, novelty, flexibility
SA8 Determination	Path of will	Community and social responsibility	To protect and maintain justice	Courage, confidence Responsibility, contribution	Magnanimity, decisiveness, determination, justice, freedom, willpower, assertiveness, strength, confidence, zeal
SA9 Cooperation	Path of harmony	Wholeness and balance	To achieve inner peace, be in harmony with universe	Harmony, peace Balance and moderation Patience and listening	Patience, acceptance, receptivity, tolerance, courtesy, universality, peace, harmony, naturalness, wholeness, tranquillity

Appendix 13A.2 Managerial Implications of Spiritual Anchors in Teams and Organisations

Team role	Key priorities	Focus on	Key contributions
1) Conductor Auditor	Order Efficiency Control	*details *rules, procedures *right/wrong *standards	*set rules and standards *ensure compliance to norms *carry an internal yardstick *planning
2) Carer Helper	Service Satisfaction People	*relationships *empathy *people *satisfaction	*improve relationships *build connections *increase group cohesion *increase member morale/satisfaction
3) Producer Motivator	Competition Environment Adaptation	*task success *motivation *survival *adaptation *speed	*increase motivation *scan environment and adapt *watch for the competition *evaluate, improve individual and organisational performance
4) Artist Innovator	Culture Meanings Identity	*aesthetics *meaning *originality *creativity	*search for meaning *strive for distinctive identity *enhance self-awareness *foster creative thinking *contribute to diversity
5) Specialist Observer	Knowledge Cognition Learning	*information *understanding *expertise *analysis	*create and manage knowledge *assigned 'expert role' *enhance organisational learning and problem-solving
6) Cautious Questioner	Power Politics Risk	*reliability *risks/threats *trust *conflicts	*foresee threats *Devil's advocate *foster loyalty and commitment *protect norms

Continued

Appendix 13A.2   Continued

Team role	Key priorities	Focus on	Key contributions
7) Explorer Innovator	Vision Change Flux	*ideas *innovation *opportunities *enthusiasm	*foresee opportunities *accelerate innovation *enact and lead change *foster individual and group creativity
8) Pioneer Captain	Strategy Results Profits	*initiative *entrepreneurship *implementation *control	*set strategic directions *find areas of investment *take initiative and risks *control/measure results
9) Coach Mentor	Dialogue Stakeholders Legitimacy	*balance *harmony *synthesis *the big picture *teamwork	*resolve conflicts among members and stakeholders *negotiate and build shared consensus *prevent polarisation *enhance cooperation and synergy

whole persons at work (Kahn, 1992, Hall and Mirvis, 1996), so it is important to acknowledge people as spiritual beings too (Garcia-Zamor, 2003). Organisations should think more broadly about the different kinds of contributions people can make, and to develop multiple reward systems as well as multiple career paths to meet the diverse spiritual needs of employees in organisations. Using this research as a starting point, organisations and practitioners can learn about the meanings and values individuals attach to spirituality at work and discover the multiplicity of spirituality experiences and spiritual values at work. This will help them to understand and accommodate the diverse spiritual needs and values of employees by designing organisational structures, policies, and programmes to support positive expressions of spirituality at work.

Bibliography

Arslan, M., 'The Work Ethic Values of Protestant British, Catholic Irish and Muslim Turkish Managers', *Journal of Business Ethics*, 31 (2001) 321–339.

Ashmos, D.P. and Duchon, D., 'Spirituality at Work: A Conceptualization and Measure', *Journal of Management Inquiry*, 9(2) (2000) 134–145.

Barnett, C.K., Krell, T.C., and Sendry, J., 'Learning to Learn about Spirituality: A Categorical Approach to Introducing the Topic into Management Courses', *Journal of Management Education*, 24(5) (2000) 562–579.

Barrett R., Liberating the Corporate Soul: Building a Visionary Organisation (Butterworth. Heinemann, 1998).

Bolman, L.G. and Deal, T.E., *Leading with Soul: An Uncommon Journey of Spirit* (San Francisco, CA: Jossey-Bass, 1995).

Butts, D., Spirituality at Work: an Overview, *JOCM*, 12(4), 328–331.

Capra, F., 'A Systems Approach to the Emerging Paradigm' in M. Ray and A. Rinzler (eds), *The New Paradigm in Business* (New York: Tarcher Books, 1993).

Cavanagh, G., 'Spirituality for Managers: Context and Critique', *Journal of Organizational Change Management*, 12(3) (1999) 186.

Conger, J., *Spirit at Work: Discovering the Spirituality in Leadership* (San Francisco, CA: Jossey-Bass, 1994).

Corkery, M. and Hagerty, J.R., 'Continuing Vicious Cycle of Pain in Housing and Finance Ensnares Market', *Wall Street Journal*, 14 July (2008).

Dent, E.B., Higgins, M.E., and Wharff, D.M., 'Spirituality and Leadership: An Empirical Review of Definitions, Distinctions, and Embedded Assumptions', *The Leadership Quarterly*, 16(5) (2005), 625–653.

Duchon, D. and Plowman, D.A., 'Nurturing the Spirit at Work: Impact on Unit Performance', *The Leadership Quarterly*, 16(5) (2005) 807–834.

Elkins, D.N., Hedstrom, L.J., Hughes, L.L., Leaf, J.A., and Saunders, C., 'Toward a Humanistic-phenomenological Spirituality: Definition, Description, and Measurement', *Journal of Humanistic Psychology*, 28 (1988) 5–18.

Fornaciari C.J. and Dean, K.L., 'Making the Quantum Leap: Lessons from Physics on Studying Spirituality and Religion in Organizations', *Journal of Organizational Change Management*, 14(4) (2001) 335.

Fry, L.W., 'Toward a Theory of Spiritual Leadership', *The Leadership Quarterly*, 14 (2003) 693–727.

Garcia-Zamor, J., 'Workplace Spirituality and Organizational Performance', *Public Administration Review*, 63(3) (2003) 355–363.

Giacalone, R.A. and Jurkiewicz, C.L., *Handbook of Workplace Spirituality and Organizational Performance* (Armonk, NY: M.E. Sharpe, 2003).

Gibbons, P., 'Spirituality at Work: Definitions, Measures, Assumptions, and Validity Claims' in Biberman, J. and M. Whitty (eds) *Work and Spirit: A Reader of New Spiritual Paradigms for Organizations* (Scranton, PA: University of Scranton Press, 2000).

Glaser, B.G. and Strauss, A.L., *The Discovery of Grounded Theory: Strategies for Qualitative Research* (London: Wiedenfeld and Nicholson, 1967).

Gozdz, K., 'Toward Transpersonal Learning Communities in Business', *American Behavioral Scientist*, 43(8) (2000) 1262–1285.

Greenhalgh, H., 'Poor ethical standards causing financial crisis', *Financial Times*, 13 October (2008).

Hall, D.T. and Mirvis, P.H., 'The New Protean Career: Psychological Success and the Path with a Heart', in D.T. Hall and Associates (eds), *The Career is Dead-Long Live the Career* (San Francisco, CA: Jossey-Bass, 1996).

Heuvel, K.V. and Schlosser, E., 'America Needs A New New Deal', *Wall Street Journal*, 27 September (2008).

Hicks, D.A., 'Spiritual and Religious Diversity in the Workplace: Implications for Leadership', *Leadership Quarterly*, 13 (2002) 379–396.

Hicks, D., *Religion and the Workplace: Pluralism, Spirituality, Leadership* (Cambridge: University Press, 2003).

Howard, S., 'A Spiritual Perspective on Learning in the Workplace', *Journal of Managerial Psychology*, 17(3) (2002) 230–242.

Hutton, W., 'Without Real Leadership, We Face Disaster', *The Observer*, 12 October (2008).

Kahn, W.A., 'To Be Fully There: Psychological Presence at Work', *Human Relations*, 45(4) (1992) 321–349.

Khurana, R., Searching for a Corporate Savior: The Irrational Quest for Charismatic CEOs (Princeton, NJ: Princeton University Press, 2002).

Kinjerski, V.M. and Skrypnek, B.J., 'Defining Spirit at Work: Finding Common Ground', *Journal of Organizational Change Management*, 17(12) (2004) 26–42.

Konz, G., and Ryan, F., 'Maintaining an Organizational Spirituality: No easy task', *Journal of Organizational Change Management*, 12(3) (1999) 200–210.

Kouzes, J.M. and Posner, B.Z., *The Leadership Challenge* (San Francisco, CA: Jossey-Bass, 1995).

Krishnakumar, S. and Neck, C.P., 'The What, Why, and How of Spirituality in the Workplace', *Journal of Managerial Psychology*, 17(3) (2002) 153–164.

Leigh, P., 'The New Spirit at Work', *Training and Development*, 51(3) (1997) 26–33.

Lips-Wiersma, M. and Mills, C., 'Coming out of the Closet: Negotiating Spiritual Expression in the Workplace', *Journal of Managerial Psychology*, 17(3) (2002) 183–202.

Maccoby, M., 'Narcissistic Leaders: The Incredible Pros, the Inevitable Cons', *Harvard Business Review*, 78(1) (2000) 69–77.

Marques, J., Dhiman, S., and King, R., Spirituality in the Workplace: What It Is, Why It Matters, How to Make It Work for You (Fawnskin, CA: Personhood Press, 2007).

McMakin, J. and Dyer, S., *Working from the Heart: A Guide to Cultivating the Soul at Work* (San Francisco, CA.: Harper Collins, 1993).

Markow, F. and Klenke, K., 'The Effects of Personal Meaning and Calling on Organizational Commitment: An Empirical Investigation of Spiritual Leadership', *International Journal of Organizational Analysis*, 13(1) (2005) 8–27.

Milliman, J., Ferguson, J.J., Trickett, D., and Condemi, B., 'Spirit and Community at Southwest Airlines: An Investigation of a Spiritual Values-based Model', *Journal of Organizational Change Management*, 12(3) (1999) 221–233.

Milliman, J., Czaplewski, A.J., and Ferguson, J., 'Workplace Spirituality and Employee Work Attitudes: An Exploratory Empirical Assessment', *Journal of Organizational Change Management*, 16(4) (2003) 426–447.

Mitroff, I., and Denton, E., A Spiritual Audit of Corporate America: A Hard Look at Spirituality, Religion, and Values in the Workplace (San Francisco, CA: Jossey-Bass Publishers, 1999).

Nursi, B.S., *Collection of Words, Flashes and Letters* (Istanbul: Sozler Publications, 1925).

Parameshwar, S., 'Spiritual Leadership through Ego-transcendence: Exceptional Responses to Challenging Circumstances', *The Leadership Quarterly*, 16 (2005) 689–722.

Patton, M.Q., *Qualitative Research and Evaluation Methods* (Thousand Oaks, CA: Sage Publications, 2002).

Riso, D.R. and Hudson, R. , *Personality Types: Using the Enneagram for Self-Discovery* (New York, NY: Houghton Mifflin Co., 1996).

Riso, D. R.and Hudson, R., *Understanding the Enneagram: The Practical Guide to Personality Types* (Boston: Hougton Mifflin, 2000).

Schein, E.H., *Career Anchors: Discovering Your Real Values* (San Francisco, CA: Jossey-Bass Pfeiffer, 1990).

Schroth, R.J. and Elliot, L., *How Companies Lie: Why Enron is just the Tip of the Iceberg* (New York, NY: Crown Business, 2002).

Steenland, S. and Dreier, S., 'It's a Moral Meltdown, Too', *Newsletter of Center for American Progress*, 7 October (2008).

Stiglitz, J.E., *Globalization and its Discontents* (New York, NY: WW. Norton and Company, 2002).

Tischler, L., 'The Growing Interest in Spirituality in Business: A Long-term Socio-economic Explanation', *Journal of Organizational Change Management*, 12(4) (1999) 273–280.

Uzunoglu, S., 'Transformation and Self-Development in Sufism', *Sizinti*, 22(3) (1999) 176–181.

Waddock, S.A., 'Parallel Universes: Companies, Academics, and the Progress of Corporate Citizenship', *Business and Society Review*, 109(1) (2004) 5–30.

Wagner-Marsh, F., and Conley, J., 'The Fourth Wave: The Spiritually-based Firm', *Journal of Organizational Change Management*, 12(4) (1999) 292–301.

Whyte, D., The Heart Aroused: Poetry and Preservation of the Soul in Corporate America (New York: Currency Doubleday, 1994).

14
Global Ethical Leadership and the Future

Carla Millar and Eve Poole

In this final chapter, we look at the skills, characteristics and competences an ethical leader is likely to need in the future. We also discuss the particular ethical challenge of leading in a global and an increasingly knowledge-based world. Finally, we reflect on future directions in leadership ethics.

Looking to the future, what kind of skills will be needed by a leader, and what does this mean for leadership ethics? As more economies in the developed world make the transition from being largely driven by manufacturing to being predominantly services-based, and as the Internet and digital revolutions both accelerate and percolate globally, leaders will need a heightened ability to handle extraordinary amounts of data – management information, news, trends – and convert it to practical wisdom for decision-making in the blink of an eye. While information will be cheap and quick, wisdom will be harder to come by. As experience will date much more quickly than it does now and is hard to hand over to others, the emphasis on the quality of a leader's education will come back into vogue. In the future we may be able to download data straight into our brains, or take drugs to accelerate our learning, so it is what a leader does with information that will make the difference in the future.

Like the Red Queen in *Alice Through the Looking Glass* (Carroll, 1871/1999), leaders will be running to stay in the same place, so they will need to sprint to lead the field. Resilience skills will therefore be paramount. Leaders won't be able to sustain performance without extraordinary commitment to the health and well-being of themselves and those around them. As globalisation matures, leaders will need to be reflexively good at reading cultures locally and globally, and adjusting their style, messages, and business models accordingly. While much regulation and legislation will standardise globally, local operating conditions will still vary enormously as communities get more particular in the face of growing global homogenisation. The world is shrinking and getting faster, so leaders will be extremely comfortable with virtual tools. A successful multi-country track record will be vital for the future leader's credibility.

While the cult of the charismatic leader may currently be out of vogue, the war for talent will mean that the future leader will need to be highly charismatic as a matter of course, to attract flighty global talent, who are loyal to their personal vocation and only to an organisation while its goals align with their own. As more industries migrate up the value curve and more work is automated, technical skills will be less distinctive than tacit knowledge, beautiful manners, and skilful conversation, in a variety of global settings and through diverse media. Perhaps 'Finishing Schools' will again be popular, but this time for finding Boards not husbands.

As time marches on, leaders will have to become manifestly better global citizens, at ease with 24/7 transparency. Data will be better, so their performance will be more exactly managed, communicated, and rewarded or punished. Character and the virtues will be of more importance than current transaction-based analysis, tested by the use of story on the international grapevine. The current drivers of employer of choice and inside-out branding will have reached maturity, as leaders realise how expensive secrecy is, and how damaging both to brand and reputation are breaches in trust, so they will naturally commit to good public behaviour throughout the supply chain and more widely in society.

So, the leader of the future will need wisdom, resilience, world-friendliness, charm, and integrity, which together create a kaleidoscope of ethical challenge. This resonates with the words of Sun Tzu in Chapter 1 (Sun Tzu, 500 BC/2002). A further ethical challenge is presented by the wider lifecycle context, as more countries become service-led economies, creating more knowledge-based organisations in an increasingly knowledge-based society. This context is fraught with danger, particularly if that society remains unswervingly loyal to the 'neutral' amorality of neo-classical economic theory which would airbrush ethics out of the equation. The intangible and tacit nature of many products and assets in a global knowledge-based society (Polanyi, 1957; Itami and Roehl, 1987) challenges the traditional models of responsible leadership (Maak and Pless, 2006) and global corporate citizenship (De Jongh, 2009; Knippenberg and de Jong, 2010; Gosling and Huang, 2010), as does the spectre of an information and technology apartheid between the rich and the poor. Dilemmas concerning the patenting of crops and drugs are just the tip of the iceberg, arguing, in spite of the Chicago School model, for the growing relevance of discussions about moral agency and its boundaries. Such discussions need to take place both within firms and across the supply chain; throughout the wider stake-holder community and down the generations.

For today's leaders, the intangibility of knowledge assets makes decision-making in organisations vague and ambiguous. In traditional manufacturing-based economies, transactions are comparatively trans-parent and the value received can be demonstrated to match the value paid in a tangible way. There is little scope for doubt about the hon-esty of the parties if a given product can be shown to function in the prescribed manner and to match the quality reflected in the price. But, in a knowledge economy, beauty is more manifestly in the eye of the beholder. Intangible services may be accompanied by an array of sug-gestive tangibles (the notorious 'freebies' on Concorde), but the actual value to the customer of the service rendered is less easy to quantify. A similar type of uncertainty occurs when leaders need to operate out-side their normal habitat – abroad, in an unfamiliar environment, and dealing with unfamiliar stakeholders. This leaves room for ambiguity on both sides, creating fertile ground for ethical ambivalence, particu-larly in a business context dominated by shareholder value. In such an environment, trust becomes increasingly crucial, and the effects of real or perceived breaches in this trust are magnified. Where there are fewer anchors, there can be ethical drift, which can have wider societal impli-cations. The recent credit crunch is but one infamous example of this.

This trust is not just about business-to-consumer trust or about leader–follower trust. As Abimbola and Abimbola argue in Chapter 8 of this collection, the web of relationships which surrounds an organ-isation adds ambiguity, as shareholders delegate to Boards who delegate to executives who delegate to staff and to outsource partners, adding distance and deniability at every stage. The multiplying of agency com-plexity throughout the system requires exponential trust, embedded in a strong positive organisational culture, supported by robust corpor-ate governance procedures. This trust includes the need for the par-ties to be reconciled with information asymmetry. Leaders have more information than followers and followers need to accept this, just as patients have to accept information asymmetry with their doctor and to trust them. Many decisions have to be made on the basis of informa-tion that cannot be shared, whether because of time pressure, commer-cial sensitivity, or just because well-honed intuitive instinct takes over.

Sustainable global corporate citizenship (De Jongh, 2009; Maak and Pless, 2006) needs trustworthy leaders, and will require increasingly innovative approaches to responsible leadership (Doh and Stumpf, 2005; Waldman and Gavin, 2008; Pless and Maak, 2009). All followers require a degree of predictability from their leaders, and see ethical integrity as a warranty of this (Moorman and Grover, 2009).

Given this need for integrity, Boddy's alarming findings in Chapter 2 about the likely incidence of Corporate Psychopathy at senior levels in organisations are particularly striking. Notwithstanding the methodological issue with his research that perhaps we all have a tendency to assume that any senior people we don't like are pathological, his findings certainly argue for urgent and meticulous research into this field. In the face of rapid developments in neurological research, there is a pressing need for ethicists to sift through the available evidence and to reflect anew on what makes us human, if only to help HR professionals steer a safe course through discrimination, harassment, and human rights legislation. Perhaps the estimate of a mere 3.5 per cent incidence of psychopathy at a senior level does not appear unduly concerning until one considers the impact senior leaders have on their organisations. Research on the impact of senior leaders has already been cited, but wider perspectives from Kleiner's Core Group Theory (2003) and Janis's GroupThink (1972) suggest that, were any of this 3.5 per cent to be board-level, their influence would cast a disproportionately large shadow over the culture and decision-making of the entire organisation.

This perspective makes Manner's findings in Chapter 3 about correlations between CEO characteristics and successful corporate social responsibility initiatives doubly interesting. Ethicists like Nigel Biggar have argued elsewhere for a renewed affirmation of the vital role the humanities play in moral formation (Biggar, 2009), and studies suggesting a link between exposure to economic theories and moral corrosion are legion, particularly when coupled with seniority, within a large organisation, in a competitive market (Frank et al., 1993, Ford and Richardson, 1994). But what is particularly intriguing is Manner's finding about women. This chimes in with an alternative view of stress, one which also argues for the particular suitability of women to occupy senior leadership positions.

Reflecting on the fact that most of what we know about stress is based on male sampling, in 2000 Taylor et al. revisited the topic, and found that female physiology drives a different reaction to stress, dubbed 'tend and befriend' rather than the traditional 'fight or flight' response. Their research suggested that, when exposed to stress, female chemistry instead drives 'nurturant activities', designed to promote safety and reduce distress, while simultaneously creating and maintaining social networks to aid this process (Taylor et al., 2000). While this has often been caricatured as the female habit of phoning a friend for a gossip, the general instinct it suggests may be of more service to organisations than the more traditionally male 'fight or flight' response. This is lent particular poignancy by research in game theory (Nash, 1996; Axelrod, 1990; Nalebuff and Brandenburger, 1996), which overwhelmingly suggests the merits of cooperative strategies in complex situations. In a context where the easy assumption of unbridled capitalism has been challenged by the recent financial crisis, an encouragement towards cooperation would act as a corrective to many of the scenarios described by our contributors, where executives have felt compelled to behave 'less well' because of the stress of the job and because of pressure from competition.

The conference on which many of these papers are based had as its secondary theme 'the global ethical leadership compass'. But perhaps the image of a navigational compass is a poor metaphor. Magnetic north is slowly drifting from Canada towards Siberia over disputed territories; it also wanders many miles a day, it changes depending on where on the earth you take the reading, and it could swap with magnetic south at any time. A compass magnet is also affected by local magnetic fields and, because opposites attract, magnetic north is in any case actually the South Pole. The conference venue, Ashridge, was originally founded as a monastery in the thirteenth century. It then became one of Henry VIII's palaces, and his daughter Elizabeth did much of her schooling there. When she was crowned Elizabeth I she sold the property to her Lord Chancellor, Sir Thomas Egerton, whose secretary was none other than the poet John Donne. He was ultimately sacked from his post for secretly marrying his boss's niece, but one of the poems he wrote her offers a different view of the moral compass, using the metaphor of the sort of compasses used for drawing:

> Our two souls therefore, which are one,
> Though I must go, endure not yet
> A breach, but an expansion,
> Like gold to aery thinness beat.
> If they be two, they are two so
> As stiff twin compasses are two;
> Thy soul, the fix'd foot, makes no show
> To move, but doth, if th' other do.
> And though it in the centre sit,

Yet, when the other far doth roam,
It leans, and hearkens after it,
And grows erect, as that comes home.
Such wilt thou be to me, who must,
Like th' other foot, obliquely run;
Thy firmness makes my circle just,
And makes me end where I begun.

This excerpt, from Donne's poem *A Valediction Forbidding Mourning* (1611), gives us the idea of a 'fix'd foot', which is perhaps a better metaphor for the role of ethics in business life than the heaving relativity of a navigational compass.

But whose fix'd foot? The range of perspectives in this collection talks to a mere fraction of the complexity facing any organisation operating internationally. Western capitalism was founded on Judeao-Christian values, which provided its original fix'd foot (Weber, 2002), and studies based on comprehensive World Values Survey data still suggest that any sort of religious belief is more conducive to a flourishing capitalist system than atheism (Guiso et al., 2002). Meanwhile, the Chicago School view that capitalism has somehow floated free from its roots and matured into a 'neutral' system that can be readily applied in any context does not stand up to scrutiny, and the particular Western individualistic view it assumes stands challenged by Eastern versions of hybrid capitalism. Geopolitical fractures too are emerging where once the West's version of capitalism was ubiquitous, underpinned by IMF money which came with structural adjustment strings attached. And as the West has recently made extensive use of interventionist economic policies they would once have prevented developing countries from using, countries in search of financial backing find in the arms of benefactors like China a rather different view of how a political economy should be run (Stiglitz, 2009).

But while it can no longer be assumed that one particular religious view can hold sway as the global fix'd foot, it may well be that the religions can offer a template for how best to navigate ethically though the global marketplace. This is because religion has always had to develop routines for discussion across ideological boundaries, some more ethical than others, and modern concern over religious extremism has led to a renewed interest in this debate. What is widely called 'public theology' might take as its philosophy a line from the poet W.B. Yeats: 'tread softly, because you tread on my dreams'. This is because in inter-religious dialogue it has always been understood that there are different belief systems at play, just as there are, often latently, in discussions about ethics. That the theologians have had to develop explicit processes for such discussions may offer insight into how business ethicists working globally might also want to conduct themselves, in a world where it is itself unethical to assume that capitalism is value-neutral.

One recent example of such discourse is the practice of Scriptural Reasoning, where Jews, Christians, and Muslims meet together to read from their holy books (Walker and Bretherton, 2007). The approach can most neatly by described by nomenclature borrowed from behavioural psychology, which draws a distinction between advocacy (speaking what you think, speaking for a point of view) and inquiry (looking into what you do not yet know, what you do not yet understand). While advocacy is the presentation of views already held, inquiry seeks to discover what others see, understanding that it may differ from your own point of view (Isaacs, 1999). When moving from dialogue to action, the public theologian Jonathan Chaplin has argued for 'candour in representation, restraint in decision' (Chaplin, 2008). This approach coheres with the argument from game theory that making available as much information as possible optimises the eventual outcome (Nash, 1996).

While inter-faith protocols are promising, in all discussions about ethics the religious person benefits from having to hand a particular worldview to explain their ethical stance. This is what the moral philosopher Toulmin would call their ultimate warrant or backing, in that any assertion may draw the challenge 'How did you get there?' followed by the question 'What have you got to go on?' (Toulmin, 2003). The role of the humanities in inculcating good moral reasoning habits has already been noted, but the issue goes deeper than that. In the West it has become fashionable to deal with multiculturalism by ironing it out under the guise of a neutral secularism. While this is of course duplicitous, it means that educators have become increasingly uncomfortable about moral formation, because in countries like the United Kingdom it used to be synonymous with an upbringing in the Christian religion. Public policy in the United Kingdom in this area flies in the face of public demand. Although they account for a quarter of the UK's primary schools, Church of England schools are routinely over-subscribed, with many parents becoming (temporarily) religious in order to get their children on the right list. While the re-introduction of moral education into schooling is politically fraught, it would appear to be more damaging not to address this key issue, given that unbridled capitalism tends to consume the very ethical resources it depends upon for its survival (Preston, 1991). Where there is no common understanding or ability to reason together, lawyers benefit, but the system collapses under the sheer weight of the regulation and contract needed to maintain order (Plant, 2001).

And where do leaders go to school? Many of them at some point end up at business schools like Ashridge. While mid-career might be considered rather late for the formation of moral character, the self-awareness of which this is a part is recognised as the cornerstone of effective leadership (Goleman, 2000), and improves with study. Like many other schools already offering leadership and ethics as a mandatory element on the MBA, we were able to feel smug when Ghoshal first issued his challenge to business schools for their complicity in creating corporate monsters (Ghoshal, 2005). The credit crunch triggered an avalanche of similar critique, so all business schools are thinking again about how embedded such teaching really is throughout the curriculum.

One obvious culprit may well be the much vaunted Harvard Case Study method. While introducing an element of ethics into case study discussions has proved useful (Cagle and Baucus, 2006), the underlying method remains ethically questionable. Stylistically, the standard case study format sets out a business dilemma of some kind, in strategy, marketing, ethics, or another discipline, and asks the class to discuss what they would do if they were CXO A or B. What this means is that, for large chunks of the MBA, the students are pretending to be someone else, building a rather schizophrenic repertoire of being hundreds of different executives in different situations in different industries across the world. While part of the well-intentioned pedagogy behind the method is to help students to learn by grappling with real issues in a multitude of environments and fast, one consequence is to train them into thinking abstractly and ideally about what the 'correct' answer might be to a particular situation. This process dislocates the decision-maker from their context as well as from their conscience. In contrast, we prefer to teach ethics by first making the students reconnect with their worldview to identify their own fix'd foot before we look at any scenarios or case studies that present an ethical dilemma. It is interesting to note the qualitatively different conversations that result, with students tending to get more creative in identifying possible 'win/win' options, rather than getting sucked into a binary win/lose good/bad decision-making dichotomy.

Within the constraints of an MBA ideology, which currently conforms to its cultural roots, the traditional approach to ethics favours an automatically utilitarian frame. However, one thing that differentiates business ethics from its formal counterpart in moral philosophy is methodology. Being located within faculties of social science, and reliant on publication for promotion, many business ethicists chase data.

While careful studies, such as those in this collection, will always shed light on the subject, particularly in the field of ethics it is crucially important not to confuse what is with what should be, and not to overstate the possibilities of data. It may be that 'the data shows that people do x', but people do not have to do x, nor perhaps should they, and there is a degree of fatalism in empiricism that does not lend itself to moral development and the nourishing of free will.

One concept of the moral philosopher Alasdair MacIntyre (2003) that is particularly resonant is his idea of 'practices'. This is one way to understand the rather complex notion of virtue ethics in the context of discussion on the formation of moral character. While decision-making based on rules or consequences will have an accumulative effect on character over time, it is a well-formed character which leads to effortlessly ethical decision-making. Character, or moral intuition, is inculcated through parenting and schooling, and through exposure to spiritual or other systems of belief. So how might its formation be accelerated, or restarted or re-formed in adulthood? While the literature on intuition is in a state of flux, given rapid advances in neurobiology, it appears that intuition is essentially lightning-quick processing, rather than 'sixth sense' messages from the ether. As such, moral character is infinitely 'trainable' through habit-forming practices. And while the use of case studies may help with this, they can have the opposite effect if they are handled lightly, and if faculty are ill-prepared or too scared to discuss ethics. More helpful are those learning processes that deal with 'real' situations, so that the consequences of decisions are actually felt. While business schools are getting increasingly creative about using experiential learning for this purpose, more needs to be done to understand how best to contribute to moral formation in adulthood.

Bibliography

Axelrod, R., *The Evolution of Co-operation* (London: Penguin, 1990).

Biggar, N., 'Saving the "Secular": the Public Vocation of Moral Theology', *Journal of Religious Ethics*, 37(1) (2009) 159–178.

Cagle, J.A.B. and Melissa S.B., 'Case Studies of Ethics Scandals: Effects on Ethical Perceptions of Finance Students', *Journal of Business Ethics*, 64(3) (2006) 213–229.

Carroll, L., *Through the Looking Glass* (London: Dover, 1871/1999).

Chaplin, J., *Talking God: The Legitimacy of Religious Public Reasoning* (London: Theos, 2008).

De Jongh, D., 'A Global Scan of Corporate Citizenship', *Management Today*, 25 (2009) 20–26.

Doh, J.P. and Stumpf, S.A.(eds), *Handbook on Responsible Leadership and Governance in Global Business* (Cheltenham and Northampton MA: Edward Elgar, 2005).

Ford, R.C. and Woodrow D.R., 'Ethical Decision Making: A Review of the Empirical Literature', *Journal of Business Ethics*, 13(3) (1994) 205–221.

Frank, R.H., Gilovich, T. and Dennis T.R., 'Does Studying Economics Inhibit Cooperation?', *Journal of Economic Perspectives*, 7(2) (1993) 159–171.

Ghoshal, S., 'Bad Management Theories Are Destroying Good Management Practices,' *Academy of Management Learning and Education*, 4(1) (2005) 75–91.

Goleman, D., 'Leadership That Gets Results', *Harvard Business Review* (Mar–Apr) (2000) 1–15.

Gosling, M. and Huang, H.J., 'The Fit between Integrity and Integrative Social Contracts Theory', *Journal of Business Ethics* (2010, forthcoming).

Guiso, L., Sapienza, P., and Zingales, L., 'People's Opium? Religion and Economic Attitudes', *National Bureau of Economic Research*, Working Paper 9237 (2002).

Isaacs, W., *Dialogue and the Art of Thinking Together* (New York, NY: Doubleday, 1999).

Itami, H. and Roehl, T., *Mobilizing Invisible Assets* (Cambridge, MA: Harvard University Press, 1987).

Janis, I., *Victims of GroupThink* (Boston: Houghton Mifflin, 1972).

Kleiner, A., *Who Really Matters* (London: Nicholas Brealey, 2003).

Knippenberg, L. and de Jong, E.B.P., 'Moralising the Market by Moralising the Firm', *Journal of Business Ethics* (2010, forthcoming).

Maak, T. and Pless, N.M., 'Responsible Leadership in a Stakeholder Society, a Relational Perspective', *Journal of Business Ethics*, 66 (2006) 99–110.

MacIntyre, A., *After Virtue* (London: Duckworth, 2003).

Moorman, R. and Grover, S., 'Why Does Leader Integrity Matter to Followers? An Uncertainty Management-Based Explanation', *International Journal of Leadership Studies*, 5(2) (2009) 102–114.

Nalebuff, B.J. and Brandenburger, A.M., *Co-opetition* (London: Harper Collins Business, 1996).

Nash, J.F., Jr, *Essays on Game Theory* (Cheltenham: Edward Elgar, 1996).

Plant, R., *Politics, Theology and History* (Cambridge: Cambridge University Press, 2001).

Pless, N. and Maak, T., 'Responsible Leaders As Agents of World Benefit: Learnings from Project Ulysses', *Journal of Business Ethics*, 85 (2009) 59–71.

Polanyi, M., *The Tacit Dimension* (New York: Anchor Day, 1957).

Preston, R.H., *Religion and the Ambiguities of Capitalism* (London: SCM Press, 1991).

Stiglitz, J.E., 'Wall Street's Toxic Message', *Vanity Fair*, July (2009) 85.

Sun Tzu, *The Art of War* (London: Penguin Books, 500 BC/2002).

Taylor, S.E., Klein, L.C., Lewis, B.P., Gruenewald, T.L., Gurung, R.A.R., and Updegraff, J.A., 'Biobehavioral Responses to Stress in Females: Tend-and-Befriend, Not Fight-or-Flight', *Psychological Review*, 107(3) (2000) 411–429.

Toulmin, S.E., *The Uses of Argument* (Cambridge: Cambridge University Press, 2003).

Waldman, D.A. and Gavin, B.M., 'Alternative Perspective of Responsible Leadership', *Organisational Dynamics*, 37 (2008): 327–341.

Walker, A. and Bretherton, L., (eds), *Remembering Our Future: Explorations in Deep Church* (Carlisle: Paternoster, 2007).

Weber, M., *The Protestant Ethic and the Spirit of Capitalism* (London: Routledge, 2002).

Index